HISTORY OF THE CHURCH IN AFRICA

ACP STUDY GUIDES

God's message to the nation (Amos)
You could be rich (Ephesians)
Fight the good fight (1 Timothy)
Happy in trouble (Philippians)
Revelation
The Spirit's power
God's message to the churches (Revelation 1–3)
How the Good News began (Mark)
Threefold secret of life (1, 2, 3 John)
Watchman in Babylon (Ezekiel)
Elijah and Elisha
The Secret of Wisdom (Job, Proverbs, Ecclesiastes)

HISTORY OF THE CHURCH IN AFRICA

A SURVEY

JONATHAN HILDEBRANDT

AFRICA CHRISTIAN PRESS

First edition 1981
Second revised edition 1987
Third revised edition 1990

ISBN 0 85352 320 7

 Maps drawn by Eric Read.

Trade orders to:
Nigeria: Challenge Bookshops, PMB 12256, Lagos, and
Fellent Ltd, PO Box 5923, Lagos
Zambia: PO Box 21689, Kitwe
Kenya: Keswick Bookshop, PO Box 10242, Nairobi
S. Africa: ACLA, PO Box 332, Roodepoort 1725, Transvaal
Zimbabwe: Word of Life Bookshops, PO Box 3700, Harare
Australia: Bookhouse, PO Box 115, Flemington Markets, NSW 2129
UK: ACP, 50 Loxwood Avenue, Worthing, W. Sussex BN14 7RA

All other orders to:
ACP, PO Box 30, Achimota, Ghana, W. Africa

Designed and Printed in England for
AFRICA CHRISTIAN PRESS
PO Box 30, Achimota, Ghana, W. Africa by
Nuprint Ltd, 30b Station Road, Harpenden, Herts AL5 4SE, UK.

Contents

Preface vii

Introduction ix

1 Africa at the time of Christ 1
2 Christianity comes to Africa 5
3 The North African Church AD 200–500 9
4 The North African Church AD 500–700 17
5 The Nubian and Abyssinian Churches 21
6 The Challenge of Islam 25
7 The Churches of Nubia and Abyssinia 1000–1600 32
8 Our heritage from the early African Churches 38
9 Progress in Africa to 1500 43
African Church History Time-Line 100–1950 55
10 Portuguese Missionary Activity 1450–1750 59
11 The 18th Century – A time of little Christian progress 70
12 Ending the slave trade 75
13 Renewed missionary activity 80
14 Expansion in South Africa 85
15 Slow progress in West Africa 89
16 Sierra Leone. Base for outreach 95
17 Samuel Crowther. West Africa's great church pioneer 99
18 Other West African areas 1840–1878 107
19 David Livingstone and the thrust from the south 111
20 New beginnings in East Africa 122
21 West-Central Africa 1840–1878 132
22 The scramble for Africa 136

23 The gospel begins to spread out in West Africa 147
24 Expansion of Christianity in West-Central Africa 1878–1914 162
25 Continued growth in Southern Africa: 1878–1914 172
26 1878–1914: A period of rapid church growth in Africa 181
27 Evaluation of the period 1878–1914 193
28 West Africa 1914–1960: Movement toward full church autonomy 199
29 West-Central Africa – Moving forward 1914–1960 211
30 South Africa 1914–1960: More church autonomy 219
31 East Africa 1914–1960: Development of the autonomous church 226
32 1960–1975. The first years of political independence 242
33 The position of the Church in Africa in 1990 247

Bibliography 267

Index 269

Preface

This book has been written to provide a basic outline of the history of the Church in the different parts of Africa. What is found in this volume is not very detailed or comprehensive, but rather only a record of the important highlights of African church history, with an emphasis on the expansion of Christianity on the African continent.

The book contains references to numerous sources where the reader may find more complete information on selected topics if more details are desired. At the end of the book is a bibliography containing additional works on the subject of Christianity in Africa.

Introduction

A man does not have to talk to many people today before he finds a common belief that Christianity is a rather recent arrival on the African continent. This assumption is usually based upon the observation that most of the denominations or local churches in Africa are less than one hundred years old. Such an assumption would seem to be justified by almost any random sampling that one might wish to make. For example, think of the churches in the area surrounding you right now: how long has each one been established? In all probability the answer is: 'less than a hundred years'.

An individual should be careful not to let such limited research lead him to the wrong conclusion. It should be remembered that Christianity has seen enormous growth in the last century. Whereas Christians in Africa in 1875 could be counted in their tens of thousands, today those Africans who testify that they are Christians are numbered in their millions. Naturally, most of the denominations and churches to care for these greatly increased numbers have been established only recently.

What, then, is the truth concerning the origin of Christianity in Africa? If there were indeed churches in Africa before 1875, where were they and when did they begin? This book has been written to answer these and other related questions. In order to give the full story, this volume starts its narrative at the time when the Church was established in Africa in the first century AD. From there it traces the development of the major movements of the Christian faith on this continent. Naturally, it would be valuable to give great detail to this coverage, but since this book is just a survey, only the highlights of nineteen centuries can be mentioned within these covers.

Some historians like to think of African church history as containing a series of disconnected incidents in history. In preparing this book I have chosen instead to emphasize more of the continuity of the development of the African Church. A good way to demonstrate this idea is for you to consider a tree. I like to think of the African Church as being like a mighty tree with many limbs and branches . The roots of the tree are grounded in Jesus Christ, who is the foundation of the Church. Above the roots is the trunk which represents the heroic first five centuries of the Church. From that main trunk spring boughs that represent the different geographical areas of Africa. These limbs in turn produce branches which represent the various new churches of Africa. Does this mean that the new churches sprang directly from the early African Church? No, there is no direct connection, but there is a relationship which in the past has often been overlooked.

During the first five centuries many African Christians suffered great persecution, yet they remained firm in their Christian faith. At the same time forms of worship, church organisation and hymns were developed in Africa which have influenced the Church throughout the centuries. During this same period great African Church leaders such as Tertullian, Cyprian and Augustine contributed theological concepts and interpretations which were eventually adopted by the global Christian Church. It is the heritage of this North African Church which has provided guidance for the new churches in Africa. As members of the invisible Church of Christ, all true Christians in Africa today share a special fellowship with those African Christians who have lived in the previous nineteen centuries.

It is hoped that this volume will give Christians in modern Africa a new appreciation for their faith as they look over the many centuries that the Church has been at work in this great continent. A study of this book should demonstrate that Christianity is not a recent arrival in Africa, nor some sort of imported religion from Europe. Rather, it is a dynamic world-wide faith that has been a part of Africa for nineteen long centuries.

Let us proceed now with the unfolding of this most interesting narrative by setting the stage for the first Christian witness in Africa.

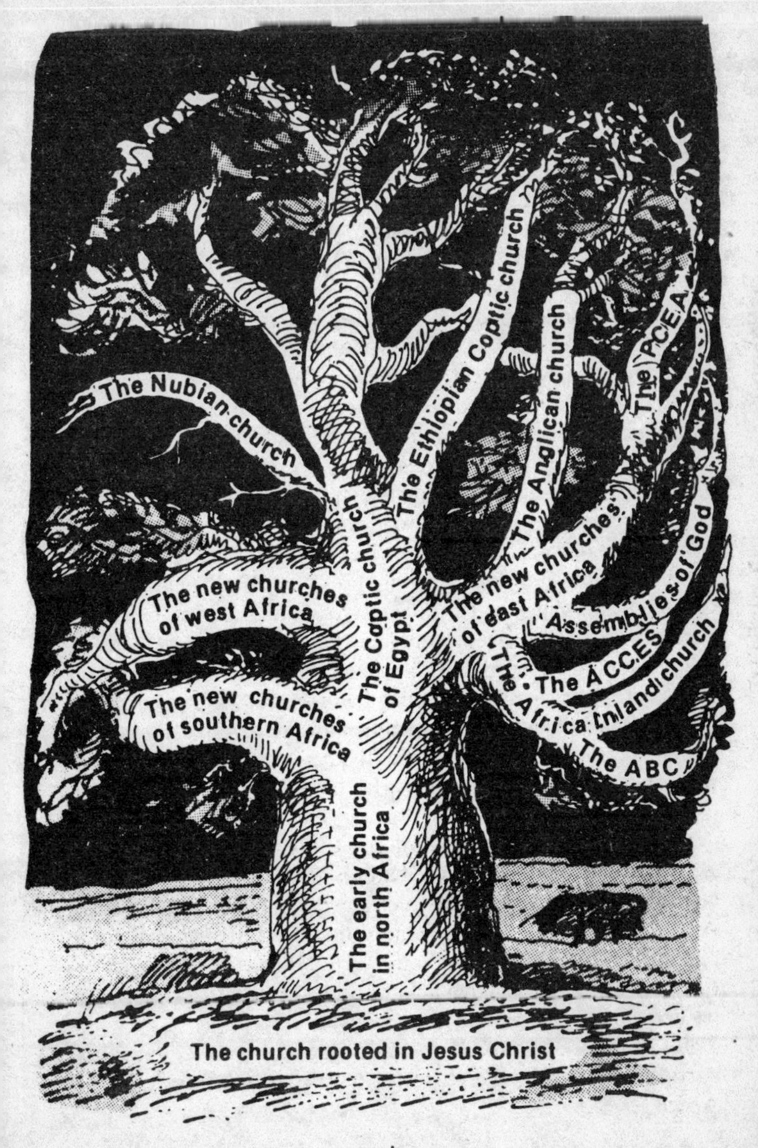
The Nubian church
The Coptic church of Egypt
The Ethiopian Coptic church
The Anglican church
The PCEA
The new churches of west Africa
The new churches of east Africa
Assemblies of God
The ACCES
The Africa Inland church
The ABC
The new churches of southern Africa
The early church in north Africa
The church rooted in Jesus Christ

1

Africa at the time of Christ

Before we can begin to study the birth and early development of the Church in Africa, we have to know something about Africa in the first century AD. Today there are more than 45 countries in Africa. Some are kingdoms, some republics and other federations. There are many different tribes and peoples in Africa, too. But what about the first century AD? Did the Empire of Ghana exist then? Were there Arabs living in Kenya? Were there organized governments in North Africa?

Africa at the time of Christ was filled with many different nations which were at various levels of development. Starting in the northeast corner of Africa, there was Egypt. Egypt had been an important nation for more than two thousand years at the time of Christ. But it was no longer an independent kingdom: it was part of the Roman Empire. The Egyptians were good farmers and had a highly developed form of irrigation for their land. The country was very important as a centre of learning and the library at Alexandria was famous throughout the world.

To the west of Egypt and along the coast of the Mediterranean Sea were other nations that were also colonies of Rome. Right next to Egypt was Cyrenaica, the country from which Simon, who is mentioned in Matthew 27:32, came. Cyrenaica, like Egypt, had been very much influenced by the Greek culture from 300 BC to the time of Christ. If you look at a modern map you will find that today we shall call Cyrenaica: Libya.

Moving further west you will find the Roman province of 'Africa'. About one hundred and fifty years before Christ, this area was called Carthage. Carthage was one of the most wealthy and powerful kingdoms of that time. However, the Romans

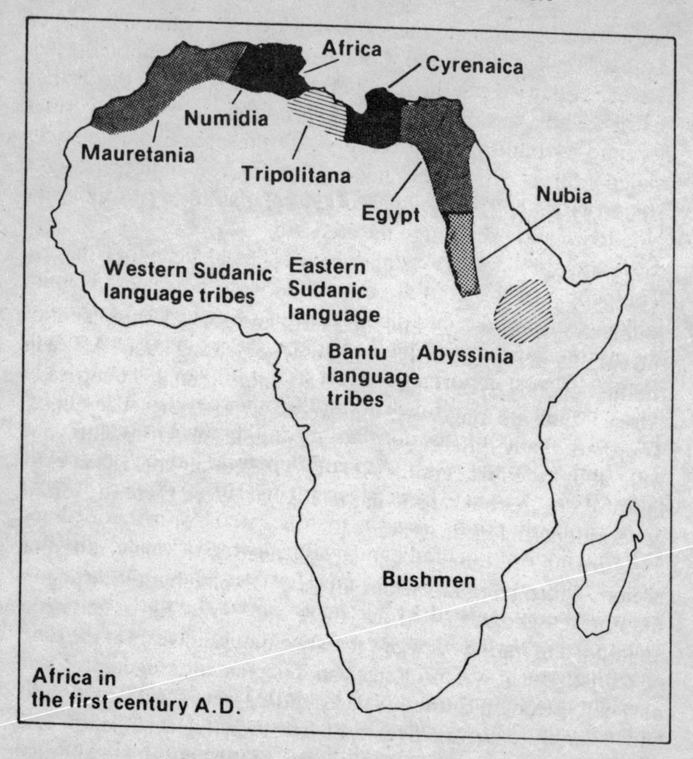

Africa in the first century A.D.

defeated it, and completely destroyed the capital city of Carthage so that it would not give them any more trouble. The farm lands of this area were very fertile, and so the Romans renamed the area 'Africa' and encouraged the Berbers of the area to settle down and start farming. Today we call this region: Tunisia.

To the west of 'Africa' was the Roman province of Numidia. This was also an area of fertile farm lands. The people in these areas were greatly influenced by the Romans. Today this area would fall in the eastern half of modern Algeria. The rest of the land westwards to the Atlantic Ocean was called: Mauritania.

But the provinces of North Africa were not the only nations in Africa at the time of Christ. There were two very large and important kingdoms to the south that we know quite a bit about. One was called Nubia and was located south of Egypt on the Nile River. Today we call the region: Sudan. Long before the birth of Christ, Nubia was the greatest gold producing area in the world of its time. Around the first century AD this area had a great city called Meroe, which was famous for its iron industry. Meroe traded with many parts of the world through trade routes along the Nile River and overland to the Red Sea.

Nearby there was Abyssinia which is the old name for Ethiopia. The people of this land are associated with the ancient Hamitic language group. Around the first century AD the city of Axum in the northern Ethiopian highlands became an important trading centre. Its most important product for export was ivory.

We do not know as much about the other parts of Africa at the time of Christ. But this does not mean there were no nations or governments in the rest of Africa. There were indeed nations and they, of course, had to have governments. However, these nations were probably not as large as the ones we have mentioned and they did not leave behind as many things which archaeologists can use to find out more about them. However, each year more and more is being learned by historians about the early history of Africa. Eventually it may be possible to get more specific information.

Right now our information is based on facts gained by the study of languages and language patterns. From these facts it is believed that there was a large concentration of people around Lake Chad at the time of Christ. These people were Negro by race and spoke what is called an 'Eastern Sudanic language'. Around the time of Christ these people had learned metal working and were also settled farmers.

In the rain forests of West Africa, bordering on the arid areas of the north were other tribes of Negro people whose language was a little different from the people around Lake Chad. We say that these people spoke 'Western Sudanic languages'. There were probably many different tribes of these people at that time.

Then to the south, in the Congo forests there was another language group, called the Bantu. Historians are not agreed as to whether this group originated in the northern Congo forests or the southern Congo forests, but for our study we can say that it was the general area of modern Zaire. At the time of Christ, these Bantu speaking Africans were quite concentrated in the forest. Some time after the first century they began a most interesting migration. They pushed east and south until by the 18th century they were the dominant peoples of East, Central and Southern Africa. We will learn a little more about their migrations later. These Bantu speaking Africans were not nomads, but settled farmers who knew how to raise different crops.

Finally the last identifiable group in Africa would be the bushmen or primitive people. They were few and quite isolated. Some lived in eastern Congo basin and some in what is now Zimbabwe (Rhodesia) and northern South Africa. These people generally had not learned farming and so were just hunters and gatherers. They were later chased into dry or mountain areas by the advancing Bantu speaking Africans.

Questions

1. Name the Roman provinces of Northern Africa at the time of Christ.
2. For what things was Nubia famous in the first century AD?
3. What city was famous for trade in Abyssinia?
4. In what geographical area were the people who spoke an Eastern Sudanic language found at the time of Christ?
5. In what general area did the early Bantu tribes live at the time of Christ?

2

Christianity comes to Africa

If we can say that the Church of Jesus Christ began its ministry of evangelism and development on the Day of Pentecost in AD 30, then it was shortly thereafter that the Gospel came to Africa.

Before His ascension, Christ said: 'But you shall receive power when the Holy Spirit has come upon you; and you shall be my witnesses in Jerusalem and in all Judea and in Samaria and to the end of the earth' (Acts 1:8). The disciples followed this instruction and waited until the Day of Pentecost when the Holy Spirit was sent and then they began to witness in Jerusalem. It is interesting to note that after Jerusalem they followed the Lord's instruction and went to Judea and then to Samaria. Following their witness in these areas the Lord had instructed them to take the Gospel to the whole world. Now it is good to note in the book of Acts that the next place that this witness went in the world was not to Europe or the rest of Asia. No, God wanted the Gospel to go next to Africa, and so He arranged for Philip to witness to an African.

> But an angel of the Lord said to Philip, 'Rise and go toward the south to the road that goes down from Jerusalem to Gaza.' This is a desert road. And he rose and went. And behold, an Ethiopian, a eunuch, a minister of Candace the queen of the Ethiopians, in charge of all her treasure, had come to Jerusalem to worship and was returning; seated in his chariot, he was reading the prophet Isaiah. And the Spirit said to Philip, 'Go up and join this chariot.' So Philip ran to him, and heard him reading Isaiah the prophet, and asked, 'Do you understand what you are reading?' And he said, 'How can I, unless some one guides me?' And he invited Philip to come up and sit with

him. Now the passage of the scripture which he was reading was this:

'As a sheep led to the slaughter or a lamb before its shearer is dumb, so he opens not his mouth. In his humiliation justice was denied him. Who can describe his generation? For his life is taken up from the earth.'

And the eunuch said to Philip, 'About whom, pray, does the prophet say this, about himself or about someone else?' Then Philip opened his mouth, and beginning with this scripture he told him the good news of Jesus. And as they went along the road they came to some water, and the eunuch said, 'See, here is water! What is to prevent my being baptized?' And he commanded the chariot to stop, and they both went down into the water, Philip and the eunuch, and he baptized him (Acts 8:26–38).

So, here in the Bible we have a record of how God arranged for the Gospel to come to Africa. God knew that the Ethopian was an important government official and that he would be able to influence many people. After this man became a Christian he, no doubt, had many opportunities to witness for Jesus Christ.

After he was baptized the Ethiopian continued on to Africa. Although the Bible calls him an Ethiopian, it is generally agreed that he was a government official in Nubia. In the first century AD the name 'Ethiopia' did not apply to the country that has that title today.

The conversion of the 'Ethiopian' minister is the longest section in the New Testament that tells about Africa or an African and the Church. However, there are other places where Africa or people from Africa are mentioned. There are two rather important entries in Acts. In Acts 11:20 we are told that people from Cyrene were quite active in the leadership of the church in Antioch. And then later in Acts 18:24–28 we are told of Apollos of Alexandria who became a Christian while on a visit to Ephesus. This man from Africa in turn became a missionary to Europe by preaching the Good News of Jesus Christ to the people of Corinth.

Tradition says that the Church in Egypt was established by the evangelist John Mark. According to Coptic Orthodox Church

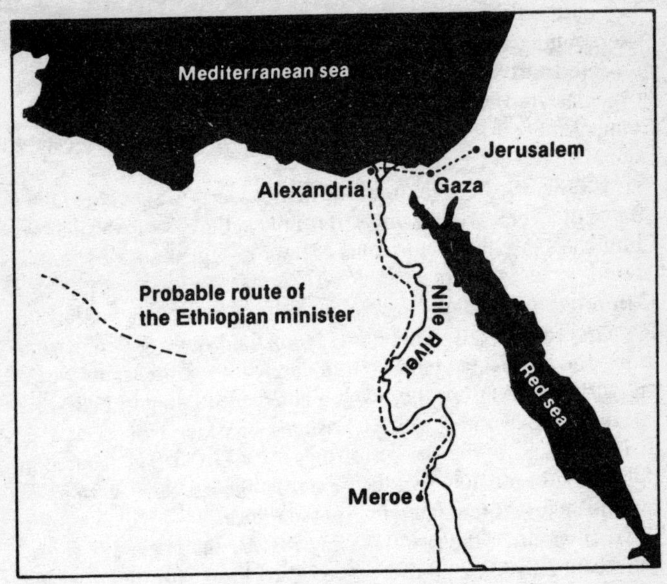

historians, after Paul and Barnabas had a disagreement about John Mark at the beginning of the second missionary journey, Barnabas and John Mark went to Cyprus to minister, after which Mark went on to Pentapolis, where he had been born, to preach. From there Mark came to Egypt and began his ministry in Alexandria. Coptic historians report that on his first day in Alexandria Mark witnessed to a shoemaker. The cobbler responded to the Gospel message and invited Mark to his house. There the entire household was saved and baptized. Anianus, the cobbler, and his family were the first converts of John Mark in Egypt and the beginning of the Egyptian Church.[1]

God blessed the witness of John Mark so that before long there were five churches in Egypt and Libya. Mark preached fearlessly against the evils of his day and the excesses of pagan religion, so that the religious and political leaders began to plot against him. On April 26, 68 AD Christians from Egypt and Libya gathered at the great Church of Baucalia in Alexandria to celebrate Easter. During the service the Roman Prefect incited some pagans to riot.

They entered the church and dragged Mark out into the streets. After pulling him through the streets with a rope, the people murdered him.[2] Although the founder of the Egyptian church had been martyred, the Church itself could not be killed so easily. Evangelism continued so that by AD 180 there was a well established Church in Egypt.

It is generally believed that the first converts in Egypt were the people of Greek origin who lived mainly in the city of Alexandria. Later the Gospel spread to the 'Copts' or Egyptians of Hamitic origin.

In addition to Egypt, the church made early progress in the Roman provinces of 'Africa' and Numidia. We do not know very much about the beginning of the Church in these areas, but we do know that by AD 180 there was a good sized group of believers. According to history, twelve Christians were killed for their belief in Jesus Christ at the city of Carthage in AD 180. The Church in this area suffered much persecution from the Roman government, but the believers remained firm in their faith.

To summarize then, we can say that by the beginning of the third century (AD 200) there were many local Christian churches in north Africa and Christianity was continuing to spread.

Questions

1. After the Gospel was taken to Samaria, to what part of the world did it go next?
2. According to Acts, who was the Ethiopian official?
3. Were there other people from Africa who played an important part in the early New Testament Church? If yes, give an example.
4. Tell something about the early Church in Egypt.
5. In what other parts of Africa were there churches that we know about before AD 200?

[1]Masri, Iris Habib, *The Story of the Copts*, (The Middle East Council of Churches, Cairo, 1978), p.14.
[2]Gregorius, Anba (Ed), *St. Mark and the Coptic Church*, (Coptic Orthodox Patriarchate, Cairo, 1968), p.19.

3

The North African Church AD 200–500

In Egypt the Church continued to grow from AD 200 to 300. This period of time saw a great increase in the number of Coptic Christians. Churches continued to grow. The local churches were organized into 'sees' or church districts and these were directed by a bishop. Around AD 300 there were more than 80 bishops in Egypt, so this would mean that there were very many local churches.

During this period of time there was persecution of the Christians by the Roman government. Sometimes many years would pass and Christians would be left alone. But then a new emperor would come to the throne and he would seek to stop the expansion of the Church by persecuting the Christians. Men who lived in the third and fourth centuries AD tell us that the Egyptian Christians set a fine record of faithfulness to Christ. The result of the persecutions was that Christians moved into other areas and began to preach the Gospel to people, so the Church actually grew larger.

During the second and third centuries there was a very important Christian school that developed at Alexandria. It was called the Catechetical School of Alexandria. The purpose of this school was to teach believers about Jesus Christ and at the same time explain the theology or beliefs of the Church. These are the same subjects that are taught at a Bible school or theological college. What is important for us to note is that this was the first such school in the world. Therefore, Africa gets the credit for having the first Bible institute or theological college in the history of the Church.

This catechetical school had many important teachers and principals. Around AD 180 a man by the name of Clement was the principal or head of the school. Clement is called a 'Church Father' since he was important in helping the Church grow during its early years. During the time that Clement was at the school, there were many people in Africa, Asia and Europe who were trying to confuse the true message of the Gospel. These men relied on earthly wisdom to find complete salvation. Clement spoke out strongly against these men and repeated the apostle Paul's words that 'the wisdom of the world is foolishness with God'. He encouraged Christians not to try to mix Greek philosophy with the Gospel message.

When Clement left the catechetical school, there was no one to lead the school. A young man who was only eighteen years old became the head of the school. This man's name was Origen. For twenty years (from around 200 to 220) he taught at Alexandria. Origen believed strongly that the Bible was the Word of God. He is important in the history of the Church because he was one of the earliest Christians to give the Church an orderly, complete statement of the Christian faith.

The Gospel also advanced in Cyrenaica and the Roman provinces to the west. In 'Africa' the Church continued to grow from AD 200 to 300. According to history, there were 70 bishops in the Church in the North African provinces around AD 220. By about AD 250 there were almost 150 bishops and by the end of the century (around AD 300) there were more than 250. It can be seen that the Church must have tripled its size during the third century.

There was an important Christian leader who lived at Carthage at the end of the second and beginning of the third century AD. His name was Tertullian. He was a brilliant lawyer before he was converted in 192. After becoming a Christian he wrote many papers and books defending the Christian faith. He was a brave man and was not afraid to attack the evils which he saw in the Roman government. He was the first Christian writer to use the term 'Trinity'. So we can trace the use of this word in our Church today to this early Christian in the African Church. In the middle of his life, Tertullian went away from the true teachings of Jesus Christ. Tertullian thought that by living a strict life (asceticism) he would be a better Christian. So he gave the rest of his life to living as a monk.

Another important church leader in Carthage was Cyprian, who became a Christian and was baptized in 246. Cyprian was a very wise man with great leadership ability. In 249 he was elected Bishop of Carthage. In 250 there was a great persecution of Christians by the Roman Emperor, and so Cyprian left Carthage and managed the affairs of the Church from a hiding place. When the persecution passed, Cyprian returned to Carthage and continued to work with the church leaders in settling such problems as what to do with Christians who renounce (give up) their faith in Jesus Christ during a persecution in order to avoid punishment and the matter of re-baptism. In 257 another persecution was started by the government and this time Cyprian was arrested and sentenced to death. He was beheaded in 258.

Cyprian has influenced our Church by his firm belief that the bishop of each national church should take care of the problems and business of his church without being told by church leaders in Rome what should be done. Cyprian said that the Bishop (or Pope) of Rome could not give orders to the bishops of any other national church.

In one area of Christian worship Cyprian departed from the usual practice of the early Church. Instead of viewing the communion service as a memorial of Christ's death. Cyprian called it a sacrifice. The Roman Catholic Church adopted this theological position of Cyprian's and still holds to it today.

In AD 303 there began the longest and most severe attempt by the Roman government to stamp out Christianity. The persecution lasted for three years in North Africa. The Church in Egypt, Carthage and the other provinces suffered very much during this time. Since the Church was larger in 303 than ever before, there were many nominal or weak Christians in the membership. When this time of testing came along many of these people renounced their faith in order to keep from being killed. After the persecution was over the leaders of the

Church had to decide how to treat such people who asked to join the Church again.

Shortly after this last persecution an event happened which greatly changed the history of the Church. In 312 the Emperor Constantine who was fighting a rival emperor for control of the Roman Empire, had a vision before a great battle. As a result of this vision Constantine became a Christian and ordered that Christians were no longer to be persecuted. In 321 Constantine made Sunday a holiday throughout his empire, so that Christians could worship God. He condemned pagan worship and encouraged people to become Christians.

The result of Constantine's conversion greatly affected the North African Church. A seeming good result was that Christians could live in peace without fear of persecution. They could also witness openly, build churches and live normal lives in their communities. However, there were some negative effects, too. When Constantine became a Christian and became favourable to Christianity many people decided it would be a good idea to pretend to be Christians in order to get special favours or attention from the government. From the time of Constantine the number of nominal or 'pretend' believers began to increase in the Church. This made it look like the Church was becoming larger, but in effect the Church was only becoming weaker. A second problem was that once the Roman Government became favourable to Christianity, people began to mix politics with religion. Thus when church leaders had an argument, instead of seeking God's guidance to settle the matter, they would ask the Emperor to help solve the problem. Another result of this peace with the government was that with no outsiders threatening them, church leaders began to fight more among themselves. This resulted in church splits and heresy.

In 319 the African Church was challenged by a new heresy. In church history this heresy is called Arianism because it was proposed by a priest from Alexandria named Arius. Arius' mistake centered around his understanding of the position of Jesus Christ. 'The Church had always believed in and worshipped Jesus Christ as God, who for man's salvation had

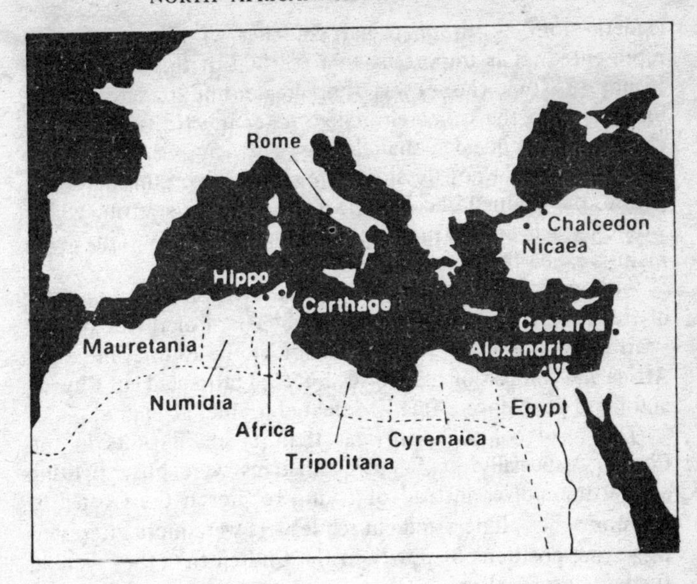

become man, but without in any way impairing his essential Godhead.'[1] Arius tried to use his human wisdom to understand the title 'Son of God'. 'He asked, "How can a son be as old as his father?" From the human impossibility of this, he proceeded to argue that the Son of God cannot be eternal.'[2] Thus Arius believed that Jesus Christ was made from nothing before the creation of the world, and that He was not the Son of God, just a very important 'being'. The leaders of the Church in Egypt recognized immediately that this teaching of Arius was wrong because if Christ is not the Son of God, He cannot make atonement for sinful man and perfectly reconcile God and man.

Arius and his followers were put out of the Church in 319. However, these people went to Caesarca and continued to preach their wrong teachings. Soon this heresy began to affect the entire Church and cause splits and quarrels almost everywhere. In 325 Emperor Constantine called all the Church leaders to a Church Council at Nicaea. At this council the leaders from all the national churches in the world were represented. It is important to note that at this meeting the Bishop of Rome (Pope) was of no greater importance than the bishops from the other churches. After much discussion the church leaders decided that the views of Arius were wrong. So that there would not be any more confusion on this matter in future, the Council decided to write a creed or doctrine which would explain Jesus Christ's position in the Trinity. This document is called the Nicaean Creed.

Although the Council condemned Arianism, the followers of this heresy did not give up their beliefs. For the next fifty years they attempted to get control of the Church in North Africa and the rest of the world. But God protected His Church and these people were finally defeated in their attempts.

The result of Arianism was that it caused splits in the Church, especially in Egypt. Christians were busy fighting among themselves instead of trying to preach the Gospel to the unreached. Elders and church leaders were more interested in getting positions of power in the Church than they were in furthering evangelism.

At about the same time that the Arian heresy grew up in Egypt, there was a Church split developing in 'Africa'. To begin with there was a competition (power-struggle) between two men for leadership of the Church in Carthage. Then the Church split into two groups: the Donatists and the true or universal Church. The Donatists taught that the Church could only exist where there was complete holiness. They also said that they, not God, would decide what was true holiness. The argument between the two sides became so great that the Emperor. Constantine made a law saying that the Donatists had to stop their preaching. However, in 362 the Donatists were allowed to continue their work again. It was not until 411 that the Donatists were finally subdued.

One of the important church leaders who helped to end the challenge of the Donatists was Augustine. He became a Christian in 387 after a period of searching for inner peace. Although he was converted in Italy, he returned to his home in 'Africa' to work as a church leader. In 395 he was elected Bishop of

Hippo. 'He was great as a preacher, as a ruler, and as a theologian; a restorer of the schism-torn African Church, and a defender of the faith against heresy.'[3] Augustine had a great mind and was able to write powerful arguments for Christian theology. 'No other Christian after Paul was to have so wide, deep and prolonged an influence upon the Christianity of Western Europe and those forms of faith that stemmed from it as had Augustine.'[4] So we see that Augustine, the Bishop from Africa, made a very great contribution to the theology and worship of the Church of Europe. More than a thousand years after the death of Augustine, missionaries from the churches of Europe brought back to Africa the contributions of Augustine. Our Church in Africa today is deeply indebted to this African Church Father of sixteen centuries ago. 'Augustine worthily completes the great trio of African saints; more humble than Tertullian, more profound than Cyprian, he combines the excellences of both.'[5]

Augustine died just as a new assault faced the Church of Africa. In 410 a group of barbarian Europeans, called the Vandals, captured the city of Rome. Then they moved through Spain and settled in Numidia. These Vandals accepted Arianism as their religion and so expelled the priests of the Christian churches in their area. In 430 they captured the city of Hippo. The Vandals remained in North Africa until the end of the century. During this time the Church in North Africa remained weak and divided.

Before the end of the fifth century the Church of Egypt was attacked by another heresy. This heresy was called Monophysitism and started shortly after 451. In 451 the world-wide Church held a council at Chalcedon to consider new questions confronting the Church. Once again a key question was put forward concerning Jesus Christ. Some bishops from Egypt believed that Jesus Christ had only one 'nature', that is, He was only God, and was never human. The view of the true Church is that Jesus Christ has two natures. This was expressed in the Chalcedon Creed which says in part: '. . . there is to be confessed one and the same Son, our Lord Jesus Christ, perfect in Godhead and perfect in manhood, truly God and truly man, . . .'[6] The bishops from Egypt (except for a few from the city of Alexandria) refused to sign the new creed. When these men returned to Egypt they split their church from the world-wide Church because they did not hold the same view of Jesus Christ. The result was the establishment of a new church which today is called the Coptic Church of Egypt. We will shortly study more about this Church in the sixth and seventh centuries.

By the end of the fifth century (499) the Church of North Africa was in a weaker position than at the beginning of the century. In Numidia there were the Vandals who supported the Arian heresy and in Egypt there were the Copts who supported the Monophysite heresy, while in other places people still supported the true Church. The Church had lost its original zeal to win souls and so the number of Christians did not seem to be increasing. It is wise to remember that the North African Church was not the only church that seemed to be 'backsliding'; the churches of Europe and Asia were also about to enter a period of ignorant and 'carnal Christianity'.

Questions:

1. Who were the three men who were called the 'trio of African saints' of the North African Church?
2. Briefly tell two important contributions to the Church by each of these three men.
3. What was the Catechetical School of Alexandria?
4. What was Arianism?
5. What church believes the doctrine of Monophysitism?

[1]Whitham, A.R., *The History of the Christian Church* (Rivingtons, London, 1968), p. 184
[2]Ibid. p. 185
[3]Ibid. p. 259
[4]Latourette, K.A., *A History of Christianity* (Harpers, New York, 1953), p. 97
[5]Whitham, A.R., *The History* . . . , p. 267
[6]Latourette, K.S., *A History* . . . , p. 171

4

The North African Church AD 500–700

The period from AD 500 to 700 was a time of persecution for the Coptic Church in Egypt. As you remember from the last chapter, the bishops from the churches of Egypt (not including the bishops of Alexandria) refused to sign the Chalcedon Creed concerning the two natures of Jesus Christ. Because of this theological difference the bishops formed a new church which is called the Coptic Church of Egypt. The Egyptian bishops had another reason for establishing the Coptic Church: they wanted an independent church which was not controlled by the Bishop of Constantinople; they wanted to manage their own church affairs.

In the way of review, it is good to remember that at the same time that the Coptic Church was separating itself from world Christianity, the churches of Europe and Asia were also beginning to divide. The two major churches were called: the Catholic (or Western) Church in Europe for which the Bishop of Rome wanted to be the leader, and the Byzantine (or Eastern) Church of Asia for which the Bishop of Constantinople wanted to speak. The Western Church and the Eastern Church did not always agree on all points of theology during the sixth century but they did not officially 'split' until later.

The Coptic Church might have rejoined the Eastern Church during the sixth century, except that a very knowledgeable man took up the leadership of those Christians who supported Monophysitism. He was a monk by the name of Jacobus. He was consecrated a bishop in about 541. 'By his extraordinary missionary zeal and untiring labours, he reorganized and strengthened the Monophysite remnant, ordaining a vast num-

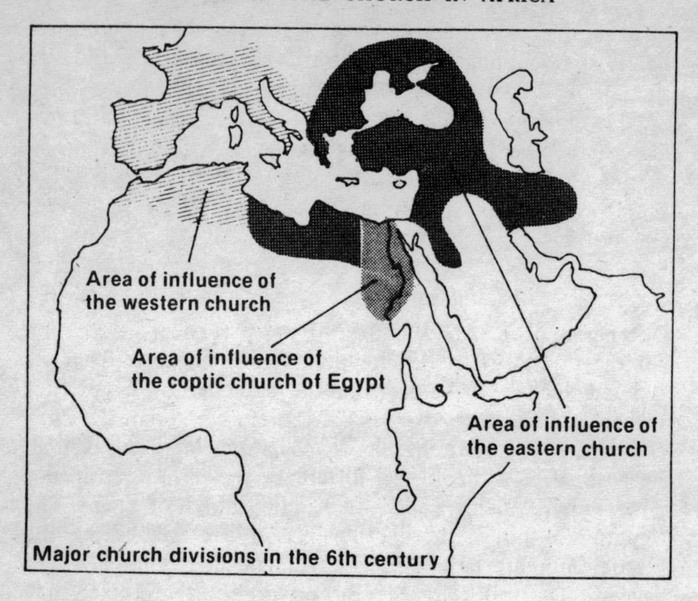

Major church divisions in the 6th century

ber of bishops and clergy, and building up a wide-spread communion. From him the Monophysites gained their later names of Jacobites.'[1] It was through the leadership and encouragement of Jacobus that the Coptic Church was able to remain separate from the Eastern Church.

During the sixth century the Coptic Church developed its theology and religious writings. An important part of the Coptic Church was the life of monasticism, i.e. becoming monks or nuns and living in monasteries away from cities and towns. Large numbers of Copts continued to join these monasteries and live simple lives of prayer and work.

During the sixth century the Coptic Church was not one united, strong national church. It was badly divided, with many sects or split-off churches. 'Towards the end of the sixth century there were said to be twenty Monophysite sects in Egypt alone. One form was tritheism, which held that in the Trinity there are really three Gods, each with a substance and a nature different from the others.'[2] This shows that the small heresy of Monophysitism that took over the Coptic Church, soon brought about even worse heresies such as tritheism.

The Emperor of the Byzantine Empire, Justinian, did not like to see the Coptic Church leaving the Eastern Church. Justinian wanted just one true or 'orthodox' church in the Empire. Therefore, in the mid-sixth century he had his government officials persecute the members of the Coptic Church. People who were followers of the Coptic Church lost their government jobs and sometimes people were even killed just because they were Coptic Christians. The persecution did not defeat the Coptic Church though; instead it strengthened it and made the Egyptians less willing to rejoin the Eastern Church.

In the seventh century (600 to 699) the Coptic Church continued to grow for a time, but before the middle of this century Muslims had invaded Egypt. At first the Arabs were kinder to the Coptic Church than the Byzantine Emperor had been. But soon taxes and indirect pressure were applied to Christians to make them convert to Islam. By the end of the century (699) the size of the Coptic Church had already begun to shrink. We will study more about the invasion of Egypt by the Muslim Arabs in chapter six.

Let us now briefly look at the Church in 'Africa'. As you remember, at the end of the fifth century that Church was badly divided by such heresies as Donatism and Arianism. But beginning in the sixth century the Eastern Church made fresh attempts to defeat these wrong beliefs. These efforts were somewhat successful. 'The re-conquest of North Africa was followed not only by the strengthening of the Catholic Church against the Arians and Donatists who flourished in that region under the Vandals. It also led to the conversion of some of the pagan Berbers, a process which continued after the death of Justinian.'[3] Thus orthodox or true Christianity was brought back into the churches of 'Africa' and Numidia.

Although the Church remained in this area until the end of the seventh century, it did not seem to become a deep part of the lives of the people. When the Muslim conquerors arrived in 697 it was only a short time before the local people gave up their Christianity for Islam. Perhaps the speed with which the people gave up their faith would indicate that they never really understood their beliefs and were not truly committed Christians.

To summarize this period of history of the Church, we can say that it was the growing period for the Coptic Church of Egypt. When the Muslims came to Eygpt, this church continued to live, but it was never as powerful as it was in the time just prior to 639. The Coptic Church still exists in Egypt today, but its followers continue to believe the heresy of Monophysitism.

In the rest of North Africa during this period there was a small revival and return to true Christian teachings. However, Christianity never seemed to become a complete part of the lives of the people, so that when the Muslims came the church was eventually defeated.

Questions:

1. Why was the Coptic Church formed in Egypt?
2. Who was Jacobus and what did he do?
3. Was the Coptic Church one unified church or were there many splits?
4. What happened to the church in 'Africa' and Numidia in the early sixth century?

[1]Whitham, A.R., *The History of the Christian Church* (Rivingtons, London, 1968), p. 321
[2]Latourette, K.S., *A History of Christianity* (Harpers, New York, 1953, p. 283
[3]Ibid. pp. 283, 284

5

The Nubian and Abyssianian Churches

In chapter two we studied the conversion of the Ethiopian minister as recorded in Acts chapter eight. It would seem that this minister returned to Nubia and witnessed to those around him. Information about the growth of the Nubian Church from AD 30 to 500 is lacking, though. About all we do know is that Origen of Egypt, who lived from 185 to 253, mentions in one of his books that the Gospel was being preached to the 'Ethiopians' but not all of them had been reached at that time. So it is not until the sixth century that we hear of intense missionary activity in Nubia.

In Abyssinia the Gospel message arrived in the fourth century. According to history, a young man by the name of Frumentius went on a journey from Tyre to India. On the return trip from India he was travelling with two of his friends on a ship in the Red Sea. The ship happened to stop at a harbour on the Abyssinian coast. As it turned out the local people were unfriendly. They made Frumentius and one of his friends slaves and killed the other friend. Frumentius was taken to the king of Axum, who made Frumentius his private secretary. As a good Christian, Frumentius worked faithfully and hard at his task. The king was very pleased with this attitude and so gave Frumentius his freedom. As a freeman, Frumentius remained at Axum and worked for the king. He also banded together with a group of traders who were Christians to start a church. After many years of service Frumentius went to Alexandria to ask the church there for a pastor. 'It was agreed that no more suitable appointment than that of Frumentius himself could be made; he was consecrated bishop,

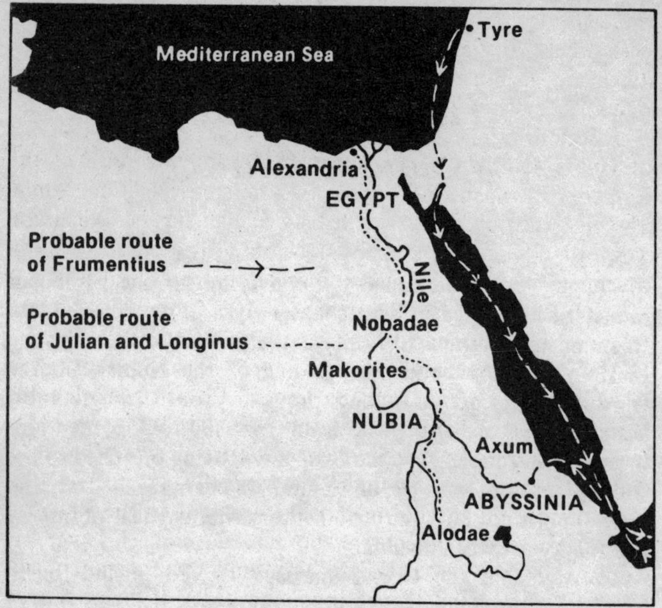

and returning to the kingdom saw many converted to the faith.'[1] According to history, Frumentius was a bishop in Axum in AD 356. He worked hard among the people of Axum and even won the King of Axum to Christ. Christianity then became the official faith of the kingdom. Later a large church was built in Axum.

Towards the end of the fifth century (around 480 or so) it is said that nine missionaries came from the Syrian Church. These people were probably followers of the Monophysite heresy. They worked among the church members of Abyssinia and taught the believers their views about the 'one nature' of Christ. Thus, from around AD 500 onwards the Church of Abyssinia was a Monophysite Church. Even today the Coptic Church of Ethiopia continues to follow the teachings of the Monophysite tradition.

Some time during the sixth century the Bible was translated into the Ge'ez language used by the people of Axum. Thus in the centuries to come when the Muslims made communication with other Christian churches difficult, the Church of Abyssinia did have the Bible in the language of the people to use for reference and study.

Also, during the sixth century the work among the people of Nubia took on a new urgency. During the reign of the Emperor Justinian (527–565), two missions went to Nubia. The first mission party was led by a man named Julian and went to Nobadae in northern Nubia.[2] They were warmly welcomed by the king and nobles of that area. Julian was a Monophysite, and so the many converts he won became followers of Monophysitism.

Shortly after Julian's visit another missionary group arrived in Nubia. They were from the Eastern Church and were not Monophysites. Julian had told the Nobadae not to welcome these other missionaries, so these new arrivals were forced to go further south to work among the Makorites.

In about 568 another missionary was sent to the Nobadae from Alexandria to encourage the first converts. This man was named Longinus. 'He is said to have built them a church, and ordained clergy, and taught them the order of divine service and all the ordinances of Christianity.'[3] Many people were added to the church in Nobadae.

Further south, the people who were called the Alodaei heard of the new church and asked for missionaries to come to them. So Longinus went to them and the message was well received so that many were converted in that place. 'Of the further personal activities of Longinus, how long he stayed in Nubia and whether he ever left, we do not know. Christianity in Nubia, however, struck root and flourished. Christian kingdoms resisted the encroachments of Islam for eight centuries, and in places for nearly a thousand years.'[4]

This brings to a close our brief study of the Church in this area. In this chapter we have seen how the churches in Nubia and Abyssinia were established and developed. Later on we will look again at this area and see how the churches continued. The period from 700 to 1300 is a silent time for the Church in this area and not very much is known about the history.

Questions:

1. Briefly tell about Frumentius and his contribution to the Church in Abyssinia.
2. Why was the Church in Abyssinia a Monophysite Church after the sixth century?
3. Who were the people of Nobadae? Who brought them the Christian message?
4. Tell about the work of Longinus.

[1]Groves, C.P., *The Planting of Christianity in Africa* vol. 1 (Lutterworth Press, London, 1948), p. 52
[2]Ibid. p. 49
[3]Ibid. p. 50
[4]Ibid. p. 51

6

The Challenge of Islam

In chapter three we saw how the history of the Church in both Africa and Europe was changed by the vision of Constantine in 312. From that time the development and growth of the Church was not as difficult as before. In this chapter we are going to study another event that is also of major importance to the history of the Church in Africa: the beginning of Islam.

Islam was founded by a man called Muhammad. Not much is known about the early life of this man. He was born around 570 in Mecca in Arabia. The only other facts we can be fairly certain of are '. . . that he belonged to a respected but not wealthy family, that he lost his father early in life, and grew up in a poor home, but that he later gained economic independence through his marriage.'[1] When he was a young man he made his living as a camel driver. In his travels he met people of different religious beliefs. Muhammad was honestly searching for truth and the true way of salvation. There were no Christian churches around Mecca or the central part of Arabia so that Muhammad probably never heard a clear Gospel witness.[2] Instead, the only thing Muhammad knew about Christianity were the people he met in his travels who called themselves Christians. Unfortunately these men did not give a very good witness, since they were probably Christians in name only, and so Muhammad was pushed away from Christianity rather than drawn to it. The one thing that really concerned Muhammad, though, was the idolatry of the Arabs who lived around him. Muhammad soon became convinced that this worship of many gods was wrong.

'In his fortieth year he began to have revelations, to see

visions and receive, as he believed, the inspiration of a prophet. He felt himself called to be a teacher of monotheism and a foe of idolatry in every shape.'[3] Muhammad began to preach against the idolatry of Mecca and urge the people to worship the only God, Allah. He gained a few converts in Mecca, but these were mainly the poor people of the city. The pagan priests of Mecca began to stir up the people against Muhammad, so that in 622 Muhammad was forced to flee to Medina in order to find safety. This trip is very important in the religious calendar of the Muslims and is called the Hegira or flight of the prophet.

In Medina Muhammad made greater progress and soon built up a large number of converts to his religion. At the same time Muhammad became a powerful political ruler. As he gained power, he came to see that his new religion could be a worldwide religion if it were strong and powerful. 'He began to preach the new faith in a definite and authoritative form and to claim for it an absolute and universal acceptance. He marshalled his followers as a religious army, whose mission was to convert or subdue the world . . . '[4] Not many years passed until Muhammad had enough followers and a strong enough army to return to Mecca and defeat the pagan leaders of the city and claim it as the holy city of Islam. Muhammad died in 632 before Islam really began to spread out and conquer. However, by 632 Muhammad had finished writing the Qur'an and had deeply influenced his followers so that they really believed that he was God's special messenger and that they must follow his instructions.

'Few single sentences can have had a greater impact on world history than the message preached by Muhammad to the Arab tribes between AD 622 and 632, the message which became the foundation of the Muslim creed – *la ilaha illallah muhammadun rasulullah:* "there is no god but God; Muhammad is the Messenger of God". In the doctrine of the one God and the paramouncy on earth of his Messenger, the Arabs found a brotherhood to transcend the divisions and conflicts among their tribes; . . . '[5] In the years after 632 the Arabs were to go forth from Arabia in a fanatical belief that they had to destroy all forms of idolatry and false religion. Not only did the conquest of these Arab armies affect the history of the world as mentioned above, it brought a great change to the Church in Africa.

Before we look at the invasion of Africa by the Muslims, it is important that we note the attitude or feelings of Muslims towards Christians at the beginning of the great conquest. Generally, at this early stage of Islam, the Muslims were not anti-Christian. Although the early Muslims were very severe with pagans, this does not mean they also persecuted Christians with the sword. It seems that Muhammad had taught his followers that Christians were 'People of the Book', which meant that Christians had the Bible and worshipped only one God. However, if the Muslims met Christians who wanted to keep their own government and politics (such as the Byzantines) the Arabs fought them until they could be pushed out of the land.

It was in 639 that Africa was first invaded by Arab armies. In that year 'Amr ibn al-'As brought an army of only a few thousand men to Egypt. By this time the Arabs had defeated the Byzantines in Syria, Mesopotamia and Persia. 'Amr found it relatively easy to defeat the Byzantines in Egypt, because the majority of the population, the Copts, did not like the rulers from Constantinople. We must remember that the Byzantine rulers of Egypt did not want the Copts to have a separate Coptic Church, and so there had been persecution of the Coptic Christians. Thus when the Arabs arrived, the Copts decided that they could not be any worse than the Byzantines. 'Once the main Byzantine army in Egypt had been defeated (640), 'Amr was able to conclude a treaty with the Copts, who agreed to pay regular taxes to the newcomers in return for freedom to practise their Christian religion, and protection for their goods, lands and water rights.'[6] In 641 the Byzantines left Alexandria and so all of Egypt was left to the Arabs to rule.

It did not take the Arabs long to conquer Cyrenaica, but from there to Carthage their progress was slowed. This was because there was five hundred miles of waterless desert

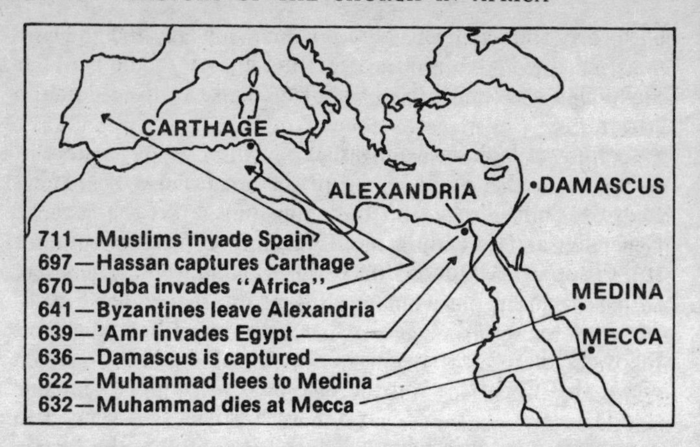

between Cyrenaica and 'Africa'. It was not until 670 that an invasion of 'Africa' was attempted. 'By the end of the century, however, both the sedentary tribes and the Byzantine armies had been overcome . . . Carthage was captured, and the new Arab city of Tunis began to rise in its place.'[7] At first the Berber Christians of the area were hostile to the Arab conquerors, but the new Arab leaders began to persuade them to become Muslims. 'The Berber tribes were now won over more and more to alliance and friendship and Islam.'[8]

By 710 the Arabs had completed their conquest of North Africa. All the land from Egypt to Morocco and the Atlantic Ocean was under their control. It is now time for us to see how this Muslim government brought about the decline of the North African Church.

Although the Muslims were tolerant of the Christians when they first conquered Egypt, after they had settled down they began to put pressure on the Christian population. Soon the Covenant of Omar appeared which placed restrictions on Christians. These restrictions included '. . . payment of tribute, hospitality to Muslims, prohibition of erection of new churches or monasteries, avoidance of all advertisement or display of Christian practice (no cross, for example, to be shown publicly), . . .'[9] As the years went by these restrictions were enforced more and more heavily.

The one pressure which seems to have influenced most weak Coptic Christians to convert to Islam was the poll-tax. If a Copt became a Muslim he did not have to pay the poll-tax any more. By 717 so many Egyptians were becoming Muslims in order to keep from paying taxes that the government could not get enough money to support itself. So around 718 Caliph Omar II said that from that time on if anyone became a Muslim he would no longer be free from the poll-tax. This resulted in fewer people wishing to become Muslims. But, 'The governor of Egypt in 744 . . . promised exemption (from the poll-tax) again to all converts, and 24,000 Christians are said to have come over in response.'[10]

By 1000 the Coptic Church was rather small compared with the number of Muslims in Egypt. How could such a large organization be reduced to such a small body? Here are some reasons: 1) The Coptic Church although large in 639, was weakened by internal fights and jealousies; 2) the freedom from paying the poll-tax was an effective temptation to weak church members to convert; 3) if a man wanted to be a government official, it was wise for him to become a Muslim; and 4) if a man wanted to marry a Muslim wife, he had to convert to Islam, because no inter-marriage was allowed. Nevertheless, in spite of these pressures the Coptic Church did not die, but continued, and today it is still in existence in Egypt.

The Church in Carthage and the areas around that city was not as successful, though. It seems that whereas the Coptic Church was a church made up of not only the people in the cities but also the people in the rural areas, in 'Africa' most of the churches were concentrated near the coast and in the urban areas. In particular, the Church of North Africa had failed completely to evangelize the Berber tribes of the interior. Only a few efforts had been made to reach these people, so the majority of these people remained pagan. When the Arabs conquered Carthage and the area of the coast, many Christians ran away and became refugees in other countries. This seriously weakened the Church. The part of the Christian population which was left did not have good leadership, and their number was not very great because the large population of Berbers had never been brought to Christ.

Then, too, the North African Church had been seriously weakened before the coming of the Arabs by different heresies and internal rivalries. People in the local churches were often confused and not sure what was the right thing to believe. In the face of this confusion the Arabs offered a straight-forward religion.

The Church in North Africa decreased quite rapidly. In 700 there were abourt thirty or forty bishops in the area. By the mid-eleventh century (1050) there were only six bishops left. And by 1300 there was only one bishop left. The last Christian villages in North Africa seem to have disappeared in the fifteenth century. 'And so the sad fact confronts us that North Africa is the land of the vanished Church. If the interpretation . . . of the historic situation be correct, then there is no more vivid warning than that to fail to share the faith with all around is to let it die.'[11]

Questions:

1. Briefly describe the life of Muhammad.
2. What was the 'Hegira' and when did it happen?
3. When did Muhammad die?
4. What is the Muslim creed?
5. What was the attitude of the Muslims towards Christians in the seventh century?
6. When was Egypt invaded by the Muslims and who led the invasion?
7. When was Carthage captured?
8. How did the Muslims pressure Egyptian Christians to become Muslims?
9. Why did the church in North Africa decline so quickly?
10. What does the last sentence in this chapter warn us about?

[1]Groves, C.P., *The Planting of Christianity in Africa*, vol. 1 (Lutterworth Press, London, 1948), p. 69

[2]Ibid. p. 70
[3]Whitham, A.R. *The History of the Christian Church* (Rivingtons, London, 1968), p. 327
[4]Ibid. p. 328
[5]Oliver, R. & Fage, J., *A Short History of Africa* (Penguin Books Ltd., Middlesex, 1962), p. 68
[6]Ibid. p. 69
[7]Ibid. p. 71
[8]Groves, C.P., *The Planting..*.' p. 79
[9]Ibid. p. 74
[10]Ibid. p. 75
[11]Ibid. p. 89

7

The Churches of Nubia and Abyssinia 1000–1600

Chapter five told us about the establishment of Christianity in both Nubia and Abyssinia and how the churches grew up to and after the beginning of Islam. At the end of chapter five it was noted that we do not know very much about these churches during the period 700 to 1300. But still there are some indications of what happened during some of these years.

NUBIA

After Egypt was conquered by the Muslims in 641, a frontier was established between southern Egypt and Nubia. A treaty was made around 650 between the Arabs of Egypt and the Nubians of Dongola, in which the Arabs agreed to leave the Nubians alone, if the Nubians would stop raiding the border towns of Egypt. This treaty was followed for about six hundred years. During this time Christianity was the faith of the Nubians.

Around AD 1000 the Nubians began to be challenged more and more by Muslim raiders. Before that time there had been conflicts, but after 1000 the challenges increased. 'The threat to Christian Nubia came less from the remote Muslim rulers in Cairo than from the nomad Arab tribes, imperfectly controlled by the administration, which gradually penetrated into Upper Egypt, . . . and ultimately, as Nubian defences weakened, infiltrated into the region of the Cataracts and beyond.'[1] So it was, that by 1100 many people in Northern Nubia had already become converts to Islam, because of the contact with these nomadic Arabs.

In 1000 there were two main kingdoms of Nubia. In the north there was the kingdom of Makurra which stretched from the Egyptian border to just south of Meroe. Its capital was Dongola. The other kingdom was called Alwa and was located south of Makurra. Its capital city was Soba. 'Soba . . . is described by Ibn Selim as a beautiful city with great monasteries, churches rich with gold, and fine gardens to embellish the whole. . . The people of the country were Christians, with bishops appointed by the patriarch of Alexandria. They used Greek writings which they translated into the vernacular.'[2]

The churches of Nubia seemed to remain strong in the twelfth century. In Makurra there were many churches and monasteries. Alwa, too, was said to have more than 400 churches at that time.

In 1275 the first serious threat to Christianity in Nubia appeared. In that year Dongola, the capital of Makurra, was captured by the Egyptians. The Egyptians put a king on the throne who would be favourable to them. This first vassal king was probably a Christian. 'It was not, however, till 1316 that we hear of the first king to be a Muslim, and even then the population remained Christian.'[3] With the government of Makurra in the hands of the Muslims, it was easier for Islam to gain in strength, which it eventually did.

In the kingdom of Alwa the Christians were threatened by the Fung people in the late fifteenth century (1480's). By 1504 Soba had been captured and the Fung began to build a new capital.

It does not seem that between 1275 and 1600 the Christians of Nubia were persecuted by imprisonment or death by the Muslims. Rather, it seems that the population began to convert from Christianity to Islam as the years and centuries passed. It must be remembered that there was not too much contact between the Christians of Nubia and the Christians of Ethiopia. Then, too, all around the Christian Nubians were either pagans or Muslims. Although the Nubians had some contact with the Coptic Christians of Egypt, they did not receive the real help and encouragement they needed from the outside world for the faith to remain alive. So the change over from Christianity to Islam was slow, but nevertheless by the seventeenth century it would seem that the Church in Nubia had died out.

Although the Nubia Church does not exist today, we must give it an important place in our African Church history. The Church lasted more than a thousand years at a time when there was little contact with the outside Christian world. 'That it should have survived so long in a kingdom ringed round by Muslim peoples and deeply penetrated by Muslim influences is a tribute to the root it had taken in the land.'[4]

ABYSSINIA

From 600 to 1200 the Christian kingdoms in Nubia were challenged by nomad and Egyptian Muslims. But during this same period Abyssinia did not have to worry that much about the Muslims. 'The real crisis of medieval Ethiopia came not from the Muslims to the north, but from the pagans to the south. Of the details of this crisis we are almost completely ignorant. One surviving letter from an Ethiopian king of the very late tenth century to his brother monarch, George of Nubia, tells the pitiful tale of a kingdom in ruins through the invasions of a neighbouring pagan state.'[5] For two and a half centuries the Ethiopians fought to rebuild the kingdom. It was a difficult task, and if the king had failed, Christianity in Ethiopia probably would have been lost until many centuries later.

While the kings tried to build up the political kingdom, Coptic monks and hermits built up the Church among the population. It was during this time that the kings of the Zagwe dynasty built the magnificent rock-hewn churches of Roha, which are still used today by the Ethiopian Coptic Christians.

So by 1270 the kingdom had pushed its borders so far south that it could include the provinces of Amhara, Lasta, Gojjam and Darmot as part of the kingdom. Because the kingdom had grown so much, the centre of it was moved from the original northern province of Tigre to Amhara.

While the Ethiopians had been busy defeating the pagan

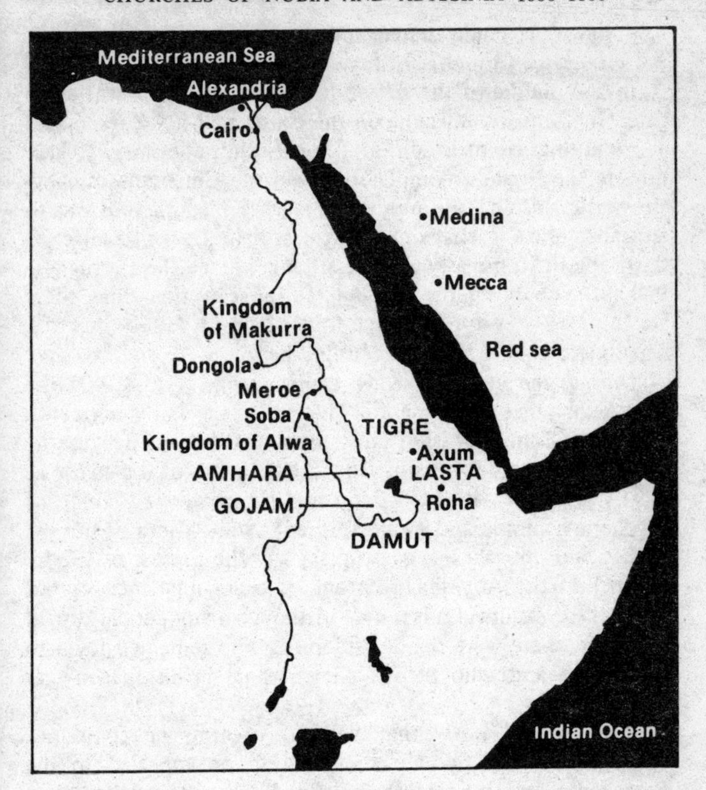

states to the south of them from 980 to 1270 the Muslims had been settling along the Red Sea coast. Thus by the late thirteenth century the Ethiopians found that they were being cut off from the sea by the Muslims. In 1270 a new king and a new dynasty were established. This new king began to battle with the Muslims and the kings who came after him were able to contain the Muslims in the fourteenth century. This new king also encouraged Ethiopian Christian leaders to read more and write more about Christianity and their church. Once again the Ethiopians used the vernacular Geéz for their writing. In this way those people who learned to read and write could understand the Scriptures and the books written by the Church.

In the middle of the fifteenth century, Ethiopia was again threatened by the Muslims on the coast. In 1434 Zara Ya'kob became king. He realized that if the Muslims continued to gain power, they would completely crush the Christians of Abyssinia. He decided the only way to save his kingdom was to appeal to the Christians of Europe for help. He sent a letter to the Pope in Rome asking for assistance. Since the Portuguese had not yet found the sea-route to India by that time, there was no easy way for the Pope to get help to Ya'kob. But still, Ya'kob was able to hold the Muslims back.

During the reign of King Lebna Dengel (1508–40) the Ethiopians met their darkest hour. In the early sixteenth century a Somali Muslim chief invaded Ethiopia. Because he had received some firearms from Arab traders at the coast, he was able to defeat the Ethiopians. He conquered much of northern Ethiopia and even captured Axum. There he burned homes and churches. '. . . So great was the success of the invader that the Abyssinian chronicles claim nine men out of ten turned Muslim at this time.'[6] Although many people turned to Islam, there were many Ethiopians who remained loyal to their faith and who helped King Dengel in his fifteen-year fight.

King Dengel knew that without firearms he could not easily defeat the Somali chief, and so he appealed to the Portuguese to send him some help. Because travel was slow and communication difficult it was not until 1541 that 400 Portuguese soldiers arrived to help the Ethiopians. By this time Dengel was dead, but King Galawdewos was still carrying on the fight against the Muslims. The Ethiopians and Portuguese fought several battles with the Muslims, until finally in 1543 the Somali chief was killed and the rest of Abyssinia was recaptured by the Christians. With this help from Portugal at just the right time, the Coptic Church of Ethiopia was saved from destruction by the Muslims.

We are now coming to the end of an important period in African Church history, since the sixteenth century marks the beginning of a new attempt at evangelism in Africa. Thus as we pause at the sixteenth century and look back over almost 1500 years of Christianity in Africa, we find that there were still Christian churches alive on the continent! The Coptic Church of Egypt, although surrounded by Muslims, was still functioning in many parts of Egypt, while the Coptic Church of Abyssinia had managed to defeat the invasion of Islam and preserve Christianity in that great land.

Nevertheless, at the beginning of the sixteenth century these two national churches had all they could do to take care of their own people. They were so busy defending their faith in their own land that they did not have time to think of going out to the unreached peoples of Africa even if they had so desired. In order for Christianity to spread to the other parts of the continent, new missionaries like Fromentius and Longinus were needed. And so it happened that in the sixteenth century Christianity began to approach Africa from a new direction. In just a few pages we will begin to explore this development in the growth of the African Church.

Questions:

1. What were the names of the two Christian kingdoms of Nubia?
2. When did the Muslim Egyptians capture the capital of Makurra?
3. From what direction did the Muslims attack the king of Ethiopia?
4. To whom did king Ya'kob appeal for help?
5. How did Portugal help the king of Ethiopia in the sixteenth century?

[1]Holt, P.M., *A Modern History of the Sudan* (Grove Press, N.Y., 1961), p. 17
[2]Groves, C.P., *The Planting of Christianity in Africa*, vol. 1 (Lutterworth Press, London, 1948), p. 107
[3]Ibid. p. 107
[4]Ibid. p. 108.
[5]Oliver R. & Fage, J., *A Short History of Africa* (Penguin Books Ltd., Middlesex, 1962), p. 94
[6]Groves, C.P., *The Planting. . .*, pp. 110, 111

8

Our heritage from the early African Churches

Before we look at the political and religious situation in Africa at 1500, it might be wise for us to think over the historic implications that can apply to us and our Church. In the Introduction I wrote that the churches of Africa today have received much from the early Church in Africa. We owe much to early African Christians and we should be aware of what they have given to us. In addition to this heritage from which we have benefited, there are some lessons that we should learn. The early Christians set many examples that would be good for us to follow. Then, too, it is often said that 'we should learn from our mistakes', so we must be ready to recognize mistakes that were made in the African Church of the past, so that we do not repeat those same mistakes in our Church of today.

An important part of our Christianity today is loyalty to Jesus Christ. In the Church of Africa today we believe that it is important to remain true to the teachings of Jesus Christ. We also believe that there can be no compromise on the teachings of Jesus concerning salvation and eternal life. As we do this we are following in the footsteps of the second and third century Christians of 'Africa' and Egypt. We have read how many were put to death by the Roman government because they believed in Christ and because they refused to give up their faith. These early African Christians realized that Jesus Christ was the only important thing in the world for them. They also realized that Jesus demands our full allegiance. 'But whosoever shall deny me before men, him will I also deny before my Father, who is in heaven ' (Matthew 10:33). These early Christians of Africa were not weak, nor were they afraid to stand up for what they believed. While our Church remains true to Jesus Christ, we can say that we are continuing this noble example.

Another concern of the early African Church was evangelism and missionary outreach. From our study it is obvious that the early Christians in 'Africa' and Egypt wanted to tell others about their faith in Jesus Christ. Before 312, they risked persecution when they witnessed or sought to lead people to the Lord, yet this did not stop them or hinder their desire to enter into evangelism. It is obvious that evangelism was a priority, otherwise the Church would not have grown so quickly or spread so far. This can only be explained by the fact that church members spread out into the villages around them to share the Good News. Today in the Church in Africa we have a great desire to see others come to a saving knowledge of Jesus Christ. When the congregations of our local churches reach out to the people around them, they are carrying on an important tradition which was practised by believers in Africa hundreds of years ago.

And then as we noted in chapter three, the modern Church in Africa is deeply indebted for the contributions made by such great African Church Fathers as Tertullian, Augustine and others. It was Tertullian who wrote plainly about the Trinity and in fact, gave us the very word 'Trinity' to express our understanding of the Godhead. Then, too, we noted that it was Augustine who made such a great contribution to Christian theology. As we look back over history, we can see that without the contributions of these African Christians our Church today would be quite different. These early African Christians made a rich contribution to our Church heritage, but not just to the heritage of Christianity in Africa, but to the Church throughout the entire world!

There are some other lessons that we can learn from these early years of the Church in Africa. Perhaps the one that you have noticed most clearly in your study is that splits and personality conflicts seriously weakened the Church. We noticed that many of the splits of the early Church were caused by heresies that crept into the Church. We saw the result of these splits and creeping heresies was the rapid disappearance of the Church in some areas. As an example we saw how Arianism and Donatism split the Church of 'Africa'. We noted that even after true Christianity was re-introduced to the area, the Church was never very strong. Then when Islam came in 697 the Church seemed to melt away. The lesson to us is clear. In our Church today we must be vigilant against any heresy that would creep into our congregation. We must always remain true to the Gospel and the basic tenets of our faith. Then too, we must avoid church splits which arise because of personality problems. All pastors and church leaders must learn to live in unity and harmony so that the Church can go on growing unhindered. 'Behold, how good and pleasant it is when brothers dwell in unity!' (Psalms 133:1).

Another important lesson is that the Bible must be translated into the language of the people, so that church members can hear and learn the Scriptures. We have seen how the Church in Ethiopia translated the Bible into Geēz and how other Christian books were put into the vernacular. C.P. Groves noted in regard to Ethiopia: 'Once again the use of the language of the people is found linked with Christian survival under stress of stormy times.'[1] This shows us the importance of keeping the Bible before the people in the congregation. Every pastor must encourage the people of his church to read and seek to learn more about the Scriptures. Then if difficult times come upon the Church, the people will be better able to remain strong for Christ.

A third lesson of history is that Christianity must be careful about how much it adapts itself to the national culture in which it is practised. When Christianity first came to Egypt, there were many Egyptians who tried to mix the Gospel with their traditional religion. Groves notes in relation to the Church in Egypt from the second to the fifth century that: 'Mummification (preserving of dead bodies by use of spices and wrapping in special cloth) was continued by Egyptian Christians until the beginning of the fifth century. . . Apparently offerings of food were still made to the dead by Christians, a survival of the Egyptian idea of the necessity of magical food for the deceased.'[2] Eventually, these things were stopped by Egyptian Christians but until that happened the Church could not give a strong witness. This serves as a warning to the churches in Africa today to avoid those men who want to mix African traditional religions with Christianity in order to make it 'authentic'. While there are some good aspects of contemporary African culture which should be a part of our expression of what we believe, we must be careful not to just adopt everything that is suggested. Otherwise the result will be a weakened Church which has mixed magic and superstition with some of the ideas of the Bible, such as happened in the second and third century in Egypt.

Finally, it is good for pastors to remember that their work may be the most important aspect of building up and continuing the Church. Many people think that church growth results from large evengelistic crusades, or Christian magazines or Christian films, etc. But this is usually not the case. The Church is helped the most by faithful pastors and elders. A secular historian has made this observation about the growth of the Ethiopian Church. 'Christianity triumphed, not through the sedentary propagation of a learned faith, but rather as a Church of ascetic monks and hermits who established their influence by personal sanctity and by denial of the world.'[3] According to this writer the Coptic Church in Ethiopia grew, not because of the words of a few great preachers, but rather because local pastors (monks) lived upright and pure lives. These same people were not interested in gaining wealth or fame for themselves, but rather they only wanted to have good Christian testimonies. This should be a lesson to all men who want to be pastors: the way they live and act will have a greater influence upon people around them than if they preach wonderful sermons on Sunday, but live a poor Christian life during the week.

Therc are many more conclusions or lessons that we could draw from this period of history. However, these are sufficient to show us why it is important to know Church history. They should also make us want to be sure that our own Church remains pure and strong.

[1] Groves, C.P., *The Planning of Christianity in Africa*, vol. 1 (Lutterworth Press, London, 1948), p. 110
[2] Ibid. P. 41
[3] Oliver, R. & Fage, J., *A Short History of Africa* (Penguin Books Ltd., Middlesex, 1962), p. 94

9

Progress in Africa to 1500

At the beginning of the sixteenth century Africa was indeed a continent of contrasts. In the north were the great cities of Muslim Africa which traded with many places in the world. In the heart of West Africa were the states which succeeded the great kingdoms of the thirteenth, fourteenth and fifteenth centuries. In southern Africa, Africans had built great stone cities like Zimbabwe and were sending gold to Safola for export to India and Arabia. In East Africa there were many trading cities on the coast; Arab traders bought ivory from the interior and shipped it to the East. Yet further into the heart of Africa were tribes which only had a knowledge of agriculture and some metal working. These tribes did not have a form of writing, in contrast with some of the other areas of Africa. These tribes practised their own traditional religions, for they had not been contacted by either Muslim or Christian missionaries. With such great contrasts it is impossible to describe Africa at that time in just a few words. And yet we must have some idea of the condition of Africa during this period in order to appreciate how the Church grew and prospered later.

Starting first in the north for the period from 800 to 1500, it can generally be said that this was the 'Golden Age of North Africa'. During this time the kingdoms of North Africa were somc of the most important in the world. But this success brought with it much trouble. The countries of North Africa were continually being attacked by different groups of Muslims and Berbers. In fact, by 1000 Islam already had many different schisms. Each group of Islam tried to compel the

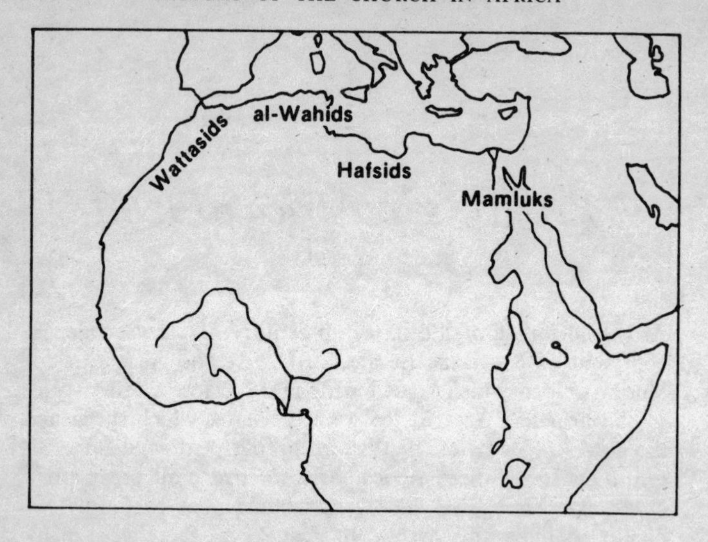

other groups to follow their interpretation of the religion.

From 1000 to 1300 different Berber religious groups ruled North Africa and parts of West Africa. However, by 1300 the control of the Berbers was coming to an end. The result was that by 1500 North Africa was split into four main parts. There was Egypt in the East, ruled by military leaders from the Middle East; next was the area which we now call Libya and Tunisia, ruled by the Hafsids; then there were the al-Wahids who controlled the area we now call Algeria and in the west the Wattasids were in control.

In West Africa from 800 to 1500 there were three great kingdoms and many smaller states that influenced history. First of all, it is important to remember that the southern part of the Sahara desert during the period 1000 to 1500 was not as dry as it is today. Therefore most of the people during this time lived in the area of the Niger River basin and few lived in the thick rain forests of the coast. Today, we find that the great population belt of West Africa is in the region along the coast and inland from it, with fewer people living along the upper Niger River.

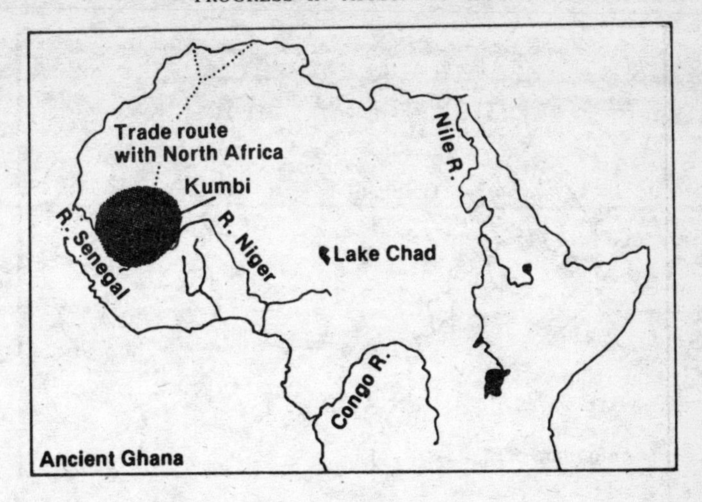

The first great kingdom of West Africa was called Ghana. It started as a trading state in the eighth century. Soon the state became quite powerful and controlled a large area of territory between the Senegal and Niger Rivers. Because the kingdom was so far from the ocean, the people had no way of getting salt which they needed for their diet. So the people of Ghana traded gold and ivory to North Africa in return for salt. The traders from North Africa were Muslims, but the people of West Africa at this time were pagans. When the Muslim traders came to Ghana the king made them live in a separate town, six miles from the capital of Kumbi. The traders obeyed the king, because he was strong and his empire was well organized.

Ghana became quite wealthy, so that other people wanted to get her wealth for themselves. In 1054 Muslim Berbers from Morocco attacked the empire, but it was not until 1076 that the capital was captured. The Berbers were unable to control the Empire of Ghana, because the Africans did not want them. So for many years there was no strong government in that region of West Africa.

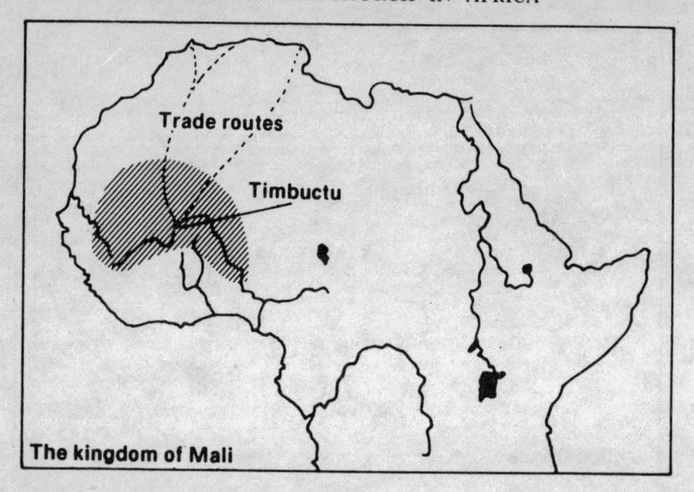

The kingdom of Mali

After the fall of Ghana, a tribe to the west began to grow in strength: it was the Mandinka. In about 1230 Sundiata Keita became the king of the Mandinka. In a battle with the rulers around the former kingdom of Ghana, Sundiata was victorious. This marks the beginning of the Kingdom of Mali. The kings who followed Sundiata Keita battled with the tribes around them, so that Mali became even larger.

In 1312 the most famous king of Mali came to the throne. His name was Mansa Musa. He made the kingdom even richer by extending trade with North Africa. Mansa Musa was a devout Muslim. During this time many pagans converted to Islam, yet in West Africa the number of pagans was much greater than the number of Muslims. After Mansa Musa died in 1337 the kingdom of Mali began to decline. By 1500 it had disappeared.

The beginning of another great kingdom came in 1375 when the people of Songhay regained their independence from Mali. They established a strong state along the middle part of the Niger River. In 1464 Sunni Ali became the Emperor of Songhay and set out to make the empire larger. In 1468 he

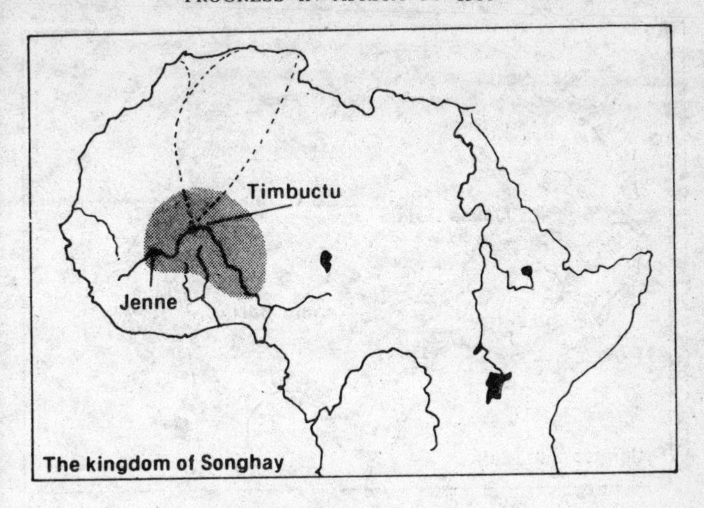

The kingdom of Songhay

captured Timbuktu, which was an important trading city on the Niger. The next city he captured was Jenne which was important for its trade in gold and kola nuts. 'Ali had no use for Islam, the religion of urban communities. . . He treated Islam as a joke as the account of the mockery he made of the prayers showed.'[1] Ali died around 1492.

Shortly after his death Muhammad Ture became the king of Songhay. He is sometimes called Askia the Great because of the way he built up and strengthened the kingdom. He developed the central government of his empire so that it ran smoothly and well. He enlarged the empire by defeating other tribes around Songhay. 'Muhammad's political astuteness led him to reverse the attitude of Ali towards Islam. . . Although Muhammad made use of Islam to reinforce his authority there is little evidence to support the claim that he initiated a wave of islamization.'[2] Thus, although Muhammad Ture was a Muslim he did not force people to become Muslims; he only encouraged them by his own example. In 1591 the Empire of Songhay came to an end when a band of Moroccans captured the capital.

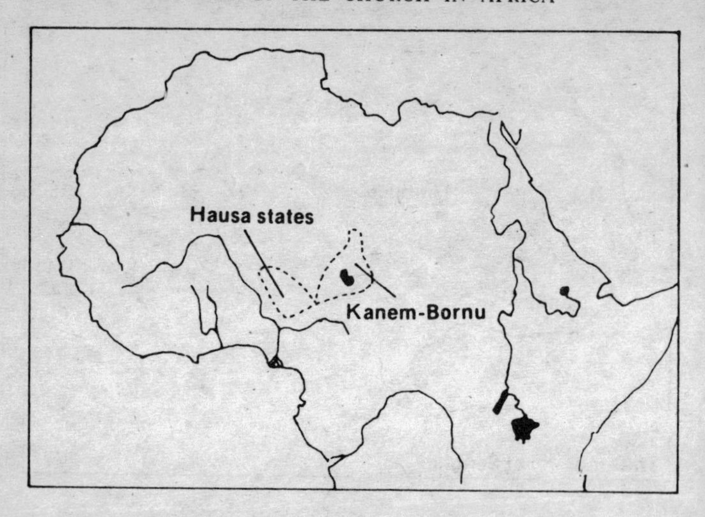

To the East of these kingdoms is an area of West Africa which is called 'The Central Sudan States'. There were many smaller kingdoms and states in this area during the period of 800 to 1500. The best known are called Kanem-Bornu and the Hausa states. The Hausa states occupied the area that we call Northern Nigeria today. Kanem-Bornu was situated to the east of the Hausa States. There is not enough space to tell about the governments of these states. But we should note one or two facts about how Islam entered these areas. 'Islam it is clear was establishing itself (in Kanem-Bornu) between 1085 and 1240. . . '[3] However, it seems to have mainly been the religion of the leaders and the people of the cities. The people of the rural areas continued to be pagans. It was not until two or three centuries later that large numbers of people could be counted as Muslims. 'Islam was later in reaching the Hausa states than those lying east and west, Kanem and Songhay, both more important terminals of caravan routes (that went to Muslim North Africa).'[4] It was not until the fifteenth century that Islam began to take hold in the cities. 'The arrival of clerics (Muslim missionaries) from Western Sudan and

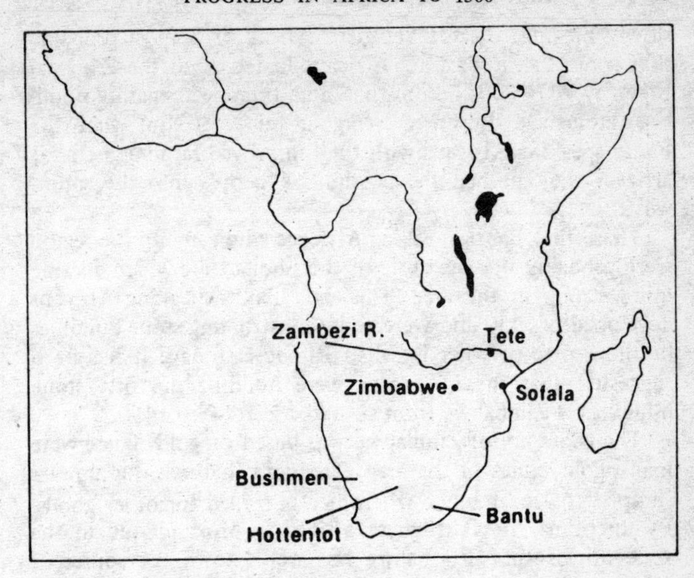

Bornu in the fifteenth century aided the accomplishment of the urban religious revolution in Kano Town.'[5]

To summarize about West Africa around 1500, we may say that most of the population still lived quite far inland from the coast, with only a few people living in the coastal rain forests. By 1500, Islam had been in most places of central West Africa for about three or four hundred years. As we have noted, though, it was only beginning to be accepted by the people in the rural areas.

Turning our attention to Southern Africa now, let us look at the state of political and religious affairs in that region. Actually, very little is known today about the people who lived in Africa south of the Zambezi before AD 1000. But as you may remember, when we looked at Africa in the first century (in chapter one) we said that the concentration of Bantu-speaking Africans in the Congo River basin were preparing for a period of great migration in which many tribes would move to the east and south. Therefore, we can assume that from AD 100 to 1500 Bantu-speaking Africans were slowly moving towards Southern Africa. It is most probable that some Bantu-speaking Africans had crossed the Zambezi River by AD 1000. Before that time there were mainly primitive 'stone age' Bushmen living in this area. But when the Bantu-speaking Africans with their improved farming methods arrived, they pushed these primitive people into the south-west.

These first Bantu-speaking Africans who came to the region were probably the ancestors of the Shona tribe which became quite strong in the area. The early Bantu-speaking Africans developed quickly and were soon constructing stone buildings in the centre of what is called Rhodesia today. It has been suggested that these Africans were building the first stone buildings at Zimbabwe from around AD 1080 to 1450.[6]

The economy of Zimbabwe was based on gold. There were many gold mines in the area. The gold that was dug up was shipped to Mozambique where it was traded for other goods. By the time the Portuguese arrived in Mozambique in the sixteenth century, Zimbabwe was well known as a source of gold.

There were probably other tribes in the area of Rhodesia and Mozambique, but they did not leave as much evidence of their progress as did the Monomatapa of Zimbabwe.

Farther south it is probable that other Bantu tribes had settled. However it is difficult to prove this point. Some historians believe that by 1500 there were Bantu tribes settled all the way down on the southern coast of South Africa. '. . . accounts show that at this time (1500), contrary to the beliefs of most present-day white South Africans, South Africa was by no means empty of Bantu inhabitants. . . east of the Kei (River), (were) peoples who can be identified as Xhosas and Tembus and Pondos and the Nguni ancestors of the Zulus. . . '[7] This is about all we know of the people of South Africa at the beginning of the sixteenth century. It must be assumed that they were not as advanced as the kingdoms of West Africa at that time. For all the tribes south of the Zambezi River, we can say that the only religion practised was African traditional religion.

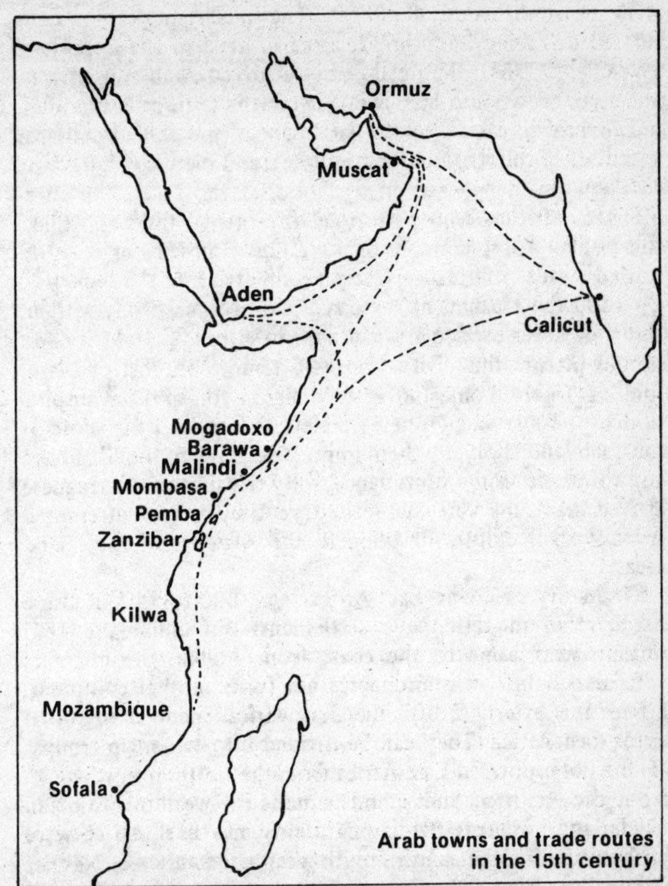

Arab towns and trade routes in the 15th century

Finally, let us survey Eastern Africa from 800 to 1500. Looking first at the coast, up to AD 1000 that area was mainly inhabited by Africans. 'The number of Muslims who had so far settled on the coast must have been small; as late as about AD 1150 the towns of the mainland from Barawa south are described as pagan.'[8] However, in the twelfth and thirteenth centuries Arabs came from the Persian Gulf area to settle along the coast. They began to build trading towns and mix with the

Africans at the coast. By 1400, 'The inhabitants can be considered as falling into three classes in most of the important settlements. The ruling class was of mixed Arab and African ancestry, brown in colour, well read in the faith of Islam. Such would probably be also the landowners, the skilled artisans, and most of the religious functionaries, and merchants. Inferior to them (in many cases in a state of slavery) were the pure-blooded Africans who performed the menial tasks and tilled the fields. Apart from both were the transient or recently settled Arabs, still incompletely assimilated into the society.'[9] By 1500 the Muslims at the coast had become firmly settled. But they never tried to move into the interior of East Africa. 'We should picture this civilisation as a remote outpost of Islam, looking to the homeland of its religion for spiritual inspiration. . . . Their religion never penetrated beyond the shore of the mainland, nor did their impressive skills in building have any influence in the hinterland.'[10] By the time the Portuguese arrived the Arabs were well settled, yet they had not attempted to take their culture or Islam to the Africans of the inland areas.

The story of inland East Africa from 800 to 1500 is also a narrative of migration and settlement. But unlike the Arab settlers who came to the coast from Arabia, the migrants who settled in the interior were not from another continent. Some time after AD 100 the first African peoples began to enter East Africa. They can be divided into two main groups: 'The Nilotes entered East Africa from the north or north-west, from the southern Sudan and perhaps the western Ethiopian borderland, whereas Bantu migrations into East Africa were probably from the south, south-west and west. . . Neither Nilotes nor Bantu-speaking Africans arrived in East Africa all at one go. Instead, we should imagine numerous Bantu and Nilotic movements throughout the length of the iron age – a period of one to two thousand years from the present (i.e. AD 100 to 1800).'[11]

There is not enough space to tell in detail about the many tribes that had settled in East Africa by the sixteenth century. One of the most well-known early civilizations of East Africa

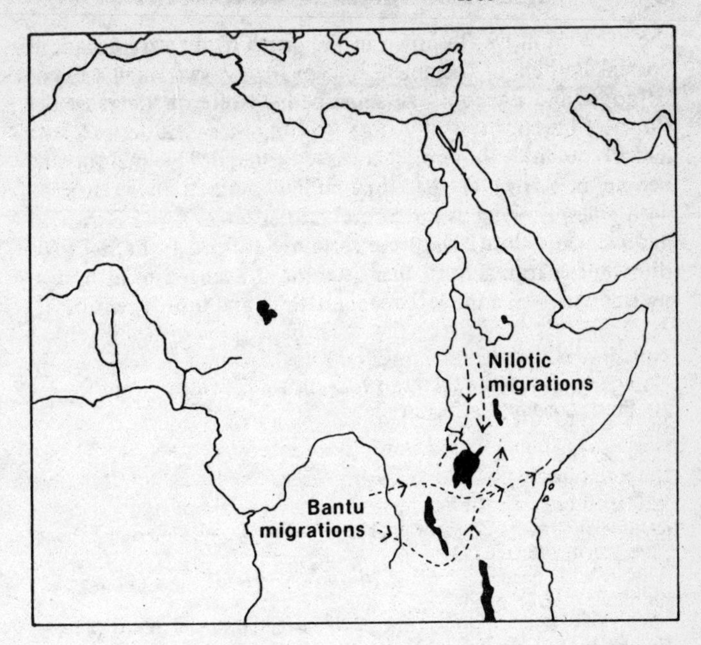

was the Chwezi, a people who were pastoralists. They came into the area of Uganda and Northern Tanzania from Sudan or Ethiopia. 'According to oral tradition and archaeological evidence, the Chwezi culture must have flourished between AD 1350 and 1500.'[12] This tribe seems to have disappeared after 1500 and other tribes settled in the area instead. It can be said that by 1500 the first Luo had begun to settle in western Kenya, and the Bantu ancestors of the Kikuyu and Akamba had left the area of the Taita Hills in order to move north. There were also Bantu-speaking Africans spread out through Tanzania. As to the religious condition of East Africa at this time, we can say that Islam was practised in most of the coastal towns, but the tribes of the interior still followed traditional religions.

To conclude our survey, we can say that at 1500 Africa was a continent that held a wide range of civilizations from the very primitive Bushmen in the south to the very advanced coastal Berbers of the north. Except for the two small areas of Ethiopia and Egypt where some people were members of the Coptic Church, most of Africa was unaware that Jesus Christ had come into the world to save sinners. The majority of people in Africa at that time followed traditional religions, with Islam ranking as the second largest religion and Christianity a distant third. The time certainly seemed to be right for the Church to make another attempt at evangelism in Africa, such as had been done in the second, third and fourth centuries.

[1] Trimingham, J.S., *A History of Islam in West Africa* (Oxford University Press, London, 1962), pp. 94, 95
[2] Ibid. P. 97
[3] Ibid. P. 115
[4] Ibid. p. 130
[5] Ibid. p. 132
[6] Summers, Roger., *Zimbabwe: A Rhodesian Mystery* (Nelson & Sons, Cape Town, 1963), p. 84
[7] Oliver, R. & Fage, J., *A Short History of Africa* (Penguin Books Ltd., Middlesex, 1962), p. 64
[8] Ogot, B.A. & Kieran, J.A (editors), *Zamani: A Survey of East African History* (East African Publishing House, Ltd., Nairobi, 1968), p. 107
[9] Ibid. pp. 113, 114
[10] Ibid. p. 117
[11] Ibid. p. 90
[12] Were, G.S. & Wilson, D.A., *East Africa Through a Thousand Years* (Evans Brothers Ltd., London, 1969), p. 47

AFRICAN CHURCH HISTORY TIME-LINE 100–1950

(Showing the relationship of selected historical events in different parts in Africa)

Date AD	*North Africa*	*West Africa*	*Central Africa*	*Southern Africa*	*East Africa*
100	The Church is growing in Egypt and being started in Carthage	Tribes speaking Western Sudanic languages were already inhabiting West Africa	Large group of Bantu-speaking Africans is concentrated in the Congo River Basin	Hottentots and stone age tribes inhabit this region. African tribes have not yet arrived	
	Catechetical School started in Egypt to train Christians				Nilotic people from the north east begin to migrate into East Africa
200	Time of Tertullian in Carthage				
250	Cyprian elected Bishop of Carthage				From the Congo River Basin Bantu-speaking Africans begin to enter East Africa
	Roman persecution of the Church		People of the Congo follow traditional tribal religions		Frumentius the Gospel to Ethiopia
300	Arianism splits the church	People of West Africa practice traditional religions			
				Hottentots and other primitive tribes continue their own tribal religions	
350	Donatists split the Church of Carthage				Ethiopian Church established with Frumentius as the first Bishop
	Conversion of Augustine				
400	Vandals invade North Africa				
450	African Churches send bishops to Chalcedon to discuss the nature of Christ				
					Syrian missionaries convince Ethiopian Church to become a Coptic Church (Monophysite)
500	Coptic Church established in Egypt on the belief that Jesus only had a divine nature				Julian brings the Gospel to Nubia

Date	*North Africa*	*West Africa*	*Central Africa*	*Southern Africa*	*East Africa*
AD		Trade increases between West Africa and North Africa			
550	Decline of the Byzantine Church in Egypt				
					Longinus comes to Nubia to tell about Jesus Christ
					Ethiopians translate the Bible into Geéz
600					
	Amr invades Egypt and brings Islam to Africa				
650					Nubians sign a treaty with Arabs of Egypt to keep peace at the border
	Uqba invades province of Africa				
	Hassan captures Carthage				
700	Church in Carthage and Africa begins to decline quickly because of inner weakness and Islamic pressure				Nubians keep Islam out of Nubia
750	Number of Coptic Christians in Egypt begins to decline because of pressure from Muslims				
800	Church of North Africa in rapid decline	Kingdom of Ghana expands its power. Trade with North Africa grows.			Coptic Church continues to grow in Ethiopia
850	Berber tribesmen begin to turn to Islam				Nomadic Muslims from Egypt and Christian Nubia
900		Gold and salt trade expands further between North and West Arica			Raids against Ethiopia by pagan tribes of the south greatly reduces the power of Ethiopia
1000	Majority of population is now Muslim				Arab dhows begin to visit East African Coast
	The number of bishops in Carthage and Africa has fallen from 40 in AD 650 to 6 in 1050	Kings of Ghana resist Islam			

AFRICA CHURCH HISTORY TIME-LINE 100–1950

Date	*North Africa*	*West Africa*	*Central Africa*	*Southern Africa*	*East Africa*
AD					
		Muslim Berbers attack Ghana			
		Kingdom of Ghana falls to the Berbers			
1100	Muslim Berbers try to reform governments of North Africa				Ethiopian kings defeat pagans and strengthen the empire
1150					Arabs begin to establish trading posts along the East African coast
1200		Sundiata Keita builds the Kingdom of Mali			
1250	Berbers begin to lose control of North Africa				A new dynasty is established in Ethiopia. New king encourages Christians to remain strong.
	Egyptian Muslims capture Nubian capital of Dongola				
1300		Mansa Musa leads Mali to height of power; makes a pilgrimage to Mecca			
1350	Hafsids become rulers of central North Africa	Kingdom of Songhay begins to gain strength			
1400	Wattasids rule western part of North Africa	Portuguese ships reach mouth of Senegal River			Zara Yakob becomes king of Ethiopia: seeks to protect Coptic Church from Muslims (1434)
1450		Sunni Ali becomes Emperor of Songhay (1464)			
1500	Church in western North Africa completely disappears		Catholic missionaries arrive in the Kingdom of the Kongo (1491)	Diaz reaches Cape of Good Hope (1487)	Muslims from the coast increase raids against Ethiopia
					Vasco da Gama reaches Mombasa & Malindi (1498)
1550	Saadians rule Northwest; they are descendants of Prophet Mohammad	Songhay defeated by band of Moroccans – last great kingdom comes to an end (1591)	Alphonso becomes first Christian king of the Kongo	Da Silveira strangled while trying to convert Monomotapa (1561)	400 Portuguese soldiers save king of Ethiopia from Muslim invaders (1541)
					First Catholic monastery built at Mombasa (1567)
1600		Europeans establish trading castles along the coast			Jesuits begin missionary work in Ethiopia to convert Coptic Christians to Catholicism (1607)
1650		Beginning of the slave trade along the coast	Catholicism begins to decline in the Kingdom of Kongo		Catholics expelled from Ethiopia (1625)

Date AD	*North Africa*	*West Africa*	*Central Africa*	*Southern Africa*	*East Africa*
1700	Various holy men establish marabouts (holy places) and extend control over most of Morocco			Schmidt of the Moravians preaches in Cape District Schmidt driven out of Cape by Dutch	Catholicism dies out in Mombasa due to hostility of Muslims
1750		Thompson begins work at Cape Coast for Anglican Church (1751) Philip Quaque begins preaching in Cape Coast (1766)	Catholicism dies out in the Congo	Second group of Moravians arrive at Cape (1792)	Slave trade on East African coast increases
1800	White Fathers begin Catholic mission in Algeria	First CMS station established in Sierra Leone (1804) Wm. DeGraft establishes first African Bible study in the Gold Coast		L.M.S. begins work in South Africa (1799) David Livingstone arrives in Cape Town (1840)	Krapf establishes first CMS station in Mombasa (1844)
1850	North Africa Mission begins work in Algeria (1881) Gospel Missionary Union begins work in Morrocco in 1895	Samuel Crowther goes on Niger Expedition Rev. Crowther ordained an Anglican Bishop (1864) European scramble for Africa Anglican Church of Sierra Leone sends out its own missionaries (1895)	Roman Catholics re-establish mission work in Congo area Large numbers of Protestant missions enter Congo Protestant missions bring world attention to Leopold's atrocities in the Congo	Rhenish Mission begins work in South-west Africa First spiritual independent church started in South Africa (1892)	Roman Catholics return to East Africa by opening a station in Tanganyika for freed slaves Ugandan Martyrs die for their faith near Kampala (1886) Africa Inland Mission takes the Gospel to interior Kenya (1895)
1900	Roman Catholics begin mission work in Libya after Italy takes control of government	Prophet Harris preaches in Ivory Coast and Gold Coast (1914)	Simon Kimbangu starts his own spiritual church in Congo	John Chilembwe leads his Baptists in revolt in Nyasaland (1915)	The Revival Movement begins in Rwanda (1928)
1950		Major denominations become independent of foreign mission bodies	New education policy helps Protestant schools expand	South African government begins to closely regulate church sponsored schools	Independent churches multiply while major denominations become independent of foreign missions

10

Portuguese Missionary Activity 1450–1750

At the beginning of the fifteenth century there was a prince in Portugal who became very interested in finding out more about the world beyond Europe. His name was Prince Henry and he has been called 'the Navigator' because of his great desire to find out more about the Atlantic Ocean. At the beginning of the fourteenth century, people of Europe did not know that there were the North and South American continents. In fact they did not know very much about Africa south of the Sahara Desert. The Atlantic Ocean looked large and frightening to the Europeans, so they always sailed their ships close to land. Only in the Mediterranean Sea did they sail freely from place to place. Because of their fear of the unknown, Europeans did not try to sail to Africa or India before the fifteenth century.

Around 1420 Prince Henry began seriously to consider how he could find out more about the oceans, particularly a sea route to the gold of West Africa and the spices of India. It must be remembered that at this time the Muslims of North Africa controlled the trade of gold from West Africa while the Muslims of the Middle East controlled the silk trade from China and the spice trade from India. Because all these things passed through Arab or Berber lands, the Muslims would charge a tax. Because of the cost of transport and this tax, gold and spices were sold at a very high price in Europe. Thus Prince Henry had a good motivation for finding a sea route which would go around the Muslims of North Africa and the Middle East.

Prince Henry sent out more than ten expeditions between

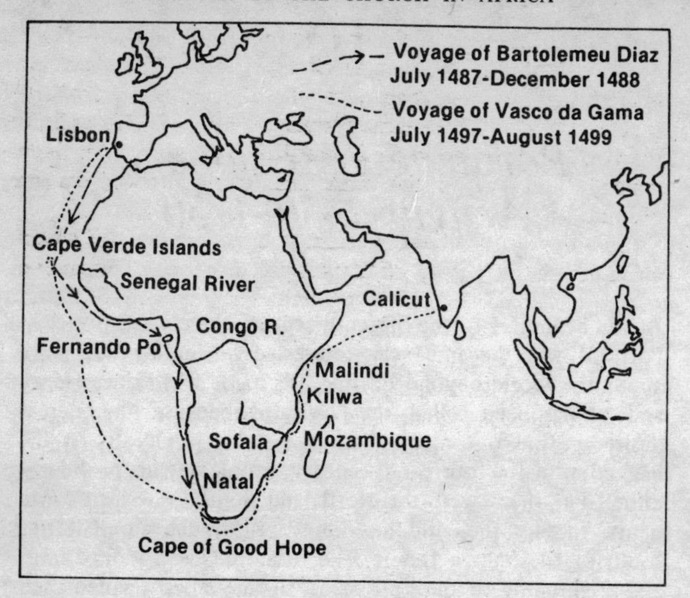

1421 and 1445. Yet it was only in 1445 that one of his captains reached the Senegal River on the coast of West Africa – progress was indeed very slow at first. Prince Henry died in 1460 before any ships actually reached the Cape of Good Hope. However, before his death, Portuguese trading ships were making regular trips down the coast of West Africa in order to trade with the Africans along the coast.

Portuguese captains continued to push further along the coast of Africa, but it was a time of slow progress. It was not until 1484 that Captain Diogo Gam reached the mouth of the great Congo River. There he met some friendly Africans, who were members of the Kingdom of the Kongo – a large tribe in that area. In 1487 Bartholomew Diaz reached the Cape of Good Hope and got to the southernmost tip of Africa before turning back for Portugal.

In July, 1497, Vasco da Gama began his historic voyage of discovery. In January 1498 he reached one of the mouths of the Zambezi river on the east coast of Africa. Da Gama sailed north visiting the different Arab towns along the coast. At Malindi he found an Arab pilot who directed him across the Indian Ocean until he reached India in May, 1498. So in 1498 the Portuguese achieved their goal of finding a route to India which would by-pass the lands that were controlled by the Muslims.

But how do all these voyages of discovery by the Portuguese affect the history of Christianity in Africa? The answer to this question is easy, if we look back at the aims of Prince Henry when he sent out his first ships for exploration. Besides finding out more about the oceans and finding out new trade routes, Prince Henry also wanted to see if there were any Christian kings in Africa. There was a rumour in Europe that there was a strong Christian king in Africa called 'Prester John'. Prince Henry wanted to find that king. In addition he wanted Roman Catholic missionaries to take the message of Christianity to the people along the African coast, where the Portuguese set up trading centres.

So it was that Roman Catholic missionaries accompanied the early trading ships of the Portuguese. In 1462 the Pope named a Missionary Prefect for all of West Africa. Many missionaries worked in this area until the end of the century, but there were few true converts. The Africans seemed more interested in Portuguese guns and power than they were in Portuguese religion. Then, too, the Portuguese spent more time and money developing trade than in furthering the work of the Church, so not as much attention was given to missionary work.

Further south the Portuguese were more successful. The story began when Diogo Cam visited the mouth of the Congo River in 1484. There he met some very friendly Africans. He decided to take some of these men to Portugal to let them see Europe. So he left some Portuguese seamen with the tribe as proof that he was not going to make slaves of these men, and then took the Africans to Portugal. These Africans were members of the Kingdom of Bakongo.

'The Kongo Kingdom was a typical "Sudanic" state, which

had been founded in the late fourteenth or early fifteenth century, by a conquering group from the south-east.'[1] It was a well developed kingdom by 1450 with a capital at Mbanza-kongo which is now the city of San Salvador in northern Angola. The population of the kingdom was estimated at two and a half million which means that it was not a small tribe – but rather a major nation.

In 1485 the Portuguese returned the Africans to Mbanza-kongo. In just one year these men had learned Portuguese and the basic facts of Christianity. The King of Portugal sent presents for the King of the Bakongo, who was called the Manikongo. The Manikongo was very impressed with the report of his men and the gifts from Europe and so he asked the Portuguese to send missionaries to help him. The first Roman Catholic missionaries arrived in 1491.

The missionaries were well received and many people were converted in the first year. Among them were the king and his wife and their eldest son. The king and queen did not seem very sincere in their decision, but the son, who took the name Alphonso, was a very dedicated Catholic. The king's second son refused to become a Christian and instead began to work against the converts. The missionaries had a difficult time, because they preached against polygamy. 'The Christian opposition to polygamy was much resented, and the devoted adherents of the old religion were much displeased. The king relapsed, Alphonso was banished, and the mission left without support or help.'[2]

A short time later there was a battle between Alphonso and the other son, in which Alphonso was victorious. He became the king of the Bakongo and established a Christian kingdom. More missionaries came to the Kongo, but their work never seems to have taken real root among the people. Nevertheless, Alphonso sent many of his people to study in Portugal as priests and government officials. In the Kongo many of the people used Portuguese baptismal names and much of the government was carried on like governments in Europe. When Alphonso died in 1543 there were many people in the land who claimed to be Catholics.

After 1543 the Kingdom of Kongo did not do so well. The Portuguese became more and more interested in getting slaves from Africa to work in Brazil. They began to buy slaves from Angola, south of the Kongo. But in order for the people of Angola to get slaves they had to make war against the other tribes around them, which included the Kongo.

Then, too, the kings who followed Alphonso were not very interested in Christianity and so the people began to turn away from the Roman Catholic Church. By 1700 Christianity in the Kingdom of the Kongo had died out. 'The mission in Congo was the first considerable Christian mission in Africa since the days of the early Church, and the first at any time south of the Sahara with any continuity of history. Yet it has disappeared. It was not overwhelmed by Islam. It seems just to have faded out.'[3]

The Congo was not the only place where the Portuguese attempted to introduce Christianity south of the Equator. On the eastern side of Africa there were many tribes that had contact with the coast because of trade. In 1560 a Portuguese missionary called da Silveira landed at Sofala with the desire to walk inland and work among the people of Monomatapa. First he went to the town of Mozambique and then inland to the trading post of Sena. There he waited for permission to enter the Kingdom of Monomatapa. At last he received permission and arrived at the capital on December 25, 1560. The king and royal household responded to da Silveira's preaching and after a short time of instruction, were baptized. When the Muslim traders in the capital saw what was happening they became afraid that the Portuguese would take the gold trade away from them. So they went to the king and told him that da Silveira was a clever witchdoctor who had put a curse on the king by baptizing him. They said the only way to stop the curse was to kill da Silveira. In March 1561 da Silveira was strangled to death at the city of Monomatapa.

After da Silveira's death other Portuguese missionaries went to Tete and parts of the Monomatapa Kingdom preaching to the people. During the seventeenth century these missionaries recorded many baptisms, but it is doubtful if

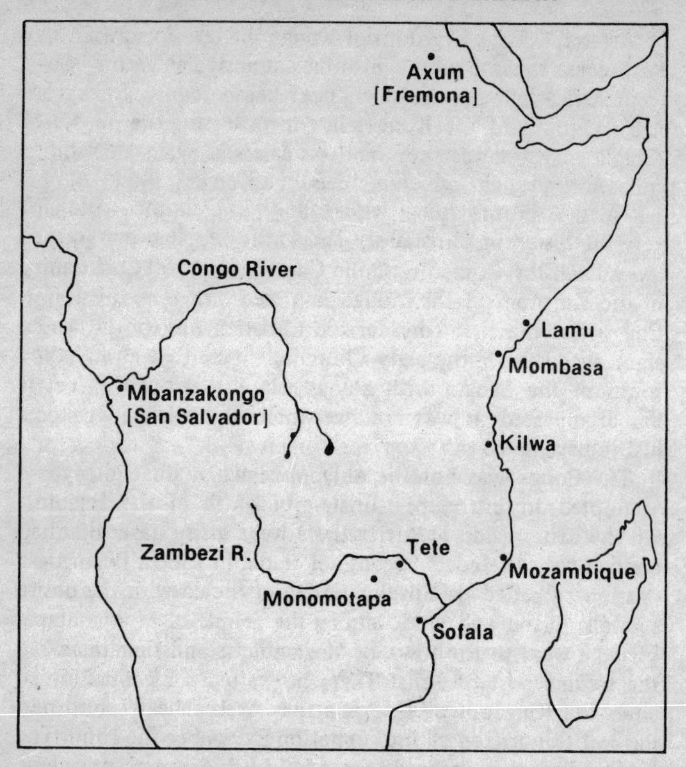

those converted really understood what they were doing. No strong or rapidly growing church developed in this area and there does not seem to be a history of large numbers turning to the Catholic Church. In 1652 the Monomatapa king was baptized which caused the Portuguese to be very happy. But still the Roman Catholic missionary effort was declining in the area and the churches began to decline also. In the eighteenth century hardly any missionaries arrived to work in the interior, and so by the end of that century the Portuguese church seems to have completely died out in the interior.

Further up the coast in East Africa the Portuguese were not as successful in converting Africans. It would seem that not as much effort was put into reaching the interior of Kenya. The Portuguese built forts at Kilwa and Mombasa to keep these towns safe for them. They could use these places as bases for their ships which went to India for trade. Several groups of Portuguese missionaries came to East Africa between 1500 and 1700, but they did not gain as many converts as the missionaries to the south claimed. In 1567 a group of Augustinian priests built a monastery at Mombasa. '. . . in 1598, three missionary priests moved to Lamu, although their work only endured for a few years. Next we hear of Augustinian friars who built a church on Mombasa island (1598) at the site of the present Old Customs House, and soon were claiming 600 converts from among the local populace.'[4] In 1607 a new Catholic mission society arrived in Mombasa. They were called the Brethren of Mercy and their main work was caring for people who had been converted from Islam. By the end of the seventeenth century the Portuguese began to lose their hold on East Africa. At the same time Catholic missionary activity began to decline. By the beginning of the nineteenth century there were no Roman Catholics left along the coast, except for some foreign traders.

The last part of our study of Portuguese missionary activity in Africa from 1450 to 1750 takes us to Ethiopia. The first Portuguese to visit Ethiopia arrived there in 1487, but the King of Ethiopia forced him to settle and live in the country. In 1520 a group of Portuguese arrived in Ethiopia and surveyed the Christian kingdom. It should be remembered that the Portuguese were looking for a Christian kingdom in Africa ruled by a king called 'Prester John'. Thus when they found Ethiopia and its Christian king they believed they had found the 'Kingdom of Prester John'. They were a little disappointed to find that the kingdom was not as strong as they had thought, and that the way the Ethiopians practised their Coptic Christianity was different from Roman Catholic ritual.

In chapter seven we recorded the arrival of the Portuguese mission in 1541 that saved the Ethiopians from defeat by the Muslims. After that time Portuguese missionaries were sent to Ethiopia. At first the kings of Ethiopia were suspicious of the

Portuguese, because they did not want their Church to become part of the Roman Catholic Church. So the first missionaries were told to work at Fremona near Axum. In 1603 a missionary called Paez arrived at Fremona to assist with the work. He had the gift of learning languages easily and was soon able to read, write and speak perfect Geéz. Paez worked hard to build up the Roman Catholic Church, but he worked quietly and slowly. His work paid off in 1622 when King Susenyos publicly proclaimed himself a Roman Catholic. Shortly after that Paez died.

A new missionary called Mendez was sent to replace Paez and direct the work. But Mendez was not very wise. He tried quickly to change the Coptic Church into part of the Roman Catholic Church. He tried to force people to be rebaptized and to re-consecrate the Coptic Churches. This only caused people to rebel. They did not want this new form of Christianity – so a civil war broke out. The king was forced to give up his throne and ask his son to become king. The son expelled all the Jesuit missionaries from the kingdom, and announced that the Coptic Church would not be changed. This made the people happy and the civil war ended.

What was the Coptic Church of Ethiopia like at the time the Portuguese visited it? We have a brief description which was written down by one of the Portuguese missionaries. It tells us a great deal about the Ethiopian church. Much of the ritual and practice of their church was like the Roman Catholic Church.

This is what the missionary, called Lobo, wrote: '. . . they celebrate with a great deal of piety, the Passion of our Lord, they reverence the Cross, they pay a great devotion to the Blessed Virgin, the angels, and the Saints. They observe the festivals, and pay a strict regard to the Sunday. Every month they commemorate the Assumption of the Virgin Mary, and are of opinion that no Christians beside themselves have a true sense of the greatness of the Mother of God, or pay her the honours that are due to her. . . Every week they keep a feast to the honour of the Apostles and angels; they come to Mass with great devotion, and love to hear the word of God.

They receive the sacrament often, but do not always prepare themselves by confession. . . ' Lobo found less acceptable the energetic and tumultuous expression of the congregation in public worship: 'No country in the world is so full of churches, monasteries and ecclesiastics as Abyssinia; it is not possible to sing in one church or monastery without being heard by another, and perhaps by several. They sing the Psalms of David of which as well as the other parts of the Holy Scriptures, they have a very exact translation in their own language. . . The instruments of music made use of in their rites of worship are little drums, which they hang about their necks, and beat with both hands. . . They begin their consort by stamping their feet on the ground, and playing gently on their instruments, but when they have heated themselves by degrees, they leave off drumming and fall to leaping, dancing, and clapping their hands, at the same time straining their voices to their utmost pitch, till at length they have no regard either to tune, or the pauses, and seem rather a riotous, than a religious assembly.'[5]

This brings to an end our survey of the Portuguese missionary activity in Africa from 1450 to 1750. But before we close this chapter we should try to answer two questions: 1) Where were the Protestant missionaries during this period? 2) Why did the Portuguese fail to establish a lasting Church?

Many people want to know why we only read about Roman Catholic missionaries trying to establish Christianity in Africa from 1450 to 1650. They want to know why the Protestants did not send missionaries; was it because they did not care? To answer this question you must recall from Church history exactly when Martin Luther started the Protestant Reformation. It was in 1517 that he nailed his questions to the church door in Wittenberg, Germany, which marks the beginning of the Reformation. But remember by the year 1517 we saw that the Portuguese had been sending missionaries to Africa for more than seventy years. So the first reason that only the Roman Catholic Church sent missionaries to Africa from 1440 to 1520 was that the Protestant Church had not yet been established in Europe.

After 1520 many Protestant churches grew up in Europe and England, yet they were often persecuted and troubled by the Roman Catholic Church. These Protestants were on the defensive from 1520 to 1700 just keeping themselves free from the Roman Catholics. Then, too, they had a big job in evangelizing and reaching the people around them who had never heard of salvation through the atoning blood of Jesus Christ. So we will see that the major thrust of Protestant missionary activity did not come until the late eighteenth century. At that time the Protestant churches were well established in northern Europe and North America and were ready to start reaching out to Africa and the other parts of the world.

The second question, 'Why did the Portuguese fail to establish a lasting Church?' is a little more difficult to answer. It would seem that much of the trouble was caused by the Portuguese's great desire for trade and wealth. They encouraged missionary work, but if they needed more slaves and the missionaries stood in the way, they would abandon the missionary effort in order to increase trade.

The second problem was that they did not fully understand the African culture in which they were working. For example, the Roman Catholics demanded monogamy of their converts, but they did not make good provision for the unwanted wives.

The church also failed because the missionaries practised mass baptisms. This means that they would baptize a large group of people, but often these people would not understand what had happened or what the baptism meant. Thus when the missionaries went away, these 'converts' did not remain Christians for long, since they did not fully understand the religion of which they were supposed to be a part. This indicates that the Portuguese never attempted to fully educate the Africans concerning the teachings of Christ.

Questions:

1. Who was Prince Henry the Navigator and why is he important to understanding African Church history?

2. Briefly tell of the missionary efforts in the Kingdom of Kongo.
3. What missionary attempted to take Christianity to the Monomatapa? What happened to him?
4. Briefly tell about Roman Catholic missionary work in Kenya from 1500 to 1700.
5. Why did the Roman Catholics fail to get control of the Ethiopian Coptic Church?

[1]Oliver, R. & Fage, J., *A Short History of Africa* (Penguin Books, Ltd. Middlesex, 1962), p. 125
[2]Groves, C.P., *The Planting of Christianity in Africa,* Vol. I (Lutterworth Press, London, 1948), p. 128
[3]Ibid. p. 130
[4]Barrett, D.B. & others (editors), *Kenya Churches Handbook: The Development of Kenyan Christianity, 1498–1973* (Evangel Publishing House, Kisumu, 1973), p. 29
[5]Groves, C.P., *The Planting. . .*, pp. 141, 142

11

The 18th century – A time of little Christian progress

In the last chapter we saw that the Portuguese Roman Catholics did most of the missionary work in Africa from 1450 to 1700. It is not until the beginning of the seventeenth century that we first begin to read about Protestant missionary efforts. However, these efforts were rather small and not very effective. In the eighteenth century there was a little more activity, but when this is compared with the nineteenth centuries, it seems very small indeed.

In West Africa the English and Dutch traders began to challenge the Portuguese during the seventeenth century. Soon the English and Dutch had established trading forts on the Gold Coast. At these forts they usually had chaplains or pastors to watch over the Christian traders. Sometimes these chaplains would make contact with the Africans around the fort. But the results of these efforts were not very lasting.

In South Africa the Dutch established a colony at Cape Town in 1652. Their main aim was trade and development of farm land in the area. At first they were interested in winning the Hottentots to Christ. The early efforts by pastors of the Dutch Reformed Church to win these people did not succeed.

Thus by the beginning of the eighteenth century we can only account for this weak Protestant missionary effort in South Africa and the Gold Coast. We must continue to remember, though, that the Protestant churches were still less than 200 years old in Europe and it would not be until the end of the eighteenth century that they would have the vision and the finances to start sending out larger numbers of missionaries.

In the early eighteenth century a group of Christians settled on a large farm in Germany. These Christians were called the Moravian Brethren who did much to get Protestant missionary efforts moving. They had a great desire that people all over the world should hear the Good News of Jesus Christ. In 1732 they sent out their first missionaries to the West Indies and in 1737 they sent their first missionary to Africa.

The missionary who was sent was called George Schmidt. Schmidt's main aim was to reach the Hottentots in the Cape area of South Africa. He had heard reports that the Dutch settlers in the area were no longer interested in evangelizing these people. Mr Schmidt began his work at a place one hundred miles to the east of Cape Town. He wanted very much to speak the Hottentot language but found that there were three kinds of clicks in their language which made it very difficult to learn and speak. He finally ended up by teaching the Hottentots to speak Dutch, so that they could understand the message he brought.

By 1742 Schmidt saw that there were several Hottentots who had received Christ as Saviour. He wanted to baptize them, but he was not an ordained pastor. So he wrote to his mission board in Germany asking for ordination. Once he received this he proceeded to baptize two Hottentots. This could have been the beginning of a strong Hottentot church in the area, except that some local Dutch pastors heard that the Germany missionary had baptized people in their church district. This made them unhappy, so they made a complaint in Cape Town that Schmidt had conducted the baptisms incorrectly and so should not be allowed to continue working in that area.

The Dutch made the work so difficult that Schmidt was forced to leave for Europe in 1744. He tried to return to South Africa to continue the work, but the Dutch would not permit it. So the missionary work among the Hottentots came to an end. It was fifty years before another missionary came to work with these people.

Another early mission society was the Society for the Propagation of the Gospel (S.P.G.), which was founded in

England in 1701. They sent most of their missionaries to North America. But in 1750 one of their missionaries who had worked in North America asked to be sent to West Africa to work among the Africans. So it was that in 1751 Thomas Thompson arrived at Cape Coast in the area we now call Ghana.

Thompson found the work rather difficult. The Africans who lived around the trading castle had watched the lives of the European traders for several years. They saw that these men did many evil things while claiming to be Christians. Therefore when Thompson arrived and started holding services for the Africans many of them were not interested in listening to his message. In addition to working with the Africans, he also sought to evangelize the traders. He found both Africans and Europeans very unresponsive. He worked hard for four years, but then he became sick and had to return to England.

The story of this early evangelistic effort at Cape Coast does not end with the departure of Thomas Thompson. In the first three years he was in the Gold Coast, Thompson had won some people to Christ. Three young men seemed very keen, so he arranged for them to go to England to study in 1754. They did well in their studies, but during their education two of these men died, leaving only Philip Quaque to complete the course. 'Philip Quaque completed his training and took Anglican orders, the first non-European since the Reformation to do so. In 1765 he was appointed by the Society for the Propagation of the Gospel as their "Missionary, School Master and Catechist to Negroes on the Gold Coast".'[1]

He arrived at his home in 1766 to begin his work. The job was not an easy one for Philip Quaque, as he had lost the fluency of his mother tongue since he had been away from his home for twelve years. At the beginning of his ministry he spoke through an interpreter while he familiarized himself again with the language.

Quaque found the people around the trading fort as difficult to evangelize as Thompson did. 'The task of winning individuals to a Christian confession was a hard one. After nine years' work, there were only fifty-two baptisms, and

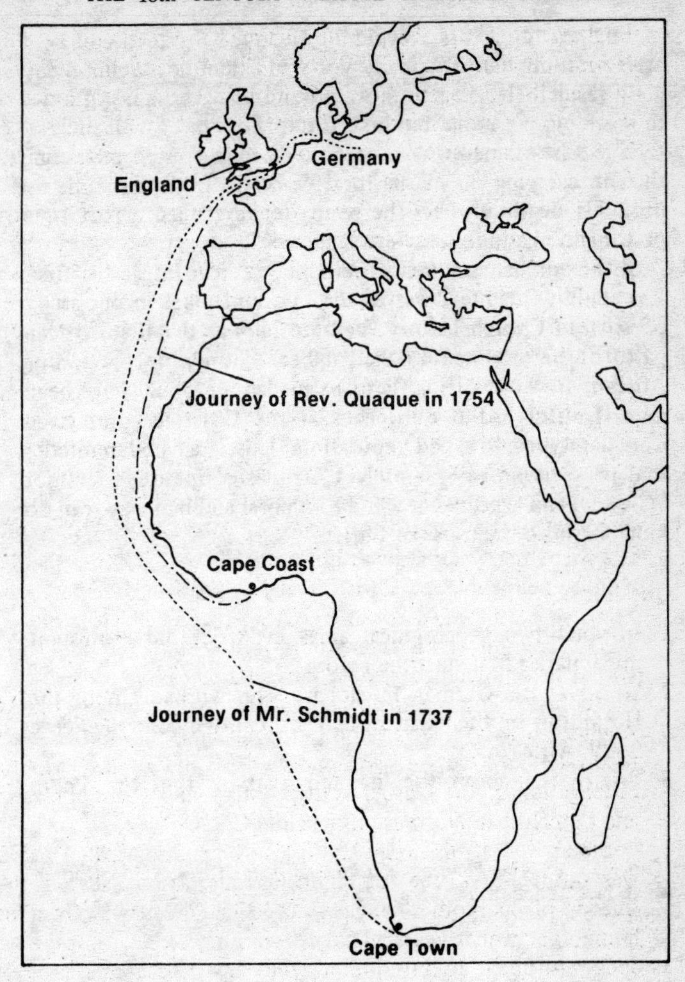

these included Europeans' and mulatto children. A principal obstacle to his work was the unworthy example of Europeans, even of the highest rank.'[2]

Like many pastors, Rev. Philip Quaque became discouraged after working hard for many years and then not seeing many good results. He tried to move around to other areas in order to reach other people, but his efforts did not meet with success. By 1790 he seems to have become more interested in trading than in carrying on his pastoral work. So from that time on until his death in 1816 he seems to have been a part time pastor and missionary at best.

Although his last years were not as fruitful as his first, Rev. Philip Quaque deserves an important place in our study of African Church history, because he was the first African pastor to be ordained by the Anglican Church to work among Africans in West Africa. Perhaps his labour would have been more fruitful if the Europeans at the Coast had not given Christianity such a bad reputation. This is a good reminder that people who call themselves 'Christians' but are in fact not believers, and who behave in an immoral and bad way, can do much harm to the cause of Christ.

Questions:

1. In what two geographical areas in Africa did Protestant missionaries first start their work?
2. Who was the German missionary who worked among the Hottentot in the eighteenth century? Why did he leave South Africa?
3. Briefly tell about the life and work of the Rev. Philip Quaque.

[1]Groves, C.P., *The Planting of Christianity in Africa*, vol. I (Lutterworth Press, London, 1948), p. 175
[2]Ibid. p. 176

12

Ending the slave trade

'Slavery – the possession of human beings as personal property – has existed in Africa, as in other parts of the world, since prehistoric times.'[1] In understanding the problem of slavery and the slave trade which faced Africa, Europe, North and South America in the eighteenth and nineteenth centuries, the student must realize that there were two concepts of slavery. The one type of slavery could be called 'limited slavery'. This was practised in most parts of Africa up to the twentieth century. It was a necessary thing because in most tribes there were no police forces nor prisons in which to put common thieves, criminals and war prisoners. Thus when a man in a tribal society did something bad against the tribe, his punishment was to be made a slave for a period of time. 'Slavery was usually for a specific period of time – commensurate with the nature of the crime or circumstances of capture – rather than being a perpetual condition, and it was also possible to earn freedom by good behaviour or purchase.'[2] When a man from another tribe was captured during a tribal war, he became a slave, but this did not necessarily mean that he would be a slave for the rest of his life. As a slave he only had to work a certain number of hours a day. In his spare time he could earn money to buy his freedom.

Now the great world problem with the slave trade developed because in the other parts of the world – mainly the Arab countries and Europe – people had a different concept or idea of slavery. When they talked of slavery they meant 'total slavery', i.e. when a man was purchased as a slave, he was a slave for the rest of his life, with little chance of freedom.

'This type of total enslavement appeared in Moslem North Africa and Egypt as early as the eleventh century, when Arab settlers' control of the Mediterranean end of the Saharan trade routes, and the spread of Islam into the savanna under the banner of the Almoravids, increased the volume of slave trading.'[3] When these Arab slave traders took an African to Turkey or the Middle East, such a man would be a slave for life.

To summarize the problem: when 'limited slavery' was practised in Africa it was not so bad, because an African still lived on his own continent, usually near the place where he was born. He lived among people who had a similar background and culture. Finally, in many cases he was able to terminate his slavery by either purchase or good behaviour. But when an Arab or European bought African slaves, he took them away from their native land and forced them to work in a foreign culture, usually for the rest of their lives.

How did the African slave trade develop? As noted above, the Arabs were already buying African slaves in the eleventh century to sell in the Mediterranean lands. 'Early Portuguese explorers and traders probably bought their first slave cargoes from Moslem traders on the coasts of Senegal and Mauritania in the middle of the fifteenth century.'[4] So it was that the earliest traders sent out by Prince Henry the Navigator bought some slaves. But before 1500, there really was not much need in Europe for African slaves. There was only a small demand for slaves as house servants.

By the end of the sixteenth century the Portuguese and Spanish had begun to develop sugar plantations in Brazil and other parts of the New World. These plantations required a large amount of unskilled labour. Slaves from Africa seemed to be the answer to this manpower need. The number of slaves that left Africa began to increase. In the sixteenth century European traders had been most interested in gold and ivory, but in the seventeenth and eighteenth centuries the demand shifted to slaves. The English and French began to develop tobacco and cotton plantations in their American colonies and these too required slave labour. By the end of the eighteenth century the volume of slaves being traded was quite high.

As the slave trade increased, the political situation in many parts of Africa became unstable. The European slave traders did not go into the countryside of Africa to buy slaves. Instead, different African chiefs would supply slaves to the Europeans at the coast. Some of these chiefs built up very large empires with the money and power they got from selling slaves. The Ashanti, Oyo and Dahomeans are three examples of tribes that made most of their money by attacking other tribes in order to capture slaves to sell at the coast. Because these tribes were always fighting to get slaves there was much unrest in Africa. When there is unrest it is difficult to aid development and it is difficult to do missionary work. During the seventeenth and eighteenth centuries we saw that there was little missionary work: the slave trade was one of the reasons why this was the case!

Slavery was a very important part of world trade, yet some people began to feel that it was wrong. It is interesting to see that the people who started the fight against slavery were truly born-again Christians in England and Europe. In the early part of the eighteenth century there had been a great Christian revival in England. This revival spread to North America. The most well-known man of this period of history was John Wesley who founded the Methodist Church. This revival brought a great change to the lives of many Englishmen and Americans. Such people were no longer selfish and interested only in themselves; they began to care about others. When God begins to change men on the 'inside', such people change on the 'outside'. As it turned out, many of these Christians who grew out of this revival began to work against the slave trade.

In England there was one group of Christians who made it one of their main aims to end slavery. This group was made up of politicians, bankers and businessmen. In 1772 they succeeded in having slavery outlawed in England. But these people did not just get the slaves freed in England and then forget about them. No, they began to develop a scheme whereby those Africans who did not have jobs in England and who wanted to return to Africa could do so. These Englishmen established a settlement in Sierra Leone in 1787 for ex-slaves, and then provided transport and money for these people to establish homes in Sierra Leone. The next twenty years were not easy for the ex-slaves. They formed a company and tried to develop honest trades in the area. Many people in England felt that if Sierra Leone could succeed in trading in items other than slaves, it would help to defeat the slave trade all along the coast.

But the group of Christians in England were not satisfied with only ending slavery in England. They realized that only if the slave ships could be stopped from buying slaves in Africa would slavery finally come to an end in the Americas. So they worked to get a bill passed in the English Parliament to stop British ships from carrying slaves. Wilberforce was the British politician who finally succeeded in getting the anti-slave bill passed in Parliament in 1807. After this great victory by the Christian abolitionists in England, other European countries decided to end the slave trade. 'The Danes had anticipated the British abolition by three years, the slave trade became illegal for the United States in 1808, and the Dutch outlawed it in 1814. Under British pressure, most of the other maritime nations followed suit after the Napoleonic wars (1815), though at first Portugal and Spain could be induced only to limit their slave trade to the seas south of the equator.'[5]

This did not mean the end of slavery all together. It would take another fifty years for the British navy finally to end the trading of slave ships on the West African coast. It would be even longer before the Arab slave traders in East Africa could be stopped from selling slaves to the Middle East.

However, this limiting of the slave trade by 1815 was a great encouragement to the new missionary effort in Africa which was just getting started. 'The success of the anti-slavery movement was not only an achievement of Christian men; it was an indispensable prerequisite for the successful planting of Christianity in Africa. . . There were still necessary those positive missionary activities that alone could communicate to Africa the Christian life and message. During the very years of the anti-slavery campaigns new missionary societies were appearing – a score or more sprang up, between 1792 and 1835, in England and Scotland, in North America, and on the continent of Europe. There had been nothing like it before. The Protestant Churches were at last awake.'[6]

Questions:

1. Explain the African practice of slavery in Africa. How did the Europeans and Arabs view slavery from the sixteenth to the nineteenth centuries?
2. Why were slaves needed in North and South America?
3. What had happened in the eighteenth century that made Christians in England concerned about the slave trade?
4. What was the purpose of the settlement in Sierra Leone?

[1]Wiedner, D.L., *A History of Africa South of the Sahara* (Vintage Books, Random House, New York, 1964), p. 45
[2]Ibid. p. 45
[3]Ibid. p. 46
[4]Ibid. p. 47
[5]Oliver, R. & Fage, J., *A Short History of Africa* (Penguin Books, Ltd., Middlesex, 1962), p. 136
[6]Groves, C.P., *The Planting of Christianity in Africa*, vol. I (Lutterworth Press, London, 1948), p. 196

13

Renewed missionary activity

In chapter eleven we saw that by 1750 there were only three or four small Protestant groups interested in missionary work in Africa. In chapter twelve we noted that in Europe and America from the period 1700 to 1790 there was a great revival among Protestants. One outcome of this revival was the desire among many Christians to end the slave trade. Another result was that Christians in America and Europe became concerned about the needs and salvation of people in other parts of the world. Because of this desire to reach out with the Gospel to other people, many different Protestant missionary societies were founded.

In 1780 different Christians began to talk about establishing new mission societies. One man who did the most to interest people in missions around 1790 was William Carey. He spoke to many different groups of Baptists in order to present the need for missionaries. 'On October 2, 1792, the Baptist Missionary Society was constituted. The first of the new missionary societies had been born.'[1] One year later, Carey and another man left England for India to become the first missionaries of this society. The reports of these men soon came to the attention of other Christians in other churches, so that in the thirty-five years that followed the founding of the Baptist mission, many other evangelical missions were established. The following is a brief list of the more important societies and the year in which they were founded.

1792 Baptist Missionary Society
1795 London Missionary Society
1796 Scottish Missionary Society

1796 Glasgow Missionary Society
1799 Church Missionary Society
1804 British & Foreign Bible Society
1810 American Board of Commissioners for Foreign Missions
1813 Wesleyan Methodist Missionary Society
1814 American Baptist Foreign Missionary Society
1815 Basel Missionary Society
1824 Church of Scotland Foreign Mission Committee
1824 United Presbyterian Missions

Naturally progress was slow at first, since all of these societies were small and they were attempting something new. But over the years the societies grew and the number of people interested in serving the Lord in different parts of the world increased.

In 1800 a successful missionary effort had not yet been established in West Africa, although several missionary societies had been founded. As it happened, before 1800 four different missionary societies tried to establish a work in Sierra Leone. For different reasons they did not succeed. Among the black settlers at Sierra Leone were many Christians. These people had become Christians when they were in England or America and so many of them continued to practise their faith. They had their own pastors and built their own churches. The mission societies did not want to help these black settlers as much as they wanted to reach the African tribes around Freetown and other parts of Sierra Leone. In 1800 there was still a lot of trading in slaves going on along the west coast of Africa. The mission societies felt that Sierra Leone, a colony of freed slaves, was the safest place to use as a base for reaching the tribes of Africa with the Gospel.

In 1804 the Church Missionary Society (C.M.S.) sent two German missionaries to Sierra Leone. These men were supposed to move to the Suso tribal area and work among the Suso. However, for several years they acted as chaplains to the settlers along the coast. Later other C.M.S. missionaries arrived to help in the work. By 1815 the missionaries had found a new ministry. The British navy was stopping ships along the coast of West Africa at that time. If a ship was found to be carrying slaves, it was forced to go to Sierra Leone and discharge the Africans. These Africans had to be settled and given a means of supporting themselves. The C.M.S. began to work among these newly released slaves that were brought to Sierra Leone.

In 1811 the first Wesleyan Methodist missionaries arrived in Sierra Leone and established a school and church work. Thus by 1815 in Sierra Leone there were the indigenous churches of the black settlers, the work of the C.M.S. and the new work of the Methodist mission.

There was another area besides Sierra Leone where the new missionary societies attempted to work, and this was South Africa, particularly the region around the Cape. In 1792 three missionaries of the Moravian Mission arrived in South Africa. Of course, the Moravians were not a new mission society, but they came to establish again the work started by George Schmidt back at the very place where George Schmidt had worked and built a school and church. They even found a woman whom George Schmidt had led to the Lord; she was more than eighty years old, but was still strong in her faith.

The Hottentots could see that the German missionaries were very interested in their welfare. 'By 1798 more than 800 Hottentots were settled on the station, of whom a quarter were members of the church.'[2] By 1802 the members had grown so large that a new church which could seat 1,000 people had to be built. By 1810 the church and station were well established.

Another mission society that started to work in South Africa was the London Missionary Society (L.M.S.). The first L.M.S. missionaries arrived in 1799 and divided into two groups. One group went east to work with the Xhosas beyond Graaff Reinet. It was a difficult time to work with these Africans as they were engaged in a conflict with the Dutch settlers in the area. By 1800 the L.M.S. missionaries saw that it was impossible to work with the Xhosas at that time, and withdrew from the area. The other group of L.M.S. missionaries began to work with the Bushmen north of Cape Town. The Bushmen did not respond very well to the Gospel message,

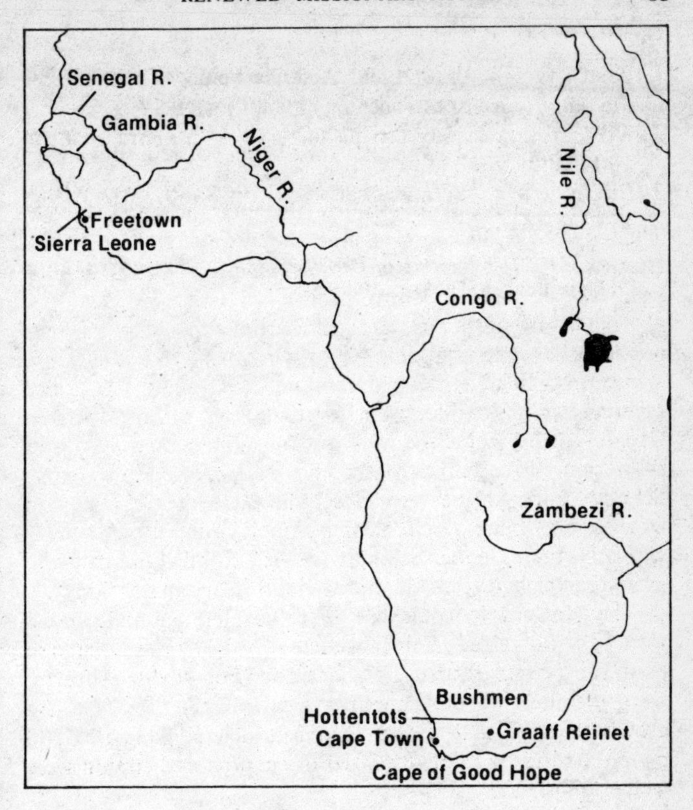

but the Hottentots in the area appreciated the message and many were saved. Many other missionaries began to arrive in Cape Town to assist the L.M.S. pioneers.

By 1815 then, we can see that the beginning of the modern Protestant missionary effort was firmly established in two areas. From these two regions missionaries could spread out with the Gospel message. Then, too, completely new areas of Africa could be entered with the use of knowledge gained in the pioneering work of missionaries in Sierra Leone and Cape Province.

Questions:

1. What event in Europe and America helped Christians see the importance of establishing mission societies?
2. What mission society established a work in Sierra Leone in 1804? Briefly tell of its work.
3. Briefly tell about missionary work in South Africa from 1792 to 1815.

[1]Groves, C.P., *The Planting of Christianity in Africa*, vol. I (Lutterworth Press, London, 1948), p. 198
[2]Ibid. p. 221

14

Expansion in South Africa

By 1815 there were a number of Protestant missionary societies working in South Africa. During the period 1815 to 1840 these societies were increased in number by new societies while at the same time the number of Christians in southern Africa increased.

From 1815 to 1840 the work of the Moravian Mission continued to expand. As the number of Hottentots at the Genadendal Mission Station increased, practical trades such as metal working were taught to the people. In 1817 the Moravian missionaries started a work among people who had leprosy. These people had been neglected by the Hottentots and settlers, and so it was the missionaries who first sought to meet their need by establishing a leper asylum.

The London Missionary Society continued to build up their work during the twenty-five years after 1815. In 1815 the L.M.S. was mainly working with the Griquas in the north. The missionaries worked in the region of Griqua Town which was 700 miles from Cape Town. From this place the L.M.S. was invited to move further north by the chief of the Bechuana, and so work was started among this tribe.

In 1817 one of the best known L.M.S. missionaries arrived in South Africa. He was Robert Moffat who was only twenty-one years old when he arrived in Cape Colony. At first Moffat worked with a much feared Hottentot chief, named Africaner. In 1820 Moffat married Mary Smith and the L.M.S. transferred him to Bechuanaland to work with the people there. The Moffats established a mission station at Kuruman on the river by that name. They remained at this place for many years.

In 1815 the Wesleyan Methodist mission began work in South Africa. They opened their work in the Namaqua area. Later in 1821 the Methodists sent missionaries into Bechuanaland.

After 1820 several other missionary societies entered the work in South Africa. It would soon become confusing if I tried to name each one and tell the area in which they worked. However, you can see by the information already given that the early missionaries were already beginning to make good progress in getting out the Gospel by 1820. As the encouraging news of their progress reached Europe and America, more missionaries came, so that by 1840 there were eighty-five Protestant mission stations in South Africa. An Englishman visited South Africa in 1840 and visted many of these stations. He then listed the different missions and the number of mission stations they had. 'He made individual reports on *twenty-six* stations of the London Mission (LMS) (eighteen in Cape Colony; two in Kaffraria; three in Griqualand, counting the outstations of Griqua Town as one; two in Namaqualand; and Kuruman in the Bechuana country); *thirty-two* of the Wesleyan Methodist Society (sixteen in Cape Colony, eight in Kaffraria, three in the Basuto, three in the Bechuana country and two in Great Namaqualand); *six* Moravian stations (five in the Colony and one at Shiloh in Kaffraria); *five* of the Glasgow Society (all in Kaffraria); *seven* Paris Society centres (three each in Basutoland and the Bechuana country, and one at the Cape); *six* Rhenish Society stations (five at the Cape, and one jointly with the L.M.S. in Namaqualand); and *three* of the Berlin Mission (one in Griqualand and two in Kaffraria). He also reported on thirteen centres of the Dutch Reformed Church in the colony.'[1] We can see by 1840, when there were hardly any missionaries in East Africa, that the Church in South Africa was already well established.

We cannot leave the work of this missionary period without mentioning the great work done by some missionaries in protecting the rights of the Hottentots and Africans in southern Africa at this time. We must remember that the Cape became a British colony in the early nineteenth century. The

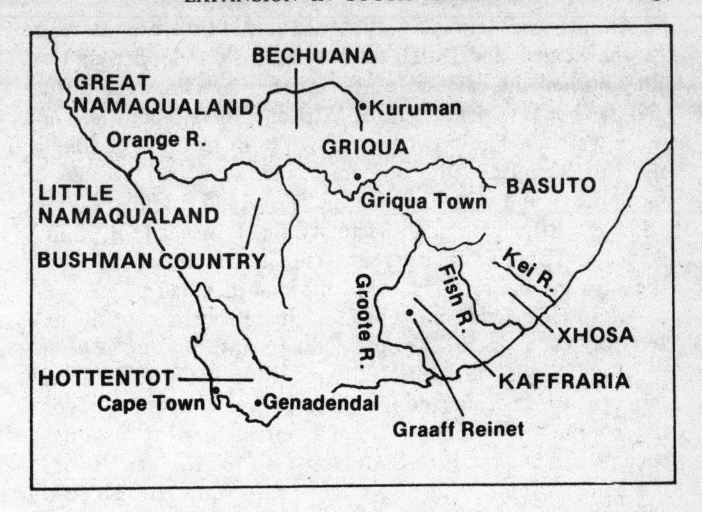

British had ended the slave trade in 1807. This meant that the Dutch settlers in the Colony had a problem in getting cheap labour to help them on their farms. The Hottentots were unwilling to work on these farms, since they did not need the money. The settlers persuaded the British governor to pass a law requiring those Hottentots who did not work on farms, i.e. those who lived on mission stations or on their land, to pay a tax in money. This, of course, forced the Hottentots to work to get money to pay the tax. At this time the famous L.M.S. missionary called Dr John Philip became aware of this unfair treatment of the Hottentots and began working to protect them. Dr Philip first tried to persuade the Governor of the Cape to protect the human rights of the Hottentots, but he was not successful. In 1828 he wrote a book called 'Researches in South Africa' in which he told about the unfair treatment the Hottentots received. As a result of Dr Philip's work, a law was passed in July, 1828, which said that the Hottentots in the Cape Province should enjoy the same rights as all other people.

Another problem in South Africa at that time was the desire by the English and Dutch settlers for more and more land. As they pushed the eastern frontier of the Cape Province farther and farther into land held by Africans, there were more and more wars. Dr Philip tried to show the British that as long as the settlers pushed the borders farther east, there would be more death and wars. But few people would listen to him. In 1835 the British Colonial Secretary finally heeded Dr Philip's advice and ordered that the settlers pull back their border with the Africans and return some of the land they had taken.

'Meanwhile hard on the heels of the retrocession of the new territory came one of the outstanding events of Cape history – the Great Trek. Between 1836 and 1840 some 7,000 Dutch farmers, it is said, crossed the Orange River, thus going beyond the confines of the Colony, and settled in what eventually became the Orange Free State; some crossed the Vaal River to the North; others went into what became Natal. British policy in the race questions was predominantly the issue that led to the Boer withdrawal.'[2]

It can be seen that in the early years of missionary work in South Africa, it was the missionaries who tried to protect the rights of the Hottentots and Africans and at the same time preserve their land for them.

Questions:

1. Who was Robert Moffat?
2. By 1840 how many Protestant mission stations were there in South Africa?
3. Briefly describe the work of Dr John Philip.

[1]Groves, C.P., *The Planting of Christianity in Africa*, vol. I (Lutterworth Press, London, 1948), p. 267

[2]Ibid. p. 258

15

Slow progress in West Africa

From 1815 to 1840 mission societies continued to work in West Africa. But during this time a large number of missionaries died because of fever and other illness. These early missionaries also faced the opposition of illegal slave traders. Although the slave trade had been outlawed, many slave ships continued to work along the coast of West Africa, illegally buying slaves from the African chiefs of the coast. But through these difficult beginnings a Church was established in West Africa.

In chapter thirteen we noted that the C.M.S. had found a new ministry in working among liberated slaves who were brought to Sierra Leone by the British navy. More missionaries were sent out in 1816 to help with this work. Before they left England they were reminded that their main task was the work of evangelism. From 1816 to 1819 the C.M.S. established nine villages for liberated Africans to settle in. A school was established and two missionary schoolmasters were brought to Sierra Leone by the British navy. More mission-masons, bricklayers, carpenters, shingle-makers, smiths and tailors. In 1827 a very important educational event occurred: Fourah Bay College was established in Sierra Leone to give further education to those people who completed work in the mission schools. Later this College was affiliated with the University of Durham so that it could grant degrees. The early missionaries were responsible for the establishment of the first university-college in West Africa.

'At the close of this period (1840) the C.M.S. reported 1,500 communicants in Sierra Leone with a regular attendance at public worship of 5,500 more. The fifty schools had 6,000 pupils on their rolls. The Wesleyan membership was approaching some 2,000 members, with 1,500 at their schools.'[1]

A little north of Sierra Leone was the Gambia. In 1821 a Wesleyan Methodist missionary by the name of Morgan landed at the mouth of the Gambia River to begin work in that area. 'But it was work among a Muslim people; Morgan laboured on for two years without a sign of success. "Mohammedans seemed to be shielded against Christianity," he wrote, "as perfectly as the crocodiles in the river were against the spear and the bullet. Preaching and school-teaching were alike unsuccessful." '[2] Morgan left the Muslims and began to work with liberated slaves at the Gambia coast. By 1836 Methodist Church membership had reached 535 and there were 230 students enrolled in their schools. But 1837 was a bad year in that yellow fever attacked the work in Gambia, killing all but one of the missionaries there.

To the south of Sierra Leone was an area of territory which was to become Liberia. Because of the success of the British settlement at Sierra Leone for freed slaves, an American group decided to establish a colony for freed slaves in Africa. In 1820 the first party of settlers landed in what is now called Liberia (a name that comes from the word 'Liberty'). At first the black settlers had a difficult time, because the local Africans were unfriendly. But after eight hard years the settlement became fairly well established. From 1829 to 1835 more than fifteen missionaries came to Liberia but most of them died before they had been in the country one year. Since Liberia was an American project, most of the missionary effort was carried on by American societies. One American church that came to work in Liberia early in the history of that country was the Methodist Episcopal Church which established its first outpost in 1833. From these early efforts came one of the largest churches in Liberia today: the United Methodist Church. Many of the early missionaries who came to Liberia were Black-American pastors, who established churches among the settlers. When more missionaries came in the mid-1830's they extended the work to the surrounding African tribes. Unfortunately, the black settlers of Liberia did not want to

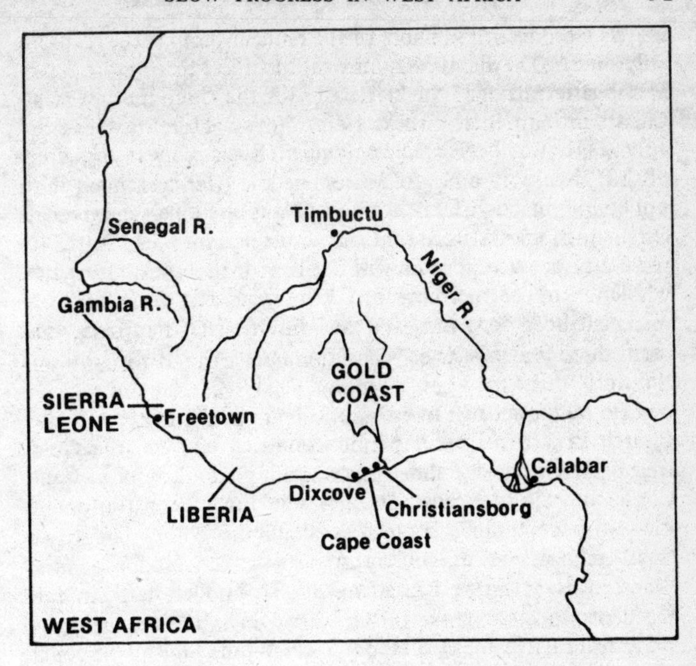

mix with the African converts, and so separate churches were established in Liberia.

Another area of missionary activity during this time was the Gold Coast, further to the east from Liberia. As mentioned in chapter eleven, there was a Christian effort made at Cape Coast in the eighteenth century, but because of the climate and the bad example of the European traders, progress had been very, very slow.

In December, 1828, a new mission society began to work in the Gold Coast. It was called the Basel Mission. This mission had been training German and Swiss Christians for missionary service for many years. Usually, these men served with other mission societies such as the C.M.S., but in 1828 they began their own work in the Gold Coast. Of the four missionaries who arrived in December, three were dead by August, 1829.

In 1831 the fourth member of the pioneer party died, temporarily ending the Basel Mission work. In 1832 three more Basel missionaries arrived. 'In March, 1832, the three men were at Christiansborg. In six weeks Heinze, the doctor, was dead; in July, Jager was buried; in September, Riis's life was despaired of, but thanks to a Negro doctor, he was given treatment that pulled him through. Once again there was one lonely survivor.'[3] Other missionaries were sent out, but they, too, died. In 1840 the Basel '. . .Committee was faced with the question of the whole future of the mission. Twelve years had gone by; nine men had been sent out, and one survived. Of baptized converts there was not one.'[4] The Committee voted to continue the work, but with a new direction, as we will read about later.

One of the most interesting incidents in the history of the Church in Africa of this period comes to us from the Gold Coast. Around 1822 the British established a school at Cape Coast to train Africans for service in the administration of the different trading companies along the coast. The Cape Coast school was run by an African, called Joseph Smith. 'Smith was a sincere Christian with an implicit faith in the Word of God. He, therefore, on his own initiative, included Bible readings in his curriculum. . .'[5] Among Smith's students was a man by the name of William de Graft. He was very much interested in his teacher's Bible readings and so asked Smith if he could have a Bible of his own. Through what he read, de Graft received Jesus Christ as his Saviour. But unlike Smith, de Graft wanted to reach out to other people and at the same time try to understand more of the message of the Bible. Soon de Graft organized his own group among the students at the school. 'De Graft called his company "A Meeting or Society for Promoting Christian Knowledge"; the first meeting was on October 1, 1831. They were systematic in their Bible reading, and stated their purpose in these words: "That, as the Word of God is the best rule a Christian ought to observe, it is herein avoided framing other rules to enforce good conduct; but that the Holy Scriptures must be carefully studied, through which, by the help of the Holy Spirit and faith in Jesus Christ, our minds will be enlightened, and find the way to eternal life."[6]

Joseph Smith did not like the idea of de Graft leading such a Bible study, so Smith asked the Governor of Cape Coast to put de Graft and another member of the Bible study group into prison because they were 'dangerous'. While in prison de Graft and his friend sang hymns and preached to the other prisoners. One man was saved because of their ministry! Within the year the Governor realized that de Graft and his friend were not bad men, and so they were released from prison.

De Graft moved to Dixcove along the coast and continued his ministry. Many people were converted and soon they asked de Graft for Bibles. Because de Graft was an African, with no connection with an overseas mission society, he did not know where to get the Bibles for these people. De Graft went to a Christian captain at Cape Coast and asked if he could get them some Bibles. This captain was very impressed when he heard of how this group of believers had grown because of the ministry of de Graft. This captain was able to get a Wesleyan Methodist missionary to come to Cape Coast in 1834. The missionary was only able to work at Cape Coast for six months before he was brought down by fever, but in that time he was able to bring together de Graft and his former teacher Joseph Smith, so that they became workers together in getting out the Gospel. Other Methodist missionaries followed and soon the Methodist Church was well established at the coast. But it must be remembered that this church was the result of the work begun by the African Christians: Joseph Smith and William de Graft in the 1820's.

By 1840, then, we can see that the Christian mission was firmly established, although still not as large as the work in South Africa. There was a good foundation built in Sierra Leone, while in Gambia and Liberia there was a Christian witness that would be continued in the years to come. Even in the unhealthy climate of the Gold Coast missionaries had been able to strengthen the church which had been established by the Africans there.

Questions:

1. Briefly tell what the missionaries in Sierra Leone did to help the liberated slaves.
2. How did the first missionary work begin in the Gambia?
3. Tell of the difficulties of the Basel Mission in the Gold Coast.
4. Who was William de Graft and what part did he play in establishing the church in the Gold Coast (modern Ghana)?

[1] Groves, C.P., *The Planting of Christianity in Africa*, vol. I (Lutterworth Press, London, 1948), p. 283
[2] Ibid. p. 289
[3] Ibid. p. 300
[4] Ibid. p. 301
[5] Ibid. p. 301
[6] Ibid. p. 302

16

Sierra Leone. Base for outreach

The first forty years of the nineteenth century had been filled with progress and invention in Europe. Inexpensive cloth and cheaper steel were being made because of the 'industrial revolution' which was well under way. The first steamship had already been launched and there were already some railways in operation in both Europe and America. This improvement in industry and communication meant that the world was trading and exchanging more items than ever before. People in Europe and America wanted to know more about places like Japan, Korea, Australia and the interior of Africa.

Although the world had made great progress by 1840, the fact remained that still very little was known about the interior of Africa by people who lived in other places. Although the Portuguese had drawn a map in the sixteenth century showing the entire coast of Africa, by the early nineteenth century much of the interior of Africa still remained hidden to people in the rest of the world. Mapmakers did not know where the source of the Nile River was; they did not know the course of the Congo or Zambezi Rivers; the size and position of Africa's interior lakes were also unknown. We should not be surprised when we read that the Church in Africa was mainly a coastal church before 1840.

From 1840 to 1878 a large number of European explorers came to Africa to find out more about the natural geography of interior Africa. While these men were making their journeys, the Church and its missionaries were not remaining idle. Indeed, this period was a time in which Christians entered many new areas of sub-Saharian Africa and began to push inland from the coast with the Good News of Jesus Christ.

THE NEW MISSIONARY THRUSTS

In the next few chapters we are going to look at the history of the Church from the viewpoint of four major thrusts or penetrations. By this I mean that we are going to see how missionaries and African Church leaders used established bases such as Sierra Leone and South Africa from which to organize expeditions to unknown and unreached areas which were nearby in order to expand the Church. We have seen in the last three chapters how Christianity was established in and around Sierra Leone and South Africa. We want to now study how people from these two areas began to move into other parts of Africa. We will also see that knowledge gained by missionaries and church leaders in these two areas enabled them to make faster progress in the new parts of Africa to which they went.

Then, too, we will see how new church outposts were established at the mouth of the Congo River Region in West-Central Africa and at Mombasa in East Africa. From 1840 to 1878 the Church made little progress in these areas. But because of the work done during this time, rapid church expansion could be made after 1880.

SIERRA LEONE 1840–1878

In the next chapter we will see how important Sierra Leone was to the missionary outreach in West Africa for thirty years after 1840. The C.M.S. used Sierra Leone as its headquarters for West Africa for several years. Most of the early African missionaries came from Sierra Leone. Sierra Leone was also a base for supplies and communication during this period of expansion of the Church. But before we look at this expansion, we should briefly assess the development of the Church in Sierra Leone itself during this period.

The Anglican Church in Sierra Leone continued to grow from 1840 to 1878. The C.M.S. had first arrived in Sierra Leone in 1804 and by 1816 had organized a local denomina-

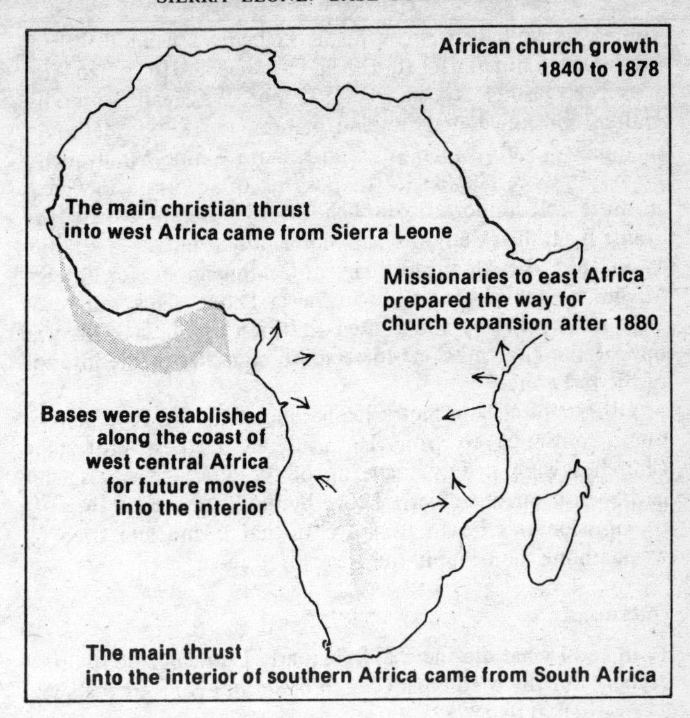

tion. Because of the continued growth, it was decided by the C.M.S. missionaries in 1854 that the Sierra Leone Anglican Church should soon become completely administered and supported by Africans. Local church affairs were turned over to the African pastors who built up the schools and churches. In 1866 the Sierra Leone Anglican Church celebrated its golden jubilee (fifty years of existence). In 1816 there had been six communicant members, but in 1866 there were 6,000.

Another early church in Sierra Leone had been the Wesleyan Methodists. This church continued to grow during the period we are now studying. The church would have grown even faster during this period, but there were not enough missionary volunteers willing to work in Sierra Leone. In addition, the Methodist Church lacked the money needed to expand the work. Nevertheless, the Sierra Leone Wesleyan Methodist church continued to grow and mature. In 1866 a Methodist missionary said: 'We must regard Sierra Leone as advancing beyond a mere Mission to the position of a Church, in a great measure self-supporting, though for the present assisted by grants from the (Methodist) Mission House Fund.'[1]

In 1855 the American Board of Commissioners for Foreign Missions established a work in Sierra Leone. This work was later taken over by the United Brethren in Christ. This was one of the first missions to establish churches in the interior of Sierra Leone.

Other churches in Sierra Leone, including the Free Methodists, continued to grow. However, all of these Protestant Churches were mainly made up of the liberated slaves who had been brought to Sierra Leone by the British navy. In 1870 the missionaries began to move further inland and tried to work among the tribes in the area.

Questions:

1. In 1854 what did the C.M.S. in Sierra Leone decide to do?
2. Why did the Methodist Church in Sierra Leone grow slowly from 1840 to 1878?

[1]Groves, C.P., *The Planting of Christianity in Africa*, vol. II (Lutterworth Press, London, 1954), p. 219

17

Samuel Crowther West Africa's great church pioneer

The thrust into unevangelized areas of West Africa during the period 1840 to 1878 could be characterized by the life of one outstanding African. His name is Samuel Adjai Crowther. Because of his great work and many contributions to the development of the Church we must take special note of Rev. Crowther as one more of the great men of African Church history.

Samuel Adjai Crowther was a member of the Yoruba tribe of Nigeria. He had been captured and sold into slavery during one of the many slave-raids of eastern Nigeria. 'As a lad, Crowther was rescued by a British boat from a slave ship, was taken to Sierra Leone, and was educated there. . .'[1] Like other liberated slaves, Samuel Crowther was greatly helped by the C.M.S. He attended their primary schools and received training as a teacher-catechist. Because of faithful service, in 1841 Samuel Crowther was asked by the C.M.S. to help the 'Niger Expedition'. This was a plan to sail up the Niger River from the mouth in the Gulf of Guinea and then to find a way to stop slave raids that were continuing in the interior of Nigeria. Samuel Crowther and a missionary took part in the expedition to see how the land could be opened up to the Gospel. Unfortunately most of the explorers who came out from England to take part in the expedition became ill with malaria, and so before the boat had moved very far up the Niger the men had to return to Sierra Leone. Although the expedition was a failure for ending slave raiding, it did serve the purpose of showing Samuel Crowther the great need of his homeland for the Gospel. Crowther wrote about his experiences on that journey in a book which is called his 'Journal'.

In 1842 the C.M.S. sent Samuel Crowther to England for theological education. In 1843 he was ordained as a pastor in the Anglican Church by the Bishop of London. 'On his return to Sierra Leone at the end of 1843 he received a great welcome and conducted in English his first service. But his mother tongue was not forgotten, and he soon took a service in Yoruba, probably the first to be taken in that language. However, he was not long to preach in Yoruba in Sierra Leone; before the year (1844) was out he had sailed for Yorubaland.'[2]

The time seemed right for the C.M.S. to expand from Sierra Leone into other parts of West Africa. Rev. Samuel Crowther seemed to be the right man to develop this work. 'In December, 1844, Crowther, Townsend, and Gollmer with their wives and four African teachers left Freetown on their momentous mission – the first effective outreach from the base at Sierra Leone, so long and patiently developed, to a field a thousand miles inland. Looked at on a map of Africa today the penetration appears slight, but at that period in relation to a slavery-infected coast and to the intermittent ferment of internal wars, it was indeed a heroic adventure.'[3]

The party arrived in the geographical area we call Nigeria today, in January 1845. Not long after that Crowther met his mother and family from whom he had been taken away years before. At first the C.M.S. worked at Badagri and then moved their headquarters to Lagos. From there the pioneers went inland to Abeokuta in Yorubaland. 'The first Christian baptisms in Abeokuta took place on Sunday, February 6, 1848, before a congregation of some 250 people. Two men and three women, of whom Samuel Crowther's aged mother was one, were received into the fellowship of the Christian Church.[4]

In August, 1851, Rev. Samuel Crowther was called to England for consultation. Since Rev. Samuel Crowther was an African and had visited much of Yorubaland, the British government wanted to get his advice concerning slave raiding. Rev. Samuel Crowther reported that slavery was still carried

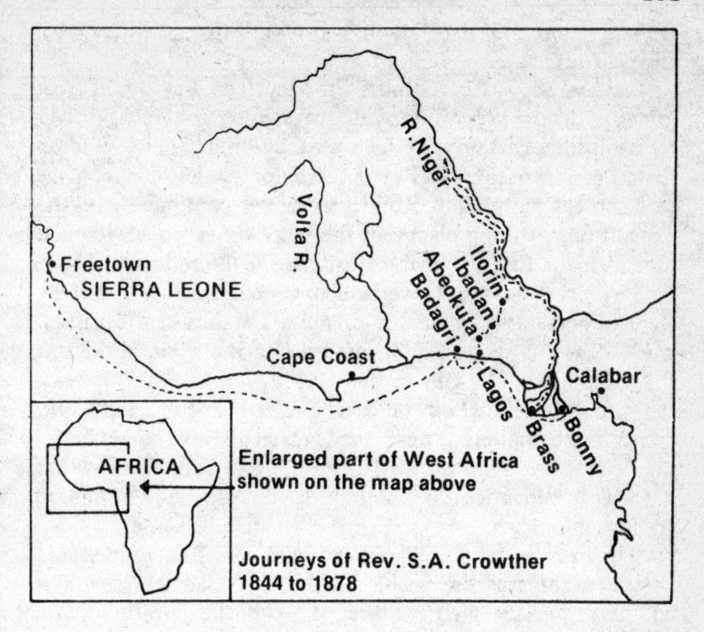

on in the area, but African church leaders and missionaries were relatively free to move around the towns.

Because of the work of Rev. Samuel Crowther and the others in his group the church continued to grow. In 1854 the Bishop of Sierra Leone visited Yorubaland to see the work. At that time he ordained the first two Africans in that area. In 1856 the C.M.S. sent Rev. Samuel Crowther up the Niger to see if it were possible to take the Gospel to that area. In his report, Rev. Samuel Crowther wrote: 'The reception we met with all along from the kings and chiefs of the countries was beyond expectation. I believe the time has fully come when Christianity must be introduced on the banks of the Niger: the people are willing to receive any who may be sent among them.'[5] After the C.M.S. read this report they assigned Rev. Samuel Crowther and Rev. J.C. Taylor (an African pastor from the Ibo tribe) to establish a 'Niger Mission' to take the Gospel to that area.

In July, 1857, Rev. Samuel Crowther and Rev. J.C. Taylor joined a British expedition which was going up the Niger river by steamship. Part way up the river they found a good location for a mission station, so Rev. J.C. Taylor was left at that place to begin the work. Rev. Samuel Crowther continued with the expedition, marking places on the map which would be good locations for future mission stations. On the return trip Rev. Samuel Crowther went overland to visit Ilorin to see if there were opportunities there for opening a station and Christian work. Since he was well educated in the Bible and also knew the teachings of the Qur'an, he could speak intelligently with the tribal leaders whom he met. Because of his great work, many opportunities were made available for the Gospel message to be proclaimed. However, Rev. Samuel Crowther needed missionaries and church leaders to staff proposed stations in order to bring the Gospel to inland Nigeria.

'The promise of the Niger Mission remained: how to secure its realization was the problem. It was to Samuel Crowther, who was already meriting the title of "the apostle of the Niger", that the Society (C.M.S.) eventually turned.'[6] After much thought as to the best way of evangelizing the Niger area, a C.M.S. missionary, Henry Venn, made a bold proposal: Rev. Samuel should be made a bishop in the Anglican Church and then assigned the leadership of an all-African mission to set up mission stations and evangelize the area. Church leaders agreed to this so that '. . . Crowther was consecrated a bishop of the Church of England in Canterbury Cathedral on June 29, 1864. The University of Oxford had previously entered his name on its roll of divinity graduates by conferring upon him an honorary doctorate.'[7]

Bishop Crowther returned at once to Nigeria and made Lagos his headquarters for expanding the Niger mission. He got catechists and schoolmasters from Sierra Leone to staff his new mission stations. He then expanded the work to the towns of Brass and Bonny. In 1864 he went to Bonny by invitation of the king. The King of Bonny who had become a

Christian while in England asked Bishop Crowther to establish a mission station in the city. 'A site was provided and money collected; the European traders gave their support, and despite dissident chiefs and pagan priests the work was set going. In 1871 Crowther's son, who had been ordained (and later became Archdeacon), took charge at Bonny. There was persecution and in 1875 the first Christian was martyred. The leading persecutor among the chiefs, Captain Hart as he was known, in 1877 granted religious liberty, and at his death the following year ordered the family idols to be destroyed. In 1867 a mission was begun at Brass where in 1875 a leading chief became a convert, and two years later the king of Brass himself renounced idolatry.'[8]

And so by 1878 Bishop Crowther's Niger Mission had opened up a former slave-raiding and trading centre to the Gospel. The Niger Mission is important in African Church history as the first organized mission of West Africans taking the Good News of Jesus Christ to Africans. Bishop Crowther continued his dynamic leadership of the Niger Mission in Nigeria until his death in 1891. There is little doubt that he was one of the greatest African Church leaders of the nineteenth century. Because of Bishop Samuel Crowther's great burden for his countrymen's salvation and his dedicated service, Nigeria had been opened up to the Gospel.

THE WORK OF OTHER MISSIONS IN NIGERIA

Although the major work in opening Nigeria to the Gospel during this period was done by Bishop Crowther and the C.M.S., there were other mission societies which also started Christian work. There is not enough space in this volume to mention all of them, but we should note a few of the important ones.

The Wesleyan Methodist Church opened a work in Badagri in 1843. Thomas Freeman and William de Graft were sent by the Methodists from the Gold Coast to Badagri to pioneer the work in that land. Within a few years they had brought African teachers to begin the task of preaching the Gospel. Freeman and de Graft actually got to Abeokuta before the C.M.S.

pioneer party. However the Methodists did not have enough men to open a work in Abeokuta in 1844, so it was not until 1848 that they established a mission station there.

In 1849 the Southern Baptist Church of the United States sent its first two missionaries to Africa. One of the missionaries, who was a Black American, was left in Liberia to minister to the Baptists there. The other man, Thomas Bowen, arrived in Badagri in 1850, from where he went inland to Abeokuta. His goal was Bohoo, close to Abeokuta, but because of tribal wars he was not able to go there for two years. Finally, he was able to establish a work there. He then returned to the United States to get more workers and funds to build up the work. However, upon arrival the new workers went down with malaria. Progress for the Baptists was slow during those early years.

Although there had been various tribal wars in western Nigeria from 1845 in 1860 these never made the work of missionaries completely impossible. Beginning in 1860 the political situation became more unstable and the number of wars increased. There was much rivalry between the chiefs (or kings) of Lagos, Ibadan and Abeokuta. '. . . in October, 1867, the Egba chiefs suddenly turned on the missionaries; Anglican, Wesleyan, and Baptist were expelled with nothing but the clothes in which they stood. It was a staggering blow. . . The expelled missionaries were confident of an early recall, but it was 1880 before a permanent return proved possible. . . But if there was much to lament, there proved also to be some ground for thanksgiving. The Church survived, chastened and purified, a saving remnant faithfully witnessing to Christian truth. In 1870 this was vividly demonstrated; Abeokuta and Ibadan were still in unfriendly relationship, when the Christians in each plighted their troth: "However great misunderstandings may be among the heathen of Abeokuta and Ibadan, let unity and peace be among us Christians of the two rival cities, for we are the followers of the Prince of Peace." Lagos now became the missionary headquarters of Yorubaland.'[9] It can be seen that after twenty years of missionary effort in the Abeokuta area, the church was fairly well established.

When the missionaries were expelled in 1867 there were enough strong local Christians in the area to continue the work of the Church.

EASTERN NIGERIA

So far we have discussed the opening of mission work in western Nigeria and the Niger Delta. To end this chapter we should note the arrival of the light of the Christian message to the area around Calabar. This city was far to the east of the other cities where mission work had been established. The Scottish Presbyterian Mission began work in this area in 1847. The region around Calabar was a very difficult place to work, because the people were deep in spirit worship. The witch-doctors were powerful men; whenever a chief died, these witchdoctors would require that a large number of slaves and servants be killed in order to please the evil spirits and provide slaves and servants for the dead king in the 'next world'.

The first Scottish missionaries to arrive went right into language study. Before long they had Scripture portions in the local language for the people. In 1862 the New Testament was translated into Efik and in 1868 the Old Testament was completed.

Through the hard work of the early missionaries the Church began to grow. 'A significant stage in the work of the mission was reached with the first ministerial ordination in 1872. Esien Ukpabio, the first baptized convert and the first African teacher, was ordained to the ministry on April 9. . .'[10]

By 1878 the Gospel was being given out from several centres in Nigeria. The Lord was blessing the work. Although there were still not very large numbers of Christians, the small churches that had been established already had African pastors.

Questions:

1. Where was Samuel Crowther born? What happened to him when he was a young boy?
2. When did Samuel Crowther first go to England? What was the purpose of this visit?

3. What was the Niger Mission? Who directed this work?
4. Why do you think Rev. Samuel Crowther is important in African Church history?
5. When did the Baptist Church begin working in Nigeria and in what area?
6. What mission began working in Eastern Nigeria?

[1] Latourette, Kenneth S., *A History of the Expansion of Christianity: The Great Century*, vol. V (Harper & Bros., New York, 1943), p. 436
[2] Groves, C.P., *The Planting of Christianity in Africa*, vol. II (Lutterworth Press, London, 1954), p. 18
[3] Ibid. p. 49
[4] Ibid. p.57
[5] Ibid. p. 74
[6] Ibid. p. 78
[7] Ibid. p. 236
[8] Ibid. p.238
[9] Ibid. pp. 235, 236
[10] Ibid. p. 240

18

Other West African areas 1840–1878

To complete this study of the period 1840–1878 in West Africa let us briefly look at the beginning of missions in a few other places along the coast.

Moving to the west, we find that a major effort was made by the Wesleyan Methodist Church in the Gold Coast (now called Ghana) to expand the work begun by William de Graft in the 1830's. In 1841 a missionary, Thomas Freeman, moved inland to Kumasi to see if it were possible to establish a Methodist mission in that capital city. Freeman received a friendly welcome by the King of Ashanti and was also given a site for the mission to build a church. Additional missionaries were sent to work at Kumasi, but some of them died or were unable to carry on the work.

Along the coast more and more people began to turn to Christianity. Naturally as the number of Christians increased, the priests of the traditional religions became frightened that they would soon have no more followers, and also no one to pay their wages. Quite often there were disagreements between the growing Church and the priests of the tribal religions. An example of this type of trouble can be found in 1849. 'A small Christian community at Asafa near Cape Coast lived close by the sacred grove of Brafo, a national god and oracle with priests in attendance. One of the priests became a Christian convert. The priests in charge, sensing the threat to their prestige and revenues, secured the support of the chiefs in defence of their shrine. The breaking point was reached when some of the Christians cut building poles in the sacred grove. The local chief who had been appointed to act for his

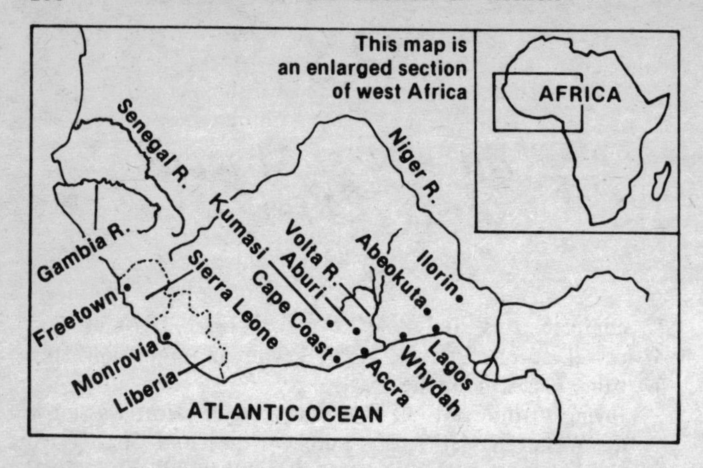

colleagues arrested ten of the Christians and burned their village. The case . . . came before the Judicial Assessor and aroused great excitement. The Court imposed fines on each side, . . .'[1]

To the east of Cape Coast, the headquarters of the Methodist Church, was Christiansborg, a Danish trading fort. (Today Christiansborg is part of the modern city of Accra, capital of Ghana). Christiansborg was the headquarters of the Basel Mission Society. In chapter fifteen we saw that by 1840 this society had only one missionary who was alive and working in the city, although many had been sent to work in that place. After 1840 the Basel Mission began a new policy of 'church planting'. They began sending their missionaries inland to Abokobi and Aburi. In 1843 they opened the first school for boys and in 1847 a school for girls. One year later in 1848 a Bible school for training catechists was opened. The Basel Mission also felt that the translation of the Scriptures was important for church growth. The work was begun around 1858 and by 1868 the entire Bible had been translated into Twi. By 1869 there were eight church districts with twenty-four local congregations with a total membership of 1,851.

From 1870 to 1874 there was a war between the British colonialists at the Coast and the Ashanti Kings. In 1874 the Ashanti were defeated. Because of the war the work of evangelism was made more difficult and the Church did not make as fast progress as it should have.

DAHOMEY

To the east of the Gold Coast was Dahomey (now called Benin). This kingdom was ruled by a very ruthless king. He made great wealth by making war on neighbouring tribes. Because his army was so strong he always defeated the tribes around and took many prisoners who were sold as slaves. The king of Dahomey was very much against the arrival of Christian workers because he knew they would seek to end slavery in his kingdom. The C.M.S. opened a witness at Whydah on the coast in 1857. The mission was operated by an African pastor called P.W. Bernasko. But because of the slave-raiding and the trouble made by the King of Dahomey, little progress was made in that area from 1857 to 1878.

LIBERIA

In Liberia for the period 1849 to 1878 progress was rather slow. The problem was made up of two parts: the unhealthy climate and the hatred between the black settlers at the coast and the tribes of the interior. Because of a lack of co-operation from the black settlers at the coast, two mission societies actually closed down their work in Liberia and went to other parts of Africa. (They were the American Baptist Missionary Union and the American Board of Missions.)

The Protestant Episcopal Church (Anglican) continued its work in Liberia. But this mission found it difficult to push into the interior. One of the missionaries explained the problem: 'Between the people on the coast of Africa (Liberia) and those in the interior, there exist, and ever have existed, the most jealous feelings. Selfishness is the cause of this.'[2] Nevertheless, in 1855 an interior mission station was opened and a group of foreign missionaries and Liberian pastors staffed it. By about 1870 the Episcopal Church of Liberia had only 446 communicant members, but twenty-two mission stations (nine Liberian and thirteen tribal).

The Methodist Church and the Disciples of Christ Church also worked in Liberia during this period, but sickness and ill health limited the work of their missionaries. In 1860 the United Lutheran Church of America started a work among one of the tribes in Liberia. In 1874 the Lutherans established the Muhlenberg Industrial Mission at which Africans were given technical education.

Questions:

1. Briefly tell of the work of the Basel Mission to the Gold Coast from 1840 to 1874.
2. Why was it difficult to establish a Christian Mission in Dahomey from 1840 to 1878?
3. Why were missionaries unable to take the Gospel to the inland tribes of Liberia in the mid-nineteenth century?

[1]Groves, C.P., *The Planting of Christianity in Africa*, vol. II (Lutterworth Press, London, 1954), p. 225
[2]Ibid. p. 221

19

David Livingstone and the thrust from the south

By 1840 the Gospel had reached many parts of South Africa. Through the efforts of Robert Moffat and others it had pushed north into Bechuanaland (Botswana). But still by 1840 there were vast areas of the interior of Africa that were unreached by the Good News. In order to open up the interior a man was needed who would be fearless and hardworking: this man also had to have a great desire to see unknown areas mapped out so that other missionaries could follow with the Gospel. The man who did that very thing was David Livingstone. Kenneth S. Latourette writes: 'More than any other one man, Livingstone was the path-breaker for Christianity in Africa south of the Sahara.'[1] Thus when we study the 'thrust from the south', we will actually be spending most of our time following the travels and work of Livingstone.

David Livingstone was born at Blantyre, Scotland, in 1813. His family was rather poor; nevertheless Livingstone was fortunate because his parents were Christians and gave him a good upbringing. When he reached the age of ten he had to stop attending school to go to work in a factory. He worked from six in the morning until eight at night to earn money to help his family. Even though he spent much time on the job, after he had completed his daily work he taught himself Latin and read scientific studies. At the age of 23 he was able to enter the University of Glasgow and further his education in the classroom.

When Livingstone entered university his desire was to prepare himself to be a medical missionary to China. However, God had other plans for him. After two years of university,

Livingstone applied to the London Missionary Society to go to China. Because of a war there, the L.M.S. suggested that he go to Africa instead. At about the same time he met Robert Moffat who was in England for a furlough. After Livingstone heard about the opportunities in southern Africa, he asked Moffat if Moffat thought he would be able to do the work. Moffat later wrote down the answer he gave to Livingstone: 'I said I believed he would, if he would not go to an old station, but would advance to unoccupied ground, specifying the vast plain to the north, where I had sometime seen, in the morning sun, the smoke of a thousand villages, where no missionary had ever been.'[2] Livingstone accepted this challenge and after being accepted as a missionary by the L.M.S., left London in 1840 for South Africa.

Once in Cape Town Livingstone lost no time travelling to Kuruman which was his assigned station. Within a few months he and another missionary walked north to find a new area for outreach. In 1843 Livingstone established a mission station 250 miles north of Kuruman at a place called Mabotsa. While at this place Livingstone was almost killed by a man-eating lion. God protected him from death, but for the rest of his life his left arm remained permanently crippled. In 1845 Livingstone married Mary, the daughter of Robert Moffat, and took her to his mission station at Mabotsa.

What kind of a person was this David Livingstone who was about to open an era of discovery? 'Various characteristics fitted Livingstone for his mission. Apparently he did not know fear. In spite of periods of gloom he was generally hopeful and had a quiet humour which lightened the tension under which he often lived. He had an indomitable will power which propelled a body often racked by fever and spent with dysentery. He was skilful in dealing with people. He was a keen and accurate observer and kept voluminous day by day records of what he saw. He always had at heart the interest of the Africans. He told the Christian story to those whom he touched on his wide travels. His Christian faith sustained him through his hardships and kept him humble. . .'[3]

In 1849 David Livingstone heard stories from the Africans

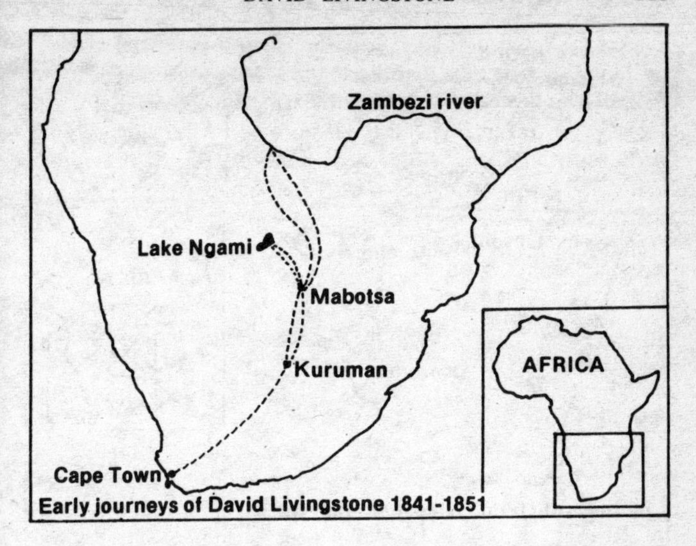

Early journeys of David Livingstone 1841-1851

about a great fresh water lake far from his mission station. Together with some Africans and fellow missionaries, Livingstone visited Lake Ngami. 'A fine river flowing into the lake from the north stirred Livingstone's imagination: "What think you of a navigable highway into a large section of the interior? . . . Is it not the Niger of this part of Africa?"'[4] When Livingstone saw the lake he began to wonder if it were possible to use one of the rivers that went into the lake as a 'road' to the north. Using this pathway he hoped to take the Gospel into a new part of Africa. Although he never found such a river, the visit by Livingstone to Lake Ngami started him on more than twenty years of exploration for the purpose of spreading the Gospel.

In 1851 Livingstone was invited by a chief far to the north to visit his tribe. He took his wife and family on that journey and all were warmly welcomed by the chief. They continued north and found the Zambezi River far in the interior of Africa. This was a great discovery for Livingstone, and he

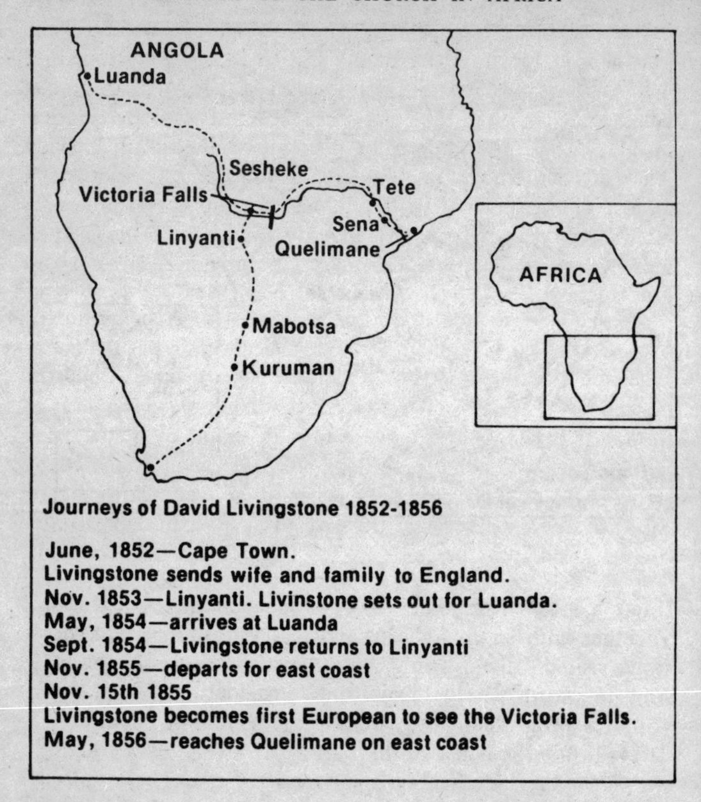

Journeys of David Livingstone 1852-1856

June, 1852—Cape Town.
Livingstone sends wife and family to England.
Nov. 1853—Linyanti. Livinstone sets out for Luanda.
May, 1854—arrives at Luanda
Sept. 1854—Livingstone returns to Linyanti
Nov. 1855—departs for east coast
Nov. 15th 1855
Livingstone becomes first European to see the Victoria Falls.
May, 1856—reaches Quelimane on east coast

hoped that such a river could be used by missionaries for their travels.

In 1852 Livingstone sent his wife and four children back to England, so that he would not have to worry about them becoming ill. He then went north to spend two or three years walking through the heart of Africa. Before starting his journey he set his objectives: '. . . to establish a mission in Barotseland or beyond, to throw some light on the problem of the slave-trade, and "also to find a way to the sea on either the east or west coast".'[5] He was unable to find a healthy place in

Barotseland for establishing a mission station, and so went on to look for an outlet to the sea. In 1853 Livingstone and his African assistants set out for Luanda, Angola, to find a land route to that sea-port. They reached their destination in May, 1854, then began the difficult twelve-month journey back in September to Linyanti. Livingstone then made a report of his journey to the L.M.S. He said that the people of the region were generally friendly and open to the Gospel, but malaria would pose the biggest hindrance in opening up the area.

In 1855 he departed for the east coast of Africa. Shortly after he started he came upon the Victoria Falls on the Zambezi and became the first European to see that wonderful sight. Livingstone then followed the Zambezi River east in hopes of finding that the river would be usable by boats which could bring missionaries up the river. He soon found many rapids and several unfriendly tribes as he went further east. In May, 1856, he reached the east coast of Africa in Mozambique. He had walked more than 1,300 miles from Linyanti to reach that place. 'The great transcontinental journey had been performed at last; the thrust from the south had achieved a penetration of the heart of Africa. . . It was an achievement that marks a watershed in the history of the continent, and which, together with Livingstone's total contribution, has meant more for the expansion of Christian missions in Africa than any other single exploit.'[6]

In 1856 Livingstone returned to England where he received a great welcome. The English were very much interested in meeting the man who had told them so much about the interior of southern Africa. While in England he told of slave-raids that were carried on in the interior of Africa to supply slaves to the Arab and Portuguese slave traders on the east coast. He believed that if a route into that part of Africa could be opened up, a cash crop like cotton could be introduced so that the people could make more money from cotton than from slave-raiding. He also believed that once the Christian message was brought to the region the slave trade would soon disappear. In 1858 he left the L.M.S. in order to direct a private expedition up the Zambezi. In December 1858, the expedition found that they could not get a steamship past the Keborabasa rapids, so Livingstone's hopes of using the Zambezi as a road to the interior were broken. But the expedition was not a failure as Livingstone directed it up the Shire River towards the north, instead. In September, 1859, the expedition found Lake Malawi which they called Lake Nyasa or 'Lake of the Stars'.

Livingstone and his followers made some voyages on the Lake and noted that there were many tribes who lived along the shore. A new mission society, called the Universities Mission, sent some missionaries to open a work in the area of the Shire River and Lake Malawi. From 1858 to 1863 they tried to establish two mission stations near the Shire. But the slave-trading tribes in the area made their work very difficult. On top of that, several of the missionaries died from fever. In 1863 the Universities Mission ended its work in that area of Africa and moved to Zanzibar. This made David Livingstone very sad, since it left almost no Gospel witness in the area.

In 1864 Livingstone once again returned to England and reported on his work. He told about the slave-trade and how the normal life of the tribes in eastern Africa was disrupted by this practice. In 1865 he returned to Africa to explore the area north of Lake Malawi and to find the source of the Nile if possible. In March, 1866, he left Zanzibar with a large party of carriers and headed for Lake Malawi. After arriving at the lake a large number of his carriers deserted him and went back to Zanzibar. On his walk from Lake Malawi to Lake Tanganyika more men deserted him. One of them took his medicine kit which he used to overcome malaria and dysentery. In April, 1867, he arrived at Lake Tanganyika. He explored the region around the Lake until he reached Ujiji in March, 1869. Here he found that the Arabs were exploiting the slave-trade in the area. Livingstone wrote: 'This is a den of the worst kind of slave-traders: the Ujiji slavers like the Kilwa and the Portuguese, are the vilest of the vile. It is not a trade, but a system of consecutive murders;

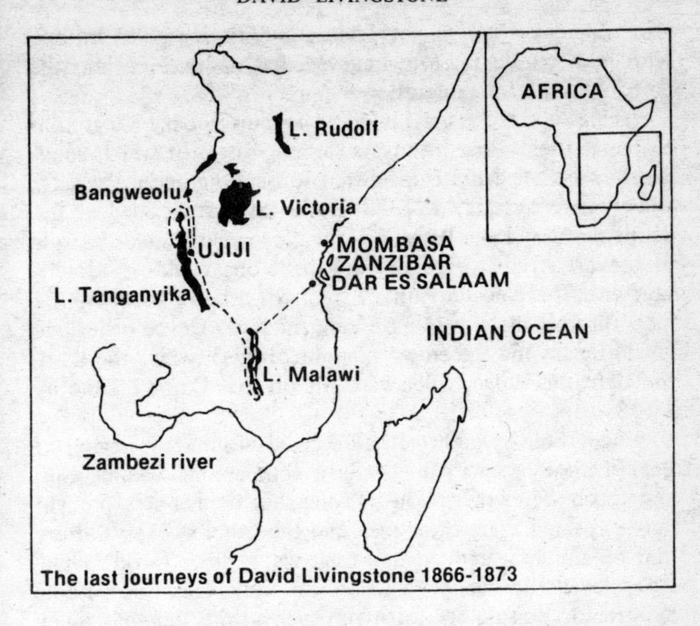

The last journeys of David Livingstone 1866-1873

they go to plunder and kidnap, and every trading trip is nothing but a foray.'[7]

From 1869 until 1871 Livingstone looked around the north of Lake Tanganyika for the Nile River but without success. He was much weakened by disease. In October, 1871, he returned to Ujiji but found that the supplies he expected there had been stolen. This was a terrible blow for Livingstone, but God had not forgotten him. 'On the morning of 10 November, 1871, Susi came dashing up to announce that an Englishman had arrived. Going out at this improbable news, Livingstone saw a large party advancing, headed by the American flag. It was, indeed, under the command of a white man, who walked up to him and said, "Dr Livingstone, I presume?" "Yes," he said, with a kind smile, lifting his cap slightly.'[8] The American was Henry M. Stanley who had led an expedition from Zanzibar to see if Livingstone were still alive. Stanley tried to get Livingstone to return to Europe with him, but Livingstone believed that within seven months he could finish his exploration.

Livingstone led a small band of men up to Lake Bangweolu to see if there were any rivers running out of it which could possibly be the Nile. During that journey he became weaker and weaker. On May 1, 1873, David Livingstone died on the south shore of Lake Bangweolu, while kneeling by his bedside in prayer. At his death David Livingstone could, no doubt, say with the Apostle Paul: 'I have fought the good fight, I have finished the race, I have kept the faith. Henceforth there is laid up for me the crown of righteousness, which the Lord, the righteous judge, will award me on that Day' (2 Timothy 4:7, 8).

Since 1869 Livingstone had walked around the region of Lake Tanganyika with his African companions: Chuma, Susi and Jacob Wainwright. When Livingstone died, a person might have expected these three men and the other workers to bury him on the spot and then go their ways. Since David Livingstone loved the men with whom he worked and because he had tried to do so much for Africa such a thing did not happen to his body. 'There seems to have been no hesitation on the part of the men in deciding that they must all return to the coast, taking the corpse with them, and that Susi and Chuma must direct their march.'[9] First they buried the heart of Livingstone near the place where he died and after preparing the body, carried it down to the coast. From there it was taken to Zanzibar and then to England. Livingstone is buried in Westminster Abbey in London.

David Livingstone had great visions of the work that could be done in Africa. His greatest dream was to see the Gospel spread far and wide in southern and eastern Africa. To that end he spent his days trying to find out about the interior of the continent so that other missionaries could follow him and so bring the Christian message. Although there were not very many missionaries working in the lands that he opened up by 1870, still his journeys had prepared the way for a great expansion of the Church in that part of Africa.

RESULTS OF LIVINGSTONE'S WORK

Because of the interest David Livingstone had raised in the area of Africa we now call Malawi, a joint mission was planned for the area in 1875. By 1876 the Livingstonia Mission, as it was called, was exploring Lake Malawi. In 1877 an African evangelist from South Africa named William Koyi arrive at the mission and began to assist the Europeans in giving out the Gospel. William Koyi reached out to the warlike Ngoni who lived on the west side of Lake Malawi. Through the work of Koyi the Ngoni were encouraged to give up a life of war and settle down to peaceful existence with other tribes. The Livingstonia Mission established schools and translated the Scriptures.

The Church of Scotland also began a mission in the area of Lake Malawi in 1876. Much of their work was like that of the Livingstonia Mission, i.e. trying to end tribal wars, stopping the slave-trade and establishing a Christian witness in the area.

OUTREACH IN OTHER PARTS OF SOUTHERN AFRICA

While David Livingstone was opening vast parts of interior Africa, the hundreds of other missionaries and African Church workers in South Africa were not idle. They continued to expand the number of churches and reach into new areas.

In 1850 a Protestant mission entered Zululand for the first time, after receiving a warm welcome from the Zulu chief. Two mission stations were established almost at once.

The mission to the Basuto which had begun in 1833 had been very successful: 'For fifteen years converts had been received in their hundreds, churches had grown in effective witness, and chiefs had become obedient to the faith.'[10] However beginning in 1848 the Basuto Church began a time of hardship. The white Boer farmers who had run away from the Cape Colony in 1836 began expanding their farms around Basutoland. They attempted to get more and more of the Basuto's land. Because this area was not governed by the British, there was no one to whom the missionaries could

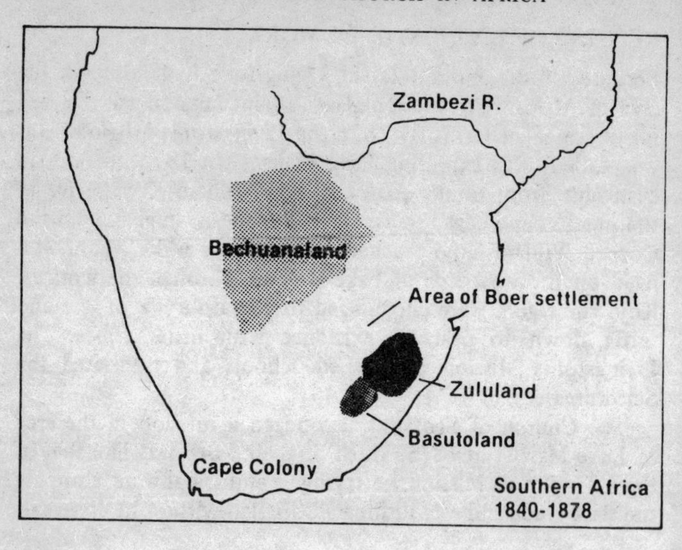

go for help in protecting the land of the Basuto. Between 1851 and 1858 there were several wars which disrupted the work of the missionaries and the church pastors, yet the Church remained firm.

In Bechuanaland the L.M.S. also experienced difficulties in the work which was caused by the migrating Boers. These Boer farmers did not like the missionaries and sought to push them away from their new Republic of Transvaal. Soon the Boers began raiding the mission stations in Bechuanaland and destroying the buildings. In January, 1853, the missionaries in Bechuanaland wrote to their directors in London about the trouble caused by the Boers: 'Mamusa (mission station) is vacated – the missionaries of Matebe and Mabotsa are driven out of the country – Koloberg is destroyed. Kuruman and Lekatlong are the only stations of our Society that yet exist in the Bechuana country.'[11] So this time the work of the Gospel was not being opposed by African tribes, but rather the while settlers of the Transvaal.

CONCLUSION

This has been a long chapter, but from it you should now have a picture of the development of the Church in Southern Africa from 1840 to 1878. Then, too, you should now understand the great service that David Livingstone did for Africa by making his many journeys in order to open the interior to the Gospel.

Questions:

1. Briefly tell about the early life of David Livingstone.
2. Where did Livingstone first work in Africa?
3. Why did Livingstone want to discover a good route into Malawi?
4. Why did Livingstone spend so much time searching around Lake Tanganyika?
5. How has the Church in Africa benefited from Livingstone's work?
6. What group of people opposed the Church in Basutoland & Bechuanaland?

[1] Latourette, Kenneth S., *A History of the Expansion of Christianity: The Great Century*, vol. V (Harper & Bros., New York, 1943), p. 349
[2] Groves, C.P., *The Planting of Christianity in Africa*, vol. II (Lutterworth Press, London, 1954), p. 120
[3] Latourette, *A History*. . . , p. 347
[4] Groves, *The Planting*. . . , p. 124
[5] Ibid. p. 163
[6] Ibid. p. 168
[7] Ibid. p. 202
[8] Simmons, Jack, *Livingstone and Africa* (Hodder & Sloughton Educational, 1955), p. 125
[9] Ibid. p. 133
[10] Groves, *The Planting*. . . , p. 147
[11] Ibid. p. 161

20

New beginnings in East Africa

Our survey of African Church history now takes us further north so that we can investigate the return of the Christian message to the coast of East Africa. The information in this chapter will briefly tell of the early missionary period and provide a background for a more detailed study of the growth of the Church in Kenya which will be dealt with later.

The early work of Protestant missionaries in East Africa was started by Ludwig Krapf and John Rebmann. Like some of the early missionaries in Sierra Leone, both Krapf and Rebmann came from Germany but were sent to Africa by the Church Missionary Society (C.M.S.).

Ludwig Krapf was born in Germany in 1810. While attending primary school he read a missionary article which caused him to consider whether God was calling him to be a missionary. After training at a missions institute in Switzerland and a university, Krapf set out for Africa in 1837. His original goal was not the coast of Kenya or Tanzania at that time, but rather Ethiopia. For five years Krapf worked with another missionary in the province of Shoa. In 1842 he went to Egypt to meet a lady coming from Germany to be his bride. After the marriage though, he was refused permission by the government to return to Shoa. Although this seemed to be a step backward for mission work in Ethiopia, we can now see that it was God's way of opening another part of Africa to the Gospel.

When Krapf found that he could not return to Ethiopia he and his wife sailed to Zanzibar, arriving there in January, 1844. He obtained permission from the Sultan of Zanzibar to

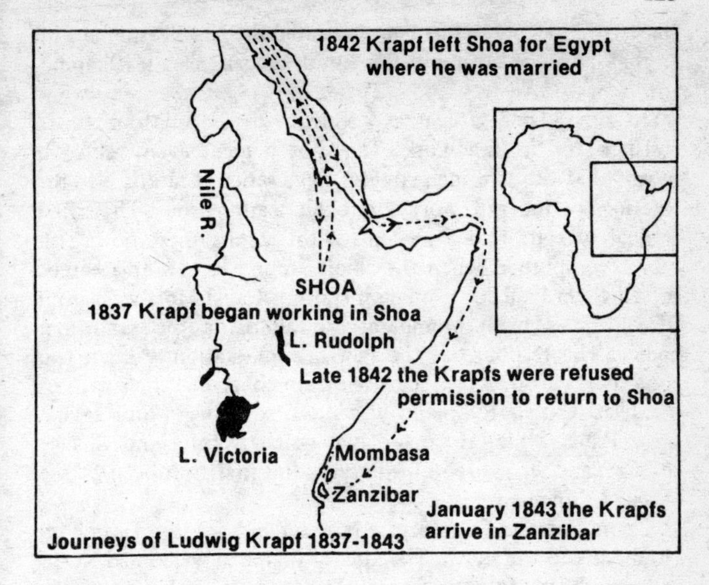

Journeys of Ludwig Krapf 1837-1843

go to Mombasa and explore the possibilities of reaching the inland Gallas. At this point we should note that Ludwig Krapf had developed a 'theory' for the evangelisation of East Africa. It was his belief that the Gallas were the 'key' tribe of East Africa: if missionaries could take the Gospel to the Gallas and these Africans became Christians, then, Krapf believed, it would be very easy to reach all the other tribes of East Africa with the Gospel. Therefore Krapf was very interested in finding the southern boundary of the Galla tribe in East Africa and then establishing a mission station among the tribesmen.

In May, 1844, Krapf and his wife established the first Protestant mission station in East Africa at Mombasa. However before they had made much progress in the work, Mrs. Krapf died in July. This was a hard blow for Ludwig Krapf, but the Lord gave him the strength to go on. At the time of his wife's death Krapf was very sick with malaria, but he recovered. He then set about learning Kiswahili. He already knew German, English, Amharic and Arabic. He learned Kiswahili so quickly that within two years he had translated the New Testament into that language. At about this time he began to learn Kikamba, too.

In June, 1846, Johannes Rebmann arrived in Mombasa to assist Krapf in the work. This was a great event, since it meant that the two men could begin a series of safaris into the interior to find out more about the nearby tribes. Their first project was to find a new place for a mission station. This was accomplished when the chiefs around Rabai Mpia agreed to sell them land for a mission station. Rabai Mpia was about fifteen miles from Mombasa, but almost a thousand feet higher. The response at the new mission station was not too good at first, but Krapf and Rebmann continued their witness for Jesus Christ. Rebmann was the first to begin long safaris from Rabai Mpia. He made two visits to Taita and Chagga country and in May, 1848, became the first European to see Mount Kilimanjaro.

Upon Rebmann's return, Krapf set out for the Usambara Mountains to the south. The king of that area welcomed Krapf and asked him to return to the tribe. Then Rebmann made another safari to the west, but this time found the people to be unfriendly toward him and so returned to Rabai.

Krapf felt that something should be done to meet the needs of the Gallas to the north. So he proposed to visit a Kamba chief whom he had met in Mombasa. Chief Kivoi was a trader in ivory. 'Setting out from Mombasa on November 1, 1849, his first objective was Kivoi's settlement, a friendly Kamba chief who had come trading to Mombasa. It was a hard march through desert country with water at rare intervals and the imminent risk of running into a Masai foraging party. They once did thirty-three miles in a single day. Three weeks' travel brought them to the plain of Yatta, an extensive lava plateau some 3,200 feet high. From this elevation they had an almost constant view of Kilimanjaro, and were traversing rolling grassland. They at length reached Kivoi's village on November 26. Krapf's statement of his missionary objective met with a sincere welcome: "I fully understand your purpose, and you shall have all your requests," said Kivoi. He invited

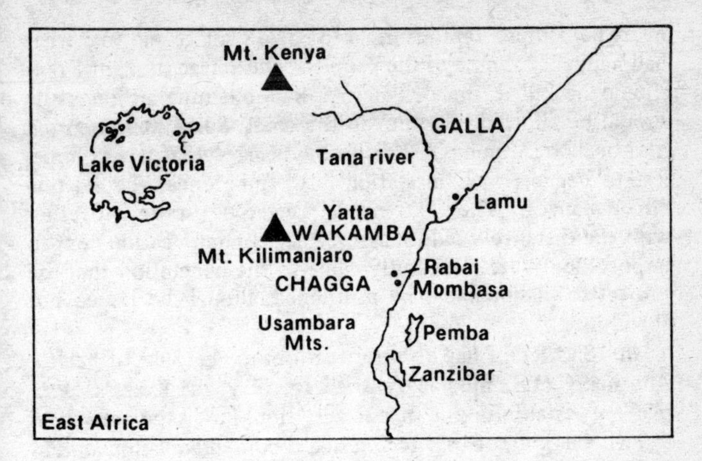

Krapf to go with him into the interior, returning to the coast in four or five months, but this had to be declined. . . Kivoi told him of another "Mountain of Whiteness", and a few days later Krapf saw Mount Kenya for the first time. . . After an absence of fifty-one days Krapf was once more back at Rabai on December 21, 1849.'[1]

In 1850 Krapf went to Europe in order to explain a new plan he had for developing mission work in East Africa. His idea was to have a 'chain of mission stations' across the heart of Africa, starting at Mombasa and reaching the Gabon River in west-central Africa. The C.M.S. liked his proposal and authorized him to establish the next two interior stations upon his return to East Africa. In July, 1851, he left Mombasa for Kivoi's village to start a settled work in Ukambani. When he reached Kivoi's village he was warmly welcomed. Kivoi, Krapf and a group of men then set out for the north, since Krapf wanted to see the Tana River. Like David Livingstone, Krapf hoped to find a big river that could be used as a 'highway' for missionaries travelling inland. However, before the party could reach the Tana it was attacked by a band of more than a hundred robbers. Kivoi and some of his men were killed; Krapf and the other men escaped, going in different directions. After many hardships Krapf returned to Kivoi's village and told what had happened. Some of the people at the village thought Krapf should be killed, since Kivoi had died, but others thought he should be allowed to return to the coast. Some men escorted him back to Mombasa. 'Krapf now realized that it was hopeless to begin a mission station in Ukamba under the existing circumstances. The extremely dangerous route, together with the distance would make regular communication next to impossible. . . He reluctantly came to the conclusion that the projected mission must be postponed, though he hoped not abandoned.'[2]

In 1853 Krapf had to return to Europe because of health. Another C.M.S. missionary tried to carry out Krapf's other plan of establishing a mission station in Usambara. Even though the king of that region had promised a mission station to Krapf, the king would not allow the second C.M.S. missionary to carry out the plan. That missionary returned to Europe in 1855 leaving only Rebmann to carry on the work. Because of political unrest on the coast caused by the Sultan's death in 1856, Rebmann did not try any further safaris, but only worked at Rabai and Mombasa until he finally left East Africa in 1875.

Thus the early 'pioneer stage' of Protestant missions in East Africa came to a close. For all their labour, these C.M.S. missionaries did not see many converts and did not advance the Gospel very far inland. However, the work had been begun and with the reports and research done by Krapf and Rebmann, other servants of the Lord could follow and continue the work.

MISSION WORK AMONG LIBERATED SLAVES

In 1863 the Roman Catholics established a large mission station on Zanzibar island. They were given a considerable amount of money by the French government to build buildings and a church. Soon the mission reached across to the mainland, where an orphanage and freed-slave work was begun at Bagamoyo. By 1873 a very large station had been established;

there was even a training centre (novitiate) for preparing women to become nuns.

The Roman Catholics were not the only missionaries interested in helping freed slaves. In 1873 Sir Bartle Frere suggested that the C.M.S. establish a haven for freed slaves in Mombasa. In 1875, the year that Rebmann was forced to return to Europe, Freretown was established by the C.M.S. The British navy brought ship loads of liberated slaves that had been found on Arab dhows in the Indian Ocean and left them at Freretown. Soon the work expanded and met a great need in helping to defeat the terrible Arab slave trade.

METHODIST CHURCH WORK

Meanwhile, in 1862 the United Methodist Free Churches decided to meet the challenge of evangelizing the Galla tribe, which Krapf had written about in his book. A party of four missionaries were brought to Mombasa by Krapf himself; Krapf helped them establish a new station sixteen miles north of Mombasa at Ribe and then returned to Europe. Three of the new missionaries soon went back to Europe leaving only one: Thomas Wakefield. Soon he was joined by Charles New and together they began the work in earnest.

They first paid a visit to the Galla tribe by taking a ship to Malindi and then walking inland. 'Eventually they reached the Galla chief of Ganda, a village of some 300 people beyond the Tana, and found that they would be most welcome if they would offer protection from the Masai. Indeed, they found this warrior tribe dreaded throughout the land, the slightest rumour of their approach causing consternation.'[3] The Methodists did not find a suitable mission station site and came to the conclusion that Krapf had been mistaken in the size of the Galla tribe and their importance in East Africa. They observed that the part of the Galla Tribe that was south of Ethiopia was rather poor and also not strong enough to defeat the Masai. Then, too, because the population of the tribe seemed so small, Wakefield and New decided that the Gallas could not be the 'key tribe' in East Africa as Krapf had suggested to them. The Methodists encouraged some Gallas to come with them to Ribe. These people were taught the Word of God, and in 1870 the first Galla Christians were baptized. It was not until 1885 that the Methodists established a mission station in the land of the Gallas. However, the first missionaries at the new station were speared to death three months after settling there, when the station was raided by some Masai. Thus once again the mission to the Gallas came to a halt.

BUGANDA RECEIVES THE GOSPEL

By 1878 the Gospel had not reached very far inland in the area of East Africa we now call Kenya and Tanzania. However, in 1877 missionaries travelled past large numbers of people in East Africa to take the Gospel to Baganda. Why did this happen? Why were the Buganda reached before the people to the east of them had been told the Good News?

The answer to these questions is found in the person of Henry Stanley. After leaving Livingstone in 1872, Stanley had a great desire to travel through more of Africa. In 1874 he arrived again at Zanzibar and by the end of the year had brought together a large expedition which crossed to the mainland. Their objective was Lake Victoria: to find out more about the geography of the region. Once at the north side of the Lake, Stanley met King Mutesa of Buganda. Stanley was not a missionary, but in his conversations with King Mutesa, he told the Christian message. Stanley was assisted in his conversations with the King by one of his employees, called Dallington Muftaa. Muftaa was a liberated slave from the area of Lake Malawi who had been helped and trained by the Universities Mission. Since he was a Christian he was eager to witness to the Kabaka. When Stanley moved on, he left Muftaa to continue his witness with the Kabaka and his court. Muftaa then sent to the coast for a Swahili Bible, slate and chalk to help with his teaching. He also asked for another teacher to assist him in his work. So it was that African Christians prepared the way for the C.M.S. missionaries who followed to enlarge the church.

Before Stanley left the Kabaka he wrote a letter which was published in an American and a British newspaper. In his letter, Stanley told of a great kingdom in the centre of Africa, which was ruled by a very strong king. He wrote that this king was very much interested in the Christian message and had asked for other people to come and tell him more. This letter made a great impression in England: almost at once five thousand pounds was given to the C.M.S. to begin a work in Buganda. Within six months of the arrival of the letter in England, the C.M.S. had collected twelve thousand pounds to start a mission station. The first eight C.M.S. missionaries for that project arrived in East Africa in June, 1876. By June, 1877, the first two missionaries had arrived at Mutesa's capital. After meeting the King the two missionaries found Dallington Muftaa faithfully teaching people about Christ. King Mutesa gave the C.M.S. a plot of land for building a mission station and soon a house was built.Then one of the missionaries sailed across Lake Victoria to meet another man who was coming to help. But while the two were on Ukerewe Island they were killed. This was a hard blow for the C.M.S. This was no reason to give up the mission, though, and so the work continued.

Mutesa told everyone that he was a Christian and even held Sunday services at his palace. These services were attended by chiefs and servants as well as the king's household. The C.M.S. missionaries were not allowed to go about the countryside evangelizing, but they were allowed to help anyone who came to them. Most of the people who came wanted to learn how to read, so that they could read the Bible for themselves.

One of the most outstanding missionaries of that time was Alexander Mackay who had gone to Buganda as soon as he had heard about the deaths on Ukerewe Island. He was a great preacher as well as a good teacher. He preached often on Sundays for the Kabaka and was not afraid to speak out against slavery, magic charms and polygamy.

Everything seemed to be going very well when in 1879 trouble appeared at the king's court. A Roman Catholic

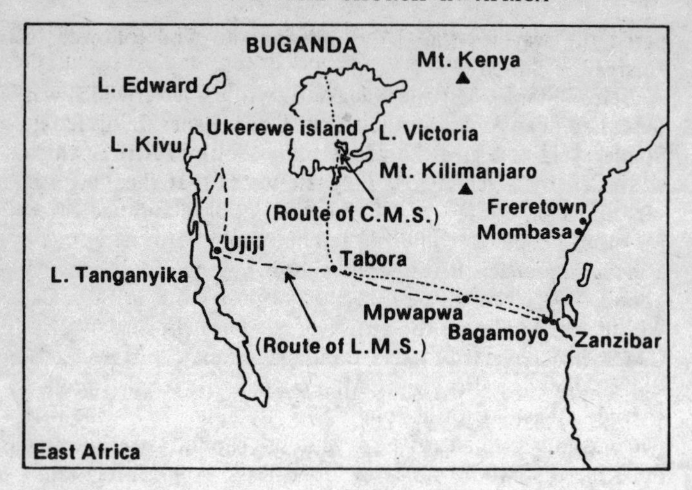

missionary arrived and asked Mutesa if he could establish a mission station in Buganda. Mackay tried to show the Roman Catholics that there were hundreds of tribes that were not reached by any missionary in East Africa. It would have been far better for the Roman Catholics to start a work in these areas instead of working in Buganda. But the Roman Catholics were not interested in reaching other areas; it seems that they only wanted to compete with the work of the C.M.S. The Kabaka decided to allow the French Roman Catholics to remain. Later on in our study we will see how this decision to start working in Buganda by the Roman Catholics led to rivalries which caused the death of many people and a delay in spreading the Gospel in that kingdom.

To the south of Lake Victoria, the L.M.S. opened a work on the shores of Lake Tanganyika. Two stations were opened in 1879, after several missionaries had died in the attempt to establish the first station at Ujiji. Nevertheless, a candle had been lit in the Lake Tanganyika area and the Gospel message was going out to the people there.

Finally, we should note the condition of the Church in Ethiopia for this period 1840 to 1878. During this time several missionaries, including Krapf, had tried to open a work in Ethiopia. There were many people in the rural areas who did not understand Christianity clearly. It was the intention of the missionaries to make the Gospel plainer to the people. However, the missionaries were opposed by the Coptic priests and the Government itself made work difficult. During the period 1860 to 1875 there was great political unrest in the country, which also hindered the work. By 1878 very few mission stations had been established in either Ethiopia or the Sudan.

Questions:

1. Where did Ludwig Krapf first start his work in Africa? Why did he leave this area?
2. Why did Krapf feel it was so important to take the Gospel to the Gallas?
3. What happened when Krapf and Chief Kivoi tried to visit the Tana River area of Ukambani?
4. What was Freretown? How did it start?
5. What efforts did the Methodists make to reach the Gallas?
6. How did Henry Stanley help to establish mission work in Buganda?

[1]Groves, C.P., *The Planting of Christianity in Africa*, vol. II (Lutterworth Press, London, 1954), pp. 104, 105
[2]Ibid. p. 107
[3]Ibid. p. 289

21

West-Central Africa 1840–1878

After the two main thrusts of African evangelism from 1840 to 1878, we studied the initial work which was begun in East Africa. To finish this period we will consider the beginning of Protestant missions in west-central Africa and the reintroduction of Roman Catholic work in the area.

CAMEROONS

The establishment of the Church in the Cameroons began in 1843 when some Baptist missionaries bought land from a local chief at the mouth of the Cameroons River. These Baptist missionaries were part of a West Indies Baptist Mission which had begun a work on Fernando Po. Many of the people in this mission were liberated slaves from Jamaica who wanted to take the Christian message back to their homeland of Africa. It was not until 1845 that the missionaries actually settled in the Cameroons and began to work.

Alfred Saker was the pioneer missionary who established the first mission station in the Cameroons. He called it Bethel. Within a short time he was reaching out to the people around him. He soon learned the Duala language and in 1848 printed the Gospel of Matthew on a printing press at Bethel. The work was not easy for Saker and his fellow workers at that time. The tribes of the Cameroons, like the tribes of the Niger delta, were held tightly in Satan's grip by their beliefs in idols and the powers of the evil spirits.

In 1858 the Spanish Roman Catholics expelled all Protestant missionaries who were working in Fernando Po. The

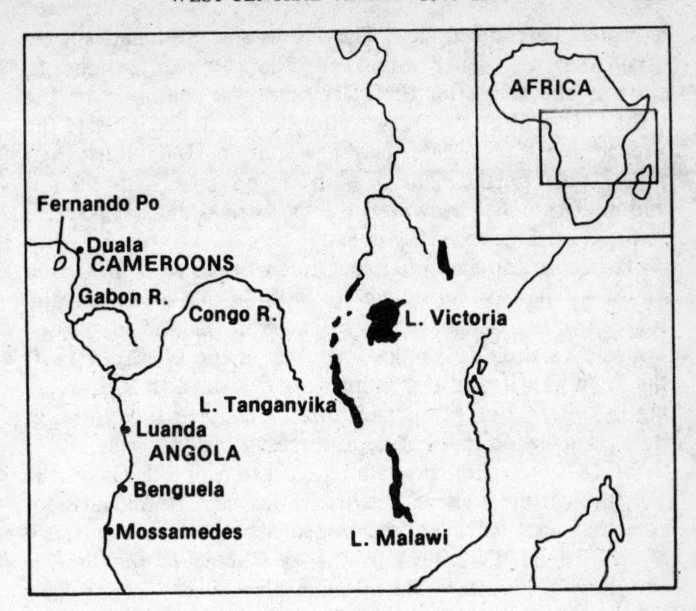

Baptist missionaries crossed the water to Cameroon and worked with Alfred Saker and the other missionaries who were working in that area. By 1872 Saker had completed his translation of the entire Bible which was printed in Duala. In 1877 Saker retired from his work in the Cameroons, but by that time the Baptist Church was well established.

GABON

The American Board of Commissioners for Foreign Missions built the first mission station in Gabon. They were well received by the local chief on the banks of the Gabon River in 1842. During the first three years the work went ahead well. But then in 1845 the French sent a gun-boat up the Gabon River. The boat bombarded the town where the mission station was, so that the chief was forced to make the land of his tribe a protectorate of France. The Protestant missionaries were afraid that the French would only allow Roman Catholics to work in the area after that. The work was continued on the Gabon River, but two new stations were started outside the French territory. These two new stations were thirty and ninety miles inland. The mission ran boys and girls schools and built churches. However, the local tribes did not respond to the Gospel message very quickly.

The American Presbyterian Church began work in Gabon in 1861. The first missionary to work in that area spent the first ten years in language study. Finally in 1874 he established a mission station 130 miles inland from the Coast. In 1870 the American Board of Commissioners decided to stop working in this area of Africa and turned over their three mission stations in Gabon to the American Presbyterian Mission.

In 1840 the Roman Catholics began work in Gabon. It was through the work of the French Roman Catholic missionaries that the French had established Gabon as a colony. Many of the Roman Catholic missionaries worked in the French government hospital. The Roman Catholics did not gain converts very quickly, even though their requirements for baptism were not as difficult to meet as the Protestants'. The problem was that the Roman Catholics were in such a rush to baptize people that the early Roman Catholic missionaries would baptize (by sprinkling) Africans who were very near death. (The Roman Catholics believe that such baptism will make the dying man a Roman Catholic and thus he will go to heaven.) However, shortly after such baptism these people usually died. The local Africans came to believe that if a person was baptized by the Roman Catholics he would soon die! After many years the French missionaries were able to overcome this fear. By 1878 the Roman Catholic Church had 2,000 members in Gabon.

THE CONGO RIVER AREA

By 1790 the Roman Catholic work in the Congo River area had about disappeared. As you remember, 1790 was about the time that Protestant missions began to work in large numbers in Africa. At a time when Protestant work was beginning to grow, Roman Catholic work in the Congo was actually dying out. Because of arguments between Portuguese, Spanish and Italian Roman Catholics, the small Roman Catholic mission had completely died out by 1850. The only Roman Catholic churches that continued to function were further south in Angola. In 1860 there were Roman Catholic missions only at the coastal cities of Luanda, Benguella and Mossamedes; the interior of Angola was unreached at that time.

In 1865 the Holy Ghost Fathers from France received permission from the Pope to establish a new Roman Catholic mission in the Congo River area. In 1866 the first two missionaries arrived in the region. As they travelled around they found a few remains of the mission work of the Portuguese of earlier centuries. By 1877 they had established four mission stations in the coastal area, which were staffed by eight missionaries. They had also built schools in which they had seventy students. By 1876, 163 baptisms had been recorded.

The Roman Catholics had successfully resumed missionary work in the Congo River area. A few years later Protestant missionaries would enter the region to proclaim the Gospel of Jesus Christ.

Questions:

1. When did the first missionaries arrive in the Cameroons? When was the Bible completely translated into Duala?
2. What two American missions began working in Gabon? When did they start their work?
3. When did the Roman Catholics again establish their work in the Congo River area?

22

The scramble for Africa

During the period 1840 to 1878 while many missionaries had been opening up new mission stations in Africa, there had been other Europeans who were busy in Africa, too. These people were the 'explorers' such as Burton, Baker and Stanley. The reports that these explorers made gave mission societies in Europe some idea of the great need of interior Africa. Unfortunately, these reports were also read by trading companies and European politicians. For the period 1878 to 1914 we are going to see that many European traders and explorers came to Africa, but their desire was not to spread the Gospel of Jesus Christ: it was rather to find wealth and/or fame for themselves. Once again we must pause in our study of the development of the Church in Africa briefly to review political events that affected further Christian development.

Today, most of Africa is ruled by independent African governments. But as we all know, not too long ago most African nations had colonial rulers. For how long have Europeans controlled African affairs? When did the colonialists come? Many students think that most of Africa was ruled by colonialists for more than a hundred years, but this is not so. 'In 1879 more than 90% of the continent was ruled by Africans. By 1900 all but a tiny fraction of it was being governed by European powers.'[1] The period 1878 to 1900 is very important for us to study, because it tells us of the take-over of Africa by the colonial powers.

The arrival of European governments in Africa was mainly brought about by one great pressure: the desire for *trade*. From 1840 to 1878 the French had established special trading forts along the coast of Africa at which only French ships could trade. Britain had a few similar forts. But for the most part the coast of Africa was open to traders of all countries who wanted to trade freely with the Africans. By 1870 some European traders began to push inland to develop more trade. Soon French traders wanted their government to protect them from competition from British traders and the British asked for protection from the French. The French and British governments began to discuss 'spheres of influence' where only the traders of one country would work, but no agreement was reached.

Then in the period 1870 to 1884 two things happened which changed the whole situation. First, King Leopold of Belgium decided that he wanted to have a private kingdom of his own in Africa. In 1876 Leopold founded an organization which he told people was to help Africans, but really was a cover for him to claim part of Africa for himself. 'In 1879 Leopold took Stanley (the explorer) into his service. During the next four years Stanley established road and river communications from the Congo estuary to Stanley Falls (Kisangani). Leopold on the Congo River, . . . was aiming at a commercial monopoly, which would attract all the trade of the Congo basin into his own river steamers and his own railway from Stanley Pool (Kinshasa) to the coast.'[2] Secondly, two German citizens were busy in 1884 signing treaties with African chiefs in Cameroons and Tanganyika so that Germany could claim territory in Africa.

With the appearance of these German and Belgium competitors things began to happen rapidly. When the French saw what Leopold was doing, they signed treaties in the Upper Congo in 1882 so that it became a French protectorate. When the British saw this they began staking out more Nigerian territory. This made the Portuguese wake up to the fact that their territories in Africa were threatened and so they made new claims to territory around Angloa and Mozambique. The Germans did not want to be left out and so they began to move into the Cameroons so that by mid-1884 they could claim that territory as their protectorate! 'Such then was the

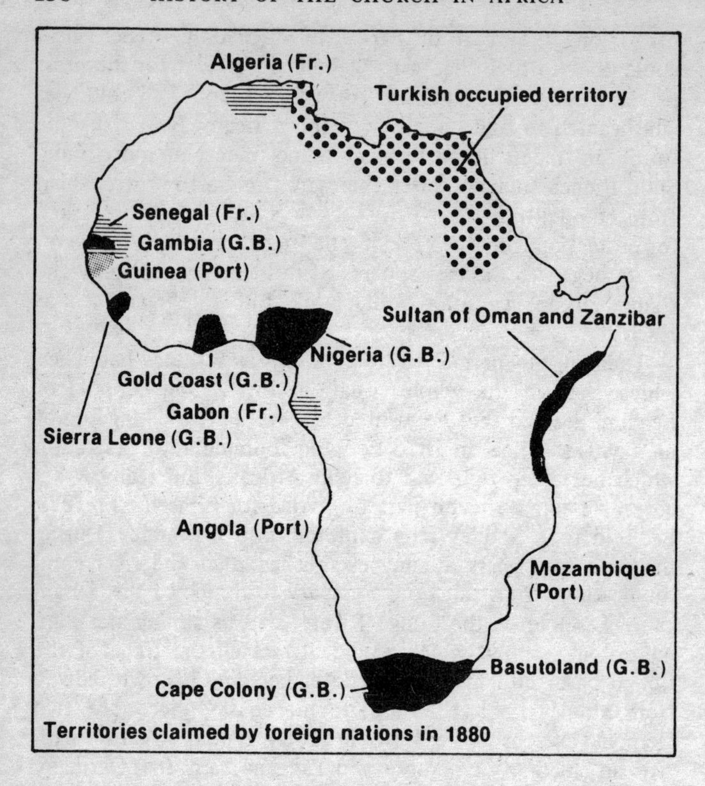

Territories claimed by foreign nations in 1880

motivation for the scramble. To the three powers already engaged on the African coastline – Britain, France, and Portugal – there was now added two more, one of them a European sovereign in search of a personal empire, the other the strongest state in continental Europe (Germany), . . In the circumstances, partition was bound to follow. Of the five powers mainly concerned, only King Leopold was positively anxious for a widespread territorial empire. Of the others, however, none was prepared to stand aside and see the continent swallowed by its rivals.'[3]

In 1884 King Leopold decided that some rules should be drawn up to cover the establishment of colonies or protectorates in Africa. Actually, this was just a clever move by Leopold to get European countries to recognize his claim to the Congo as a personal kingdom. This international conference which was held in Berlin started in November and did not end until late February, 1885. 'The outcome was the General Act of the Conference of Berlin, signed on February 26, 1885, by the fourteen European Powers, the United States abstaining. The principal provisions of the Act were concerned with two topics: the basin of the Congo, and a definition of occupation.'[4] The conference gave King Leopold the right to govern a 'Free Congo State' in the Congo River Basin. It also ' . . prepared the way for new-comers to the African scene by requiring that claims to colonies or protectorates on any part of the African coastline should be formally notified to the other powers taking part in the conference, and by insisting that such claims must be backed by the establishment of an effective degree of authority in the area concerned.'[5]

After the Conference of Berlin ended each European country began to claim different parts of Africa. 'The European powers partitioned Africa among themselves with such haste, like players in a rough game, that the process has been called "the Scramble for Africa".'[6] We should know which European country claimed what part of Africa and when, so that we can understand the next section of African Church history. It would take many pages to explain this in detail, and so what follows is only a summary for each major country of Europe.

By 1884 the Republic of **France** had already claimed Senegal, Algeria, Gabon and north Congo. In 1879 the French had pushed inland from Senegal to the Niger River. After the Conference of Berlin, their object was to claim all the interior territory of West Africa which was around the Niger River. This they did as far east as Sudan. By 1898 the French had defeated all the African chiefs of this interior region. 'By 1893 the colonies of the Ivory Coast and French Guinea had been officially established. In the same year French troops entered

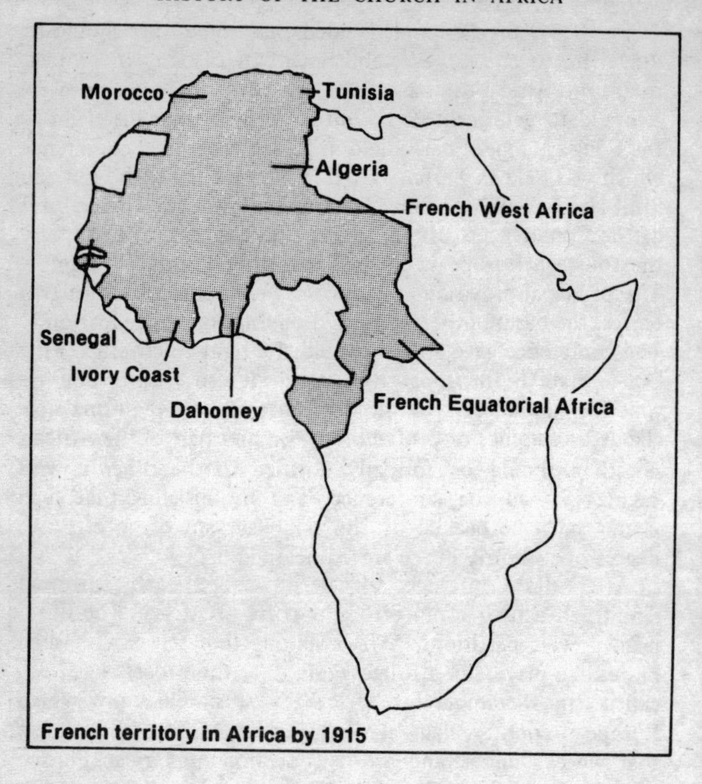

French territory in Africa by 1915

Dahomey and deposed Behanzin, the last independent King of Dahomey. Dahomey became a French colony in 1900.'[7] From Gabon and the Congo (Brazzaville) the French then began to push north, claiming territory as they went. At the same time they sent out expeditions from Algeria to push south and meet up near Lake Chad. By 1900 the French flag was flying over a great portion of North, West and Central Africa. However, one must remember that although this seems to be a major part of Africa, most of it is the Sahara Desert, with few minerals, fewer people and still less water.

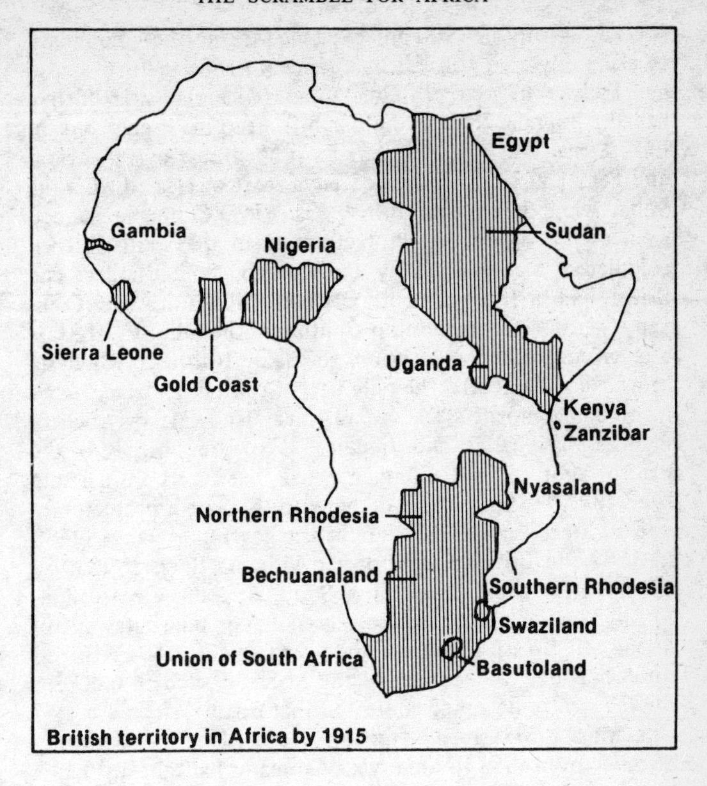

British territory in Africa by 1915

While the French were busy grabbing land, the **British** were not asleep. However, British territorial claims were sometimes made in a different way from French claims. The British used chartered companies which were private organizations that had official British protection to land that they claimed. Although Lagos and the Oil Rivers areas were British Protectorates in what we now call Nigeria, by 1885 most of central and northern Nigeria was unclaimed. Through the Royal Niger Company, this area was brought under British influence. Finally, Britain took direct control of the area from the Royal

Niger Company in 1900 and expanded the northern boundary to claim any land still left by France. In 1885 the British also had a claim to southern Gold Coast (Ghana). By 1898 they had the boundary far to the north to keep the French out. In East Africa the British declared a protectorate over Zanzibar and Pemba in 1890. Then the Kenya coast was leased from the Sultan while the Imperial British East Africa Company claimed Kenya and Uganda as Protectorates. In the south, British colonialism was assisted by the work of Cecil Rhodes. The British had in 1889 given Rhodes's British South Africa Company permission to develop Southern Rhodesia. In 1891 it was given further permission to claim Northern Rhodesia (now called Zambia). 'The only part of central Africa excluded from the company's sphere was Nyasaland (Malawi), where British missionaries and traders, who were hostile to the British South Africa Company, had been active since the later 1870's. This part of the country became a protectorate under direct control of the British government in 1891.'[8] In 1899 the British fought a war with the Boers so that by 1901 Britain could claim all of South Africa as a possession. Finally, in the north, Britain placed Egypt under its control because of British interest in the Suez Canal. In 1898 a British force defeated the armies of the Mahdi of Sudan and kept the French from gaining control of that part of Africa.

Germany tried to add territory to the land it had already claimed by 1885. In that year Germany had already taken control of the Cameroons and just a week after the Berlin Conference ended declared German East Africa (Tanganyika) to be a German possession. After their success in these areas the Germans began looking at other parts of Africa. The small strip between Dahomey and the Gold Coast was unclaimed, so Germany declared Togoland a protectorate. Germany completed her colonies in Africa by setting up a colonial administration in South West Africa.

By 1885 **Leopold** had established his claim to the Congo Free State and had received recognition of other European countries to his right to hold this land. Leopold was very greedy and wanted to gain great wealth from the Congo; but

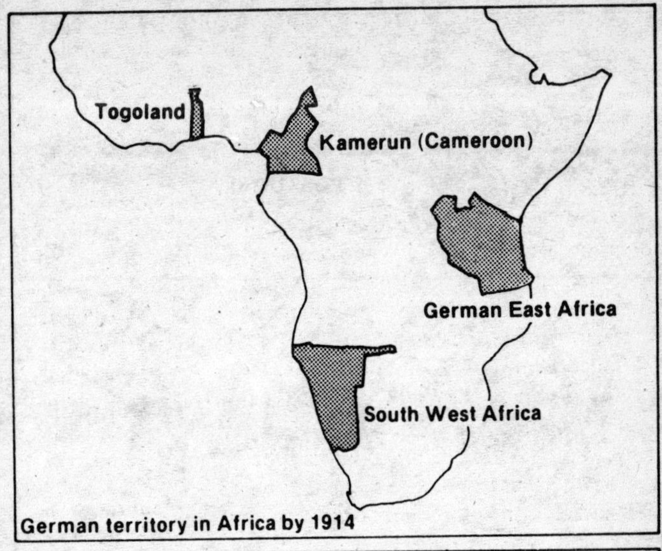

German territory in Africa by 1914

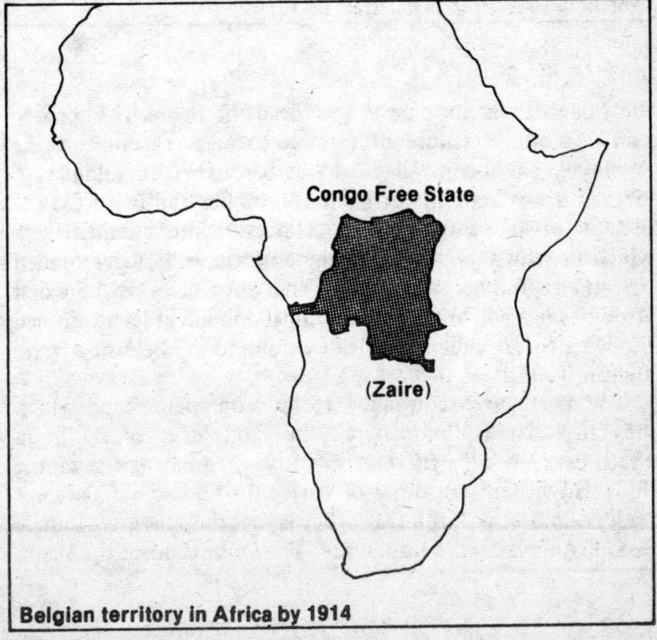

Belgian territory in Africa by 1914

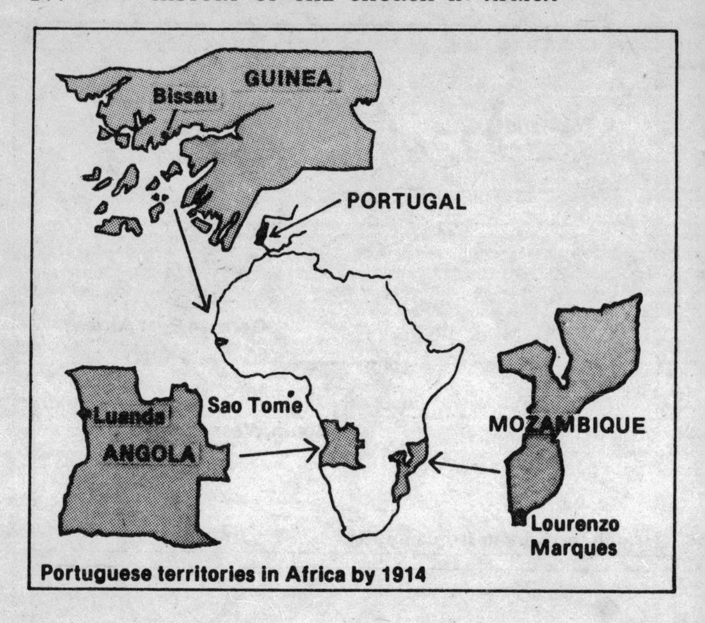

Portuguese territories in Africa by 1914

the Congo Free State never produced the riches he hoped to gain. 'Faced by failure of revenue to meet expenditure, he employed an ill-controlled and barbarous native soldiery to levy arbitrary amounts of tribute in rubber and ivory for the benefit of the state and the concessionaire companies in which he held interests. Even these measures, however, failed to produce the necessary funds, and when news of the worst atrocities leaked abroad, international opinion at length forced the King to surrender his private empire to the Belgian government in 1908.'[9]

The **Portuguese** continued to hold on to the land which they had claimed long before the Conference of Berlin in 1885. Ever since the fifteenth century when Portuguese sailing ships had visited the shores of Africa the Portuguese had kept traders and/or government officials on the coast of Guinea Bissau, Angola and Mozambique. They also claimed the island

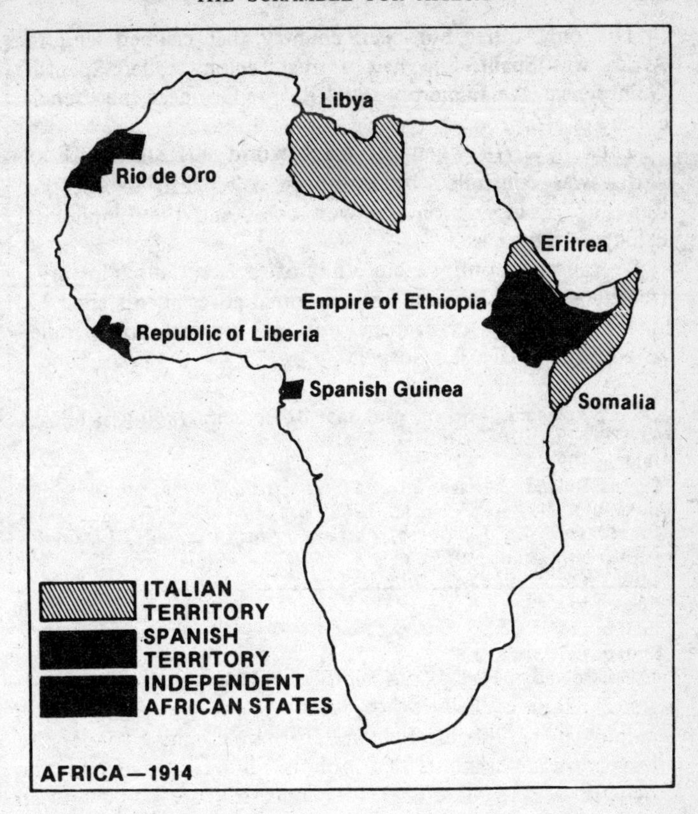

of Sao Tomé which is south of Fernando Po, off the coast of Gabon.

Italy was a little slower than the other European countries in finding territory. In 1866 she managed to occupy the Eritrean coast near Ethiopia and the part of land we call Somalia. In 1896 the Italians tried to invade and take control of Ethiopia, but Emperor Menelik decisively defeated the Italians at Adowa. In 1911 the Italians took Libya away from Turkey and made it an Italian Colony.

The only other European country that claimed land in Africa was **Spain**. She had a small colony called Spanish Guinea near the Cameroons and Rio de Oro near the French colony of Morocco.

Thus by 1914 when the First World War started all of Africa was controlled by European colonialists except the Republic of Liberia on the west coast and the Empire of Ethiopia on the east.

We can now continue our study of African Church history. We will see that in some cases colonial governments tried to hinder missionary evangelism, but in most instances people were free to preach the Gospel.

[1] Oliver, Roland & Atmore, Anthony, *Africa Since 1800* (Cambridge University Press, 1967), p. 103
[2] Ibid. p. 109
[3] Oliver, Roland, & Fage, J.D., *A Short History of Africa* (Penguin Books, Ltd. Middlesex, England, 1962), p. 186
[4] Groves, C.P., *The Planting of Christianity in Africa*, vol. III (Lutterworth Press, London, 1955), p. 9
[5] Oliver, R. & Atmore, A., *Africa. . .*, p. 111
[6] Ibid. p. 103
[7] Ibid. p. 115
[8] Ibid. p. 123
[9] Oliver, Roland, & Fage, J.D., *A Short. . . , p.* 199

23

The gospel begins to spread out in West Africa

As we start our study of the period 1878 to 1914 in the history of the Church in Africa, it is wise for us to remember that the Gospel message was still rather limited on the continent. The map on the next page shows that except for Egypt, Ethiopia and parts of southern Africa, Christianity was still generally confined to the coastal areas of Africa. However, during this period 1878–1914 we will see how men like Peter Cameron Scott and others saw the need for leaving the coastal areas and pushing inland with the Gospel. In the pages which follow we will read about the penetration of the Gospel to the interior regions of Africa.

Once again we must return to the west coast of Africa to survey the development of the Church. When we ended our study in chapters seventeen and eighteen, we had seen how Bishop Samuel Crowther and others had opened new areas in Nigeria to the Gospel. We had also seen the expansion of the work in the Gold Coast (Ghana) and Sierra Leone. As we continue our study we will find that more and more mission societies will be added to the ones we have already studied and that many of these groups will be opening up new territory to the Gospel. Perhaps the least confusing way to review developments in West Africa for the period 1878 to 1914 is to start at Senegal and then move south and east to Nigeria.

SENEGAL

The French government had claimed control over Senegal from the beginning of the eighteenth century. Because of

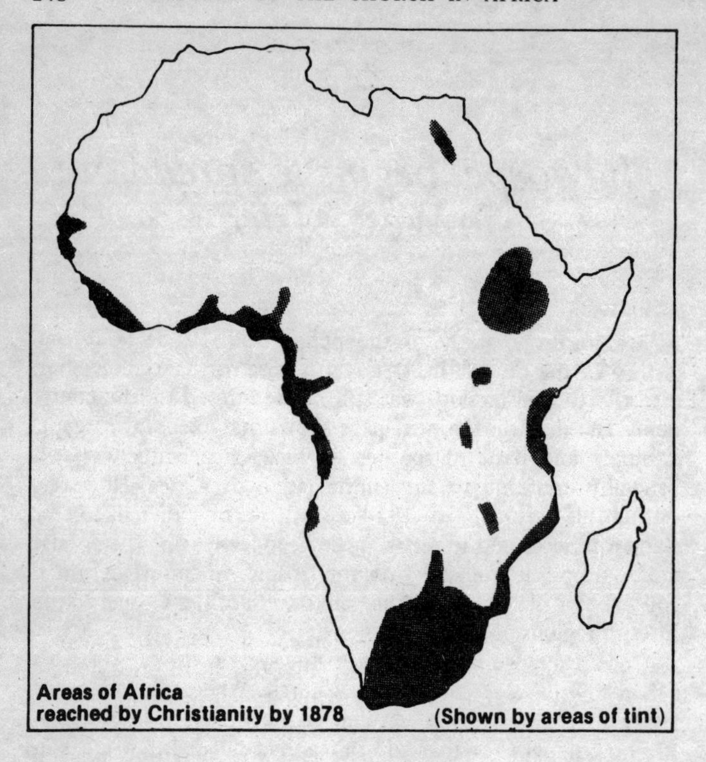

Areas of Africa reached by Christianity by 1878 (Shown by areas of tint)

French influence, the Roman Catholic Church had been encouraged to work in that area. A few Roman Catholic missionaries had come in the early nineteenth century. Although many of these missionaries died, still several mission stations were established. One problem the Roman Catholics had in gaining converts was the Muslim background of the people. Islam had been in the Senegal River area for almost eight hundred years by 1800. Nevertheless, the Roman Catholics established a seminary for training African priests and by 1902 had ten local priests. By 1914 the Catholic Church claimed 17,000 members in Senegal.

GAMBIA

Gambia is a very small country, completely surrounded by Senegal. As we have already seen, Protestant missionaries came to it in 1821. These Wesleyan Methodist missionaries continued their witness during the period 1878 to 1914, but still the influence of Islam kept the number of converts to a low number. By 1914 the Methodist Church in Gambia was not very large and still dependent on missionary help in order to continue. The Roman Catholic Holy Ghost Fathers had a small mission in Gambia, but it also had few converts by 1914.

PORTUGUESE GUINEA (GUINEA BISSAU)

Further south was Portuguese Guinea. Portuguese Roman Catholics had been working in this territory for many years, but had not achieved remarkable growth. By 1914 there were still no Protestant missionaries in the colony.

SIERRA LEONE

The Anglican Church in Sierra Leone still remained the largest denomination in that colony. In 1878 the last local mission church among the Creole in Sierra Leone which was dependent on missionaries for finances was transferred to the Sierra Leone Anglican Church. By 1890 the Anglican Church was quite large (16,000 members), but unfortunately it was becoming spiritually cold. Church members were no longer interested in evangelism and many did not live a consistent Christian life. 'Time and again it was lamented that, while external observances were meticulously kept, the moral and spiritual state of the people left much to be desired.'[1] Even so, there was some effort by the Anglican Church to move into the interior of Sierra Leone. For example, 'In 1894 the Creole congregation at Bonthe, on Sherbro Island, began evangelizing the people with whom its members were trading. It sent missionary couples out to three trading centres. By 1896 the Sierra Leone Anglican Church Mission, noting the progress of this venture of the Bonthe congregation, began to share their concern, and within a year opened two stations.'[2] By 1912

Sierra Leone Creole missionaries had established fifteen mission stations and out-stations. However, because of the Hut Tax War of 1897 and tribal animosity, the indigenous Africans came to distrust the Creole population. By 1915 it became evident that the efforts of the Creole missionaries were not getting any response from the people in the villages. Usually, the Creole missionaries filled their churches with Creole traders, teachers and government officials in the interior population centres.

During the period 1880 to 1907 the C.M.S. had sent missionaries far into the interior of Sierra Leone to do pioneer work. These stations had developed slowly. In 1907 the C.M.S. turned the stations over to the Sierra Leone Anglican Church for them to continue such evangelism. In 1912 a survey was made of the interior work done by the Anglican Creoles. The report showed that the pastors of these church stations did not show the vigour or missionary spirit needed to take advantage of all the opportunities offered.

The Wesleyan Methodist Church in Sierra Leone continued to expand. By 1880 it claimed over 14,000 members, but, like the Anglican Church, most of the members lived on the coast. In 1877 the Methodists began to move further inland and by 1908 had established a station on the western border of Sierra Leone. The Methodist missionaries had the same difficulty as the C.M.S. in mobilizing the Creole Christians to spread the Good News to the interior tribes.

A Wesleyan Methodist Missionary report of 1922 made the following evaluation: 'The freed slaves remained utter strangers to the inhabitants of the shore where they landed, their black hue did little or nothing to commend the new faith to their neighbours. The liberated Africans lodged at Sierra Leone formed an enclave by themselves through European hands, but whose gratitude went little further, and who had small idea of constituting themselves a missionary clan and being vehicles of Christ to their fellow countrymen. In this respect the Sierra Leone enterprise proved somewhat of a disappointment.'[3]

Other mission societies working in Sierra Leone during this period include: the Evangelical United Brethren, the United

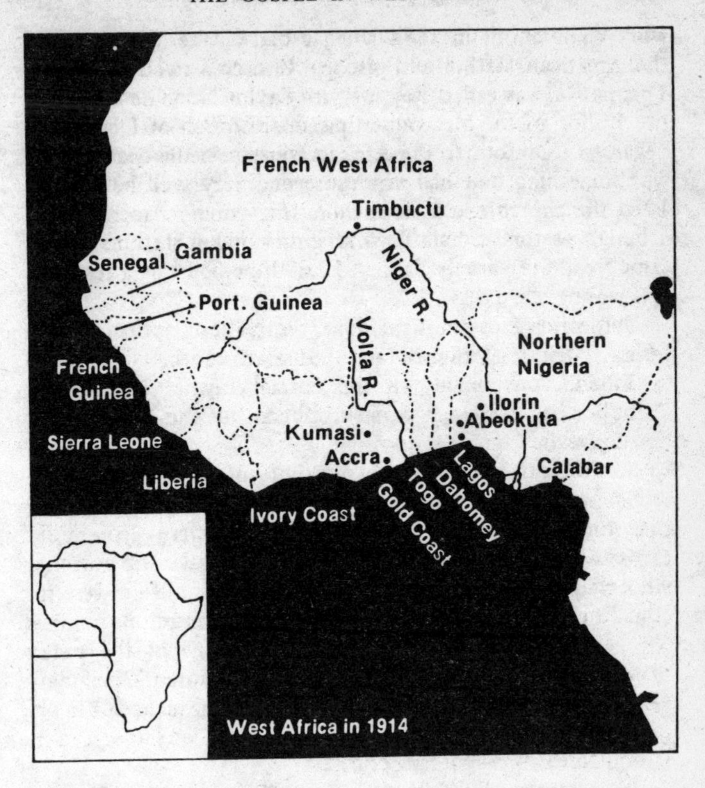

West Africa in 1914

Brethren in Christ, the American Wesleyan Methodist, and the Seventh Day Adventists.

By 1914 both the Methodist and Anglican Churches in Sierra Leone could report large memberships, but many of the pastors felt that the number of real believers was much smaller. The Sierra Leone Church was more than one hundred years old in 1914, but in great need of revival.

LIBERIA

The Protestant churches in Liberia continued their testimony during the period 1878 to 1914. A surge of interest and new work came about in 1884 when a black American pastor of the American Methodist Episcopal Church arrived in Liberia. This pastor was called Rev. William Taylor. Soon he was made the Bishop of the Methodist Episcopal Church of Liberia. He began to reach out to the African tribes near the coast, which was something that had not succeeded very well before. By 1914 the church could claim more than ninety American and Liberian pastors and staff working on mission stations. In the same year the church claimed 10,000 members as a result of this work.

The other Protestant missionary societies Baptist, Presbyterian, African Methodist and Lutheran continued to work in Liberia, but mainly in the coastal towns. The Roman Catholics had started a work in Liberia but they gained very few converts.

'In 1914, in spite of nearly a century of effort, Christianity in Liberia was only a minority movement. The descendants of the immigrants from the United States were professedly Christian, but they were mainly on the coast. The Africans who were influenced by them to adopt the culture were inclined to be open-minded to the associated religion. Beginnings (of evangelism) had been made among some of the pagan tribes. However, the vast majority of the inhabitants, including practically all those in the hinterland, were untouched.'[4]

IVORY COAST (CÔTE D'IVOIRE)

So far in our study of the growth of Christianity in Africa we have not mentioned the Ivory Coast. The reason for this is that by 1878 there still had not been a single mission station opened. In fact it was 1895 before the first missionaries arrived, and they were Roman Catholics. 'In its first three years in the colony the (Roman Catholic) society lost ten of its staff by death, but in 1901, so undauntedly did it persist, it had six stations. As French authority was extended inland, the missionaries pressed into the interior . . . A printing establishment was opened. A steamer, . . plied between the stations on the coast. In 1913 there were said to be about 2,400 native Christians.'[5]

By 1913 there was very little Protestant witness in the Ivory Coast. And then, the Lord did an amazing thing. In 1911 God spoke to the heart of William Wadé Harris, who was a member of the Grebo tribe in Liberia. William Harris became aware that God wanted him to become an evangelist and proclaim the Gospel. Harris had become a Christian while attending a Methodist mission school in Cape Palmas, Liberia, several years before this. For ten years after leaving school he was a teacher in an American Protestant Episcopal Mission School in Liberia. Harris received God's message while he was serving time in a Liberian prison for taking part in an anti-government demonstration. Upon his release from prison, he began to preach the God News to his fellow Grebo.

William Harris saw himself as being a prophet of God, whose duty was to call people to repentance, as the Old Testament prophets had done. Prophet Harris was well prepared for his new ministry because of the time he had spent at the Methodist mission school and teaching in the Episcopal mission school. He was familiar with God's message of salvation contained in the Bible. In 1913 he crossed the border into Ivory Coast to preach to people there.

In Ivory Coast Prophet Harris found village after village which had never heard the Good News of Jesus Christ. Prophet Harris did not change the Gospel message to fit into the local tribal culture so that he could attract large numbers of followers. On the contrary, he called for burning of all fetishes as proof that people were turning away from the old ways to come to Jesus.

'Although Harris gave advice about living a new life, his message during his first passage was very simple: God was good, He was love. The fetishes must be destroyed, all must be baptized and worship God in the church they were to build. He quoted from the Bible which he held before them (though he did not open it and read from it) and said that white men had sent him and would follow him to teach men to read the Bible.'[6]

The people in Ivory Coast to whom he preached were responsive and soon thousands were coming to him for baptism. Prophet Harris insisted that those who had been baptized should abstain from adultery and keep Sunday as a holy day.

Harris walked along the entire shore of Ivory Coast preaching the Gospel and then entered the Gold Coast. After preaching there for a few months he returned to the Ivory Coast. Larger numbers than before were attracted to his preaching. By November, 1914, the French colonial officials had become worried about the large following Harris was gathering. As war had started between France and Germany in Europe, the colonialists did not want an African uprising on their hands in Ivory Coast. In December, 1914, the colonial officials had Prophet Harris arrested at Kraffy.

Harris told of his interrogation by the French administrators: 'He asked me why I always continue to preach. I said to him, "I am a prophet like Elijah – to destroy the fetishes." But then they acted like pagans, they mocked me and said, "The Bible is no good." I said to them, "I stand up to witness for Jesus Christ." But they burst into laughter and said, "You are only a Kruman to row and carry hammock, that is all. You cannot teach us." But I read to them from the Bible, Acts 5:39, "If this work be of men, it will come to naught, but if it be of God you cannot overthrow it," then they began to abuse me, "Dastard, idiot of a Kruman," and they led me away to prison.'[7]

Early in 1915 Prophet Harris was escorted to a ship going to Cape Palmas and told never to return to Ivory Coast again. Back in Liberia Harris settled down, but sometimes went out on evangelistic crusades in Liberia. In July, 1917, he went to Freetown, where he preached to the Kru community for a short time. He then returned to Liberia where he continued to preach from time to time until his death in 1929.

Prophet Harris is another one of the outstanding figures of African Church history. Because he was yielded to God and moved when and where God told him, he was able to point thousands and thousands of people to Christ. People are not sure of the exact number that Prophet Harris baptized, but it is estimated than in 1915 there were between 60,000 and 100,000 people who had repented. For many years after Harris was deported, these people in Ivory Coast received little spiritual guidance. The Wesleyan Methodists sent a missionary to help meet the challenge in Ivory Coast, but in 1915 he was limited by the French government from following up those people converted by Harris. It was not until 1925 that the Wesleyan Methodists were able to consolidate those people who had responded to Harris's message.

People who knew him reported that Prophet Harris had many commendable qualities of Christian character and leadership: he kept Sunday as a day of rest; he shunned materialism; he only took gifts of food that he actually needed, giving the rest to the needy; he read and meditated on the Bible; he was not interested in building a personality cult around his preaching; and he advised people against the use of alcohol and tobacco as habits that take control of a person.

Finally, the ministry of Prophet Harris is important to African Church history for it shows us what can happen when someone obeys God's command to take the Gospel to every person. It also shows how the Holy Spirit can prepare hearts to respond to the teaching of the Word. An American professor of missions, Dr. Donald McGavran, calls the response to Harris's message a 'people movement'. In other parts of Africa, similar people-movements have occurred in which whole towns and villages have left the traditional religion and turned to Jesus Christ.

GOLD COAST (GHANA)

In 1880 the French Roman Catholic missionaries arrived in the Gold Coast to begin their work. Their arrival came more than fifty years after the Wesleyan and Basel Mission societies first began work in that area. Several of the early Roman Catholic fathers died because of disease, but the work grew. By 1906 two other Roman Catholic orders had come to work in the Gold Coast.

The Basel Mission continued its expansion in the Gold Coast. As we have seen in a previous chapter, the Basel Mission goal was to move inland. The King of Ashanti refused to give them permission to work in the Ashanti capital of Kumasi or the surrounding area. Finally in 1896 permission was given to the Basel Mission to open an Ashanti station. 'No time was lost: on February 22, Ramseyer and Perregaux entered Kumasi; it was a station of the Basel Mission at last. And more: Ashanti lay open before them; in quick succession stations were occupied – until war came in 1900. But once more the advance was resumed in 1902; the three outstations of that year had become twenty by 1914; schools had grown from one to seventeen, and communicant members increased from fourteen to 805.'[8]

The Methodist Church continued to grow. Some of this growth was due to Methodist laymen who were clerks or traders, who established churches when they were sent to new trading centres. A good example was at Kintampo, a fairly important trading centre far in the North of Ashanti, where 'one of the clerks in the Government office was a member of the Methodist congregation at Aburi. He felt it his duty to help the heathen around him to a higher faith by teaching and preaching. After a while he gave up his post under government and with it the considerable salary he was drawing and the pension which awaited him at the end of his service. He obtained a piece of ground on which he built a chapel, and when the missionary visited the place two years later he found a vigorous church already in existence, and twenty candidates for baptism presenting themselves. This was in 1910.'[9]

In 1897 friction arose in the Methodist Church between some members and the missionaries. As a result, an all African Methodist church was organized in 1898 as a self-growing, self-supporting church. The new church associated itself with the American Methodist Episcopal Zion Church, which helped by educating several promising young men who were sent to the United States. One of these young men was Dr. J.E.K. Aggrey, of whom more will be written later.

Other missions initiated work in the Gold Coast during this period. The Seventh Day Adventists began work at Sekondi in 1898; the Baptists at Cape Coast in 1898; and the Salvation Army came to Dunkwa in Agona in 1911. In 1904 the Society for the Propagation of the Gospel began work at Sekondi, beginning the first Anglican missionary work in the Gold Coast since Rev. Philip Quaque's day.

TOGO

Togo was a small territory with a population of around one million in 1914. Because Germany claimed it as a territory, most of the missions that worked in Togo before 1914 were German. The North German (Bremen) Mission actually began work in Togo in the 1850's. Their work progressed well and in 1902 they were given some additional coastal mission stations that had been administered by the Basel Mission. By 1914 the Bremen Mission numbered 7,140 baptized members. The Basel Mission later returned to Togo to open up the north-west part of the colony to Christianity in 1912. The only other major Protestant church was the Methodist Church situated along the coastal area.

The Roman Catholic Church had not made much effort to work in Togo before 1890. However, after that time much money was spent by the Roman Catholics to build churches and schools very rapidly. 'In 1892 Rome entrusted Togo to the Society of the Divine Word, which was predominately German in its personnel. In the little over two decades (20 years) before the World War of 1914–1918 intervened, the society opened a number of stations. In 1914 it had 19,740 Roman Catholic converts in its care, 198 schools with 7,911 pupils, and a staff of 47 priests, 15 lay brothers, and 30 sisters.'[10]

DAHOMEY (BENIN)

Another small territory, to the east of Togo, is Dahomey. It had less than one million people in 1914 and was ruled by the French.

The French Roman Catholic 'Society of African Missions' was the largest mission in Dahomey before 1914. The French government encouraged the French Roman Catholic missionaries, so that by 1914 the church had grown very large. The

Roman Catholics claimed 11,440 converts who were served by 34 European priests, one lay brother and 22 sisters.

The only Protestant mission in Dahomey by 1914 was the Wesleyan Methodist Missionary Society. They had a very small work and only claimed 750 church members in 1914.

NIGERIA

The territory of Nigeria had benefited from the work of Samuel Crowther and the Niger Mission. By 1890 the Gospel was going out from many centres along the coast. However, for the most part the inland areas of Nigeria were unreached.

The Anglican and Wesleyan missions were still the largest societies in Western Nigeria, although the American Southern Baptist witness was continuing to expand. By 1900, the British colonial government brought a measure of peace to the areas north of Abeokuta and so the C.M.S. began to advance northwards. When missionaries arrived in many villages they found that people who had been working in the south and who had become Christians had returned to their interior villages and were witnessing to their neighbours and thus spreading the Gospel. 'In the hinterland to the north-east, a little group of Christians who had returned to their pagan village were bitterly persecuted but refused to renounce their faith. Before long many fellow villagers were seeking baptism. When in 1912 the General Superintendent (C.M.S.) entered an area new to the Mission, he found "the nucleus of a strong African church already existing".'[11]

During the period 1878 to 1900 the Niger Mission had opened many mission stations along the Niger River. But few of the stations were further than fifteen miles from the river. After 1900 the Niger Mission began to move further and further away from the river in order to reach new areas.

In the east the Scottish United Presbyterian Mission continued its work. Beginning in the 1890's the mission began to push inland into Ibo country. The most famous missionary of this area was a single missionary lady called Mary M. Slessor. Because of her great love for the people with whom she worked she was accepted everywhere. From 1888 to 1915, when she died, she kept opening new mission stations further and further to the north in Iboland. By 1914 the Presbyterian Church in that area claimed 10,792 followers.

Although there was much missionary activity in the south of Nigeria, the great northern part of the territory remained unreached by the Gospel. Starting in the late 1890's this problem came to the attention of mission leaders in America and Europe. In 1901 the Sudan Interior Mission (S.I.M.) successfully established a work in northern Nigeria. This was the third try by the S.I.M. to enter northern Nigeria, the first two attempts being failures. The goal of the S.I.M. was to begin work in unreached areas far in the interior which had not been met by existing missions. The S.I.M. established a denomination which is today called 'The Evangelical Churches of West Africa.'

As you may remember, Islam had been moving south across the Sahara Desert since the ninth century. By 1900 many tribes in Northern Nigeria had been converted to Islam. But there still remained some tribes to the south which were pagan. The S.I.M. alone could not meet the challenge of reaching these tribes, and so in 1904 the Sudan United Mission was formed by five major denominations. The reports that reached the Sudan United Mission (S.U.M.) showed how the Muslims were trying to convert the remaining pagan tribes of northern Nigeria. 'A new dynamic aspect of the Sudan situation had been added: they "will go over to Islam". This was to become the rallying point for Christian missions in the Sudan. The call went out to "stem the tide of Islam" and give the pagan populace a fair chance to choose between Islam and Christianity.'[12] The S.I.M. and the S.U.M. wanted to take the Christian message to these border tribes so that they would know that there was an alternative to the legalism of Islam. Although these missions worked hard, Islam had been working for a much longer period of time and by 1940 most of the northern border tribes decided to convert to Islam. But in the central belt, the pagan tribes were more willing to turn to Christianity than to Islam. Still, the number of Christians remained small by 1940.

INTERIOR WEST AFRICA (NIGER, BURKINA FASO & MALI)

This territory comprised the heart of Muslim West Africa. As we have seen, Christianity was pushing into the interior of West Africa from the coast, but by 1914 it still was not as far as this vast interior region. In addition, the Muslim chiefs and kings of this area did not welcome mission officials who came to ask about opening mission stations. So it remained for the period after 1914 to see some attempts at establishing mission stations. By 1914 only a few isoated Roman Catholic mission stations existed along the upper Niger River.

Questions:

1. What was the general state of Christianity along the coast of Sierra Leone around 1914?
2. Who enabled one of the denominations in Liberia to expand into the interior in the period following 1884?
3. Who was William Wadé Harris? What did he do? Why is he important in the study of African Church history?
4. What new region in the Gold Coast did the Basel Mission enter in 1896? In what part of the country is this?
5. In 1914 what was the largest church in Dahomey. Can you give a reason why this was so?
6. Why was the Sudan Interior Mission formed? What other mission was formed to meet the same need?

[1] Groves, C.P., *The Planting of Christianity in Africa*, vol. III (Lutterworth Press, London, 1955), p. 184.
[2] Olson, G.W., *Church Growth in Sierra Leone* (Wm B. Eerdmans Pub. Com., Grand Rapids, Mi., 1969), p. 81
[3] *Wesleyan Methodist Missionary Society*, vol. 4; 1922, p. 81

[4] Latourette, S., *A History of the Expansion of Christianity: The Great Century*, vol. V (Harper & Bros., New York, 1943), pp. 452, 453

[5] Ibid. p. 448.

[6] Haliburton, Gordon M., *The Prophet Harris* (Oxford University Press, New York, 1973), p. 49
[7] Ibid. p. 104
[8] Groves, C.P., *The Planting. . .*, vol. III, p. 214

[9]Debrunner, Hans W., *A History of Christianity in Ghana* (Waterville Pub. House, Accra, 1967), p. 213
[10]Latourette, K.S., *A History. . .*, p. 445
[11]Groves, C.P., *A History. . .*, vol. III, p. 215
[12]Grimley, J.B. & Robinson, G.E., *Church Growth in Central & Southern Nigeria* (Wm B. Eerdmans Pub. Co., Grand Rapids, Mi., 1966), p. 44

24

Expansion of Christianity in West-Central Africa 1878–1914

In chapter twenty-three we ended our study by looking at developments in Nigeria. In this chapter we will continue looking at the development of Christianity, starting first with the Cameroons and then working our way south on the map.

CAMEROONS

As we noted in chapter twenty-two, the Cameroons were claimed as a colony by Germany in 1884. In the years that followed the Germans strengthened their control of the land. The German colonialists hindered the expansion of the Gospel in two ways, though. First, they were suspicious of any missionary who was not a German citizen. Mission societies with English or French missionaries found it very difficult to continue work. Then, too, the Germans required that all mission schools use German as the language of instruction. Baptist mission schools that had been working in the Cameroons for more than forty years had to change their language. However, a benefit of the German occupation was that tribal wars were not as numerous as before and communications, such as roads and post, were established. These enabled missionaries to push inland with the Christian message.

The church that suffered the most because of the Germans was the Cameroons Baptist Church established by Alfred Saker in the Duala area. Because Saker was an Englishman, he opposed the German colonialists from governing the Baptist area. In 1885 there was a war between two tribes in the area of the Baptist mission. The Germans used force to end the war, but in the process destroyed the Baptist mission station. The English Baptist mission realized that it would be very difficult for them to continue their work in Cameroons because the German government was against them and the government also required that everything on the mission stations either be done in German or the Duala vernacular. Therefore in 1886 the English Baptists invited German missionaries of the Basel Mission to take over their work. 'On December 23, 1886, there landed at Bethel in Cameroons the first Basel Mission party to enter the new field: . .'[1]

The German missionaries went right into the work, but several of the early workers died from malaria. Almost from the beginning the Basel missionaries noticed that many of the Christians in the churches had very poor moral standards. The new missionaries began preaching the importance of separation from wordly lusts. This angered some of the church members and a split in the church occurred. In 1890 a German Baptist mission came to the area and tried to work with the church members who had split off from the Basel mission. They were not altogether successful in their work, but their mission did grow later.

The Basel Mission spent the years from 1886 to 1903 adjusting to the stations and work they had taken over from the Baptists. During this time the Gospel witness was faithfully given out. Because the Basel missionaries were Germans, many Africans listened to them as they felt the missionaries were part of the new government. 'Almost as soon as the transfer (from the Baptists) was made a mass movement set in towards Christianity, possibly because the blacks associated the faith with the new order being established by the Germans. As the government built roads to the interior, the Basel Mission extended its work inland. Several tribes asked for catechists and schools, not so much because they desired Christianity, as because they wished instruction in the new culture to which they must adjust themselves. In 1914 the Basel society counted 16 head stations, 67 missionaries, 9 missionary sisters, 384 schools with 21,622 pupils, and 15,112 baptized Christians.'[2]

Another Protestant mission which we have already studied

also initiated a work in Cameroons. The American Presbyterian Board of Foreign Missions which had started a work in Gabon began to move north into the Cameroons when the French government made work difficult in Gabon. Their real work in the Cameroons began in 1890 and in 1892 they moved into the interior. Because the mission was made up of Americans whose country had no colonial interest in Africa, the German government welcomed them. The Basel Mission Society was also glad to have the Presbyterians work in south-eastern Cameroons, as they did not have enough staff to reach the whole colony. By 1914 the Presbyterian Church had 5,000 baptized members in the Cameroons.

In 1890 the Roman Catholics began work in the Cameroons. The German government allowed the Pious Society of Missions to conduct the work. Although these Roman Catholic missionaries arrived much later than the Protestant workers, because of the easier requirements for Roman Catholic baptism, the Roman Catholic Church could claim almost as many converts by 1914 as the Protestants had.

The German colonial government, like the English and French, did not allow missionaries to start work in strong Muslim areas. The colonialists thought that this might make the Muslims angry and they would start a rebellion, and so for the period 1878 to 1914 Christianity did not reach the Muslim north of the Cameroons.

GABON

As we saw in chapter twenty-one, Protestant missionaries arrived in the territory of Gabon before the Roman Catholics. But when the French colonialists took over Gabon and made it a colony, they favoured the French Roman Catholic missionaries and helped them with advice and money. In the period 1878 to 1914 the Roman Catholic Church grew much more rapidly than the Protestant churches. The Roman Catholics established a seminary to train African priests in 1856 at Libreville. But it was not until 1899 that an African

Since the beginning of the twentieth century many spiritual churches have been established. Often these groups can be identified by the special clothing they wear. This picture shows members of a spiritual church in Nigeria gathering for a meeting.

Many political leaders of independent Africa are Christians who openly practise their faith. This may be due to the fact that a majority of the schools in the first part of this century were mission schools. One professing Christian leader is President Kenneth Kaunda of Zambia, seen here speaking at a Christian convention.

Most of the spiritual churches that have grown up in Africa are patterned on Protestant doctrine or forms of worship, but a few observe Roman Catholic traditions and church government. One such group is the Maria Legio group of Western Kenya, pictured here.

Africans had already built the great stone city of Zimbabwe when de Silveira visited the Kingdom of Monomatapa in 1560 to tell the people about Christianity. This picture shows some of the ruins of Zimbabwe as they appear today.

David Livingstone walked thousands of kilometres across Africa telling the Good News of Jesus Christ and striving to end the evil slave trade. He also tried to unlock the geographical secrets of Africa's lakes and rivers. This statue of him overlooks the Victoria Falls on the border of Zambia and Zimbabwe.

This stone is on the side of a Roman Catholic Church built over the place where several Ugandan Christians were martyred in 1885-86.

Before missionaries came to Africa, blind people were left to beg or do simple, unimportant tasks around the village. Following Christ's teaching of love for all people, Christians built special schools to teach the blind how to read and write and take care of themselves. These two students were trained in Salvation Army blind schools in Kenya. They are seen here studying at a Bible College to be pastors.

Simon Kimbangu, founder of the Kimbanguiste Church of Zaire. Despite its poor quality, this picture is of historical importance as it is one of the only two known photographs of this religious leader.

With the arrival of complete autonomy for the major Protestant denominations, a new interest in traditional musical instruments has arisen in the Church. Today more and more African musical instruments are being used in worship services. Here, students at the Africa Inland Church's Scott Theological College in Kenya demonstrate some traditional and modern instruments that can be used in worship.

Dr E. K. Aggrey

Prophet William Wadé Harris

The first primary and secondary schools in many countries were established by missionaries. This picture shows a Basel Mission girls school in Ghana c. 1900.

completed the seminary course and then asked for ordination to the priesthood.

The American Presbyterian Mission which had been in Gabon before the arrival of the French colonialists was forced to give up their mission stations by the French Government. The French, like the Germans, only wanted missionaries from their own country to work in their colonies. In 1890 the American Presbyterians got the Evangelical Paris Mission Society to send teachers who could teach French in their schools. But the colonialists wanted the American missionaries to leave altogether, and so the Presbyterians gave all of the stations in Gabon to the French Protestant Society. 'In 1913 the rest was transferred to the French society. The French Protestants developed the enterprise thus acquired. In 1913 they had in five stations 1,908 Christians and 1,976 catechumens.'[3]

Before we leave Gabon we should mention one famous man who came to help the people of that territory. This man's name was Albert Schweitzer. He was the son of a pastor and as a child had heard about the need for missionaries in Africa. He attended university where he did very well. He was also one of the greatest organists of his time. The one weakness that Schweitzer had was that through his instruction and study at university he came to doubt some of the basic teachings of the Bible. Because of his beliefs he is grouped with those churchmen who are called 'Liberals'. Scheweitzer still wanted to go to Africa to help people, and so in 1913 he applied to the Paris Mission Society. 'In spite of the timorous reluctance of some of the directors of the society, who feared his radical scholarship, he was given appointment to Lamarene (Mission Station).'[4] Albert Schweitzer served as a doctor at that mission station for fifty years.

FRENCH CONGO & UBANGI-SHARI-CHAD (CONGO REPUBLIC, CENTRAL AFRICAN REPUBLIC & CHAD)

Together with Gabon, the region of French Congo and Ubangi-Shari-Chad was called by the French colonialists 'French

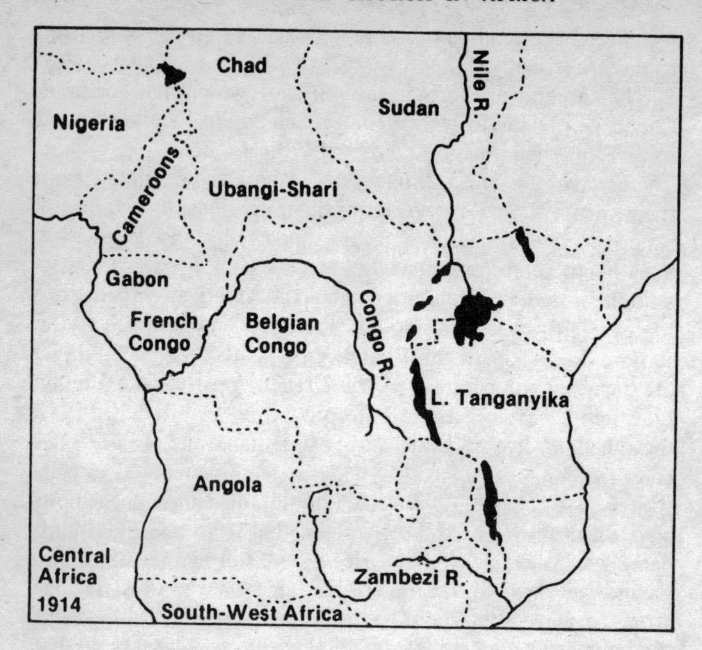

Equatorial Africa'. During the period 1878 to 1914 Protestant missions in French Equatorial Africa were mainly limited to the coastal area of Gabon. However, the Roman Catholic missionaries pushed inland.

The Pope had assigned the development of Roman Catholic work for French Equatorial Africa to the French Holy Ghost Fathers. In 1890 a new church area was formed in Ubangi. 'It, too, was entrusted to the Holy Ghost Fathers. Even before the vicariate was created, financial assistance came from the French Government.'[5] It is no wonder that the Roman Catholic Church is so important today in countries like Gabon, Congo, C.A.E. and Chad: while the French government made work difficult for non-French Protestant missionaries, they gave large sums of money to the French Roman Catholics to build up churches and mission stations. 'On the eve of 1914 there were in all of French Equatorial Africa not far from 30,000 Roman Catholics, of whom the majority were in the Vicariate Apostolic of Gabon.'[6]

BELGIAN CONGO (ZAIRE)

As we saw in chapter twenty-one the Roman Catholics preceded the Protestants in establishing a mission work on the Congo River. Because of Leopold's interests in the Congo, he wanted only Belgian Roman Catholic missionaries. The work begun by French Roman Catholics had to be modified so that Belgian missionaries could run some of the stations. Soon Leopold realized that there were not enough Belgian Catholics to do all the work, and so he allowed other Europeans to enter the Congo.

The Congo River basin had a large concentration of people in the late nineteenth century. This large number of unreached Africans attracted many Roman Catholic and Protestant mission societies to work in the area. Because King Leopold was a Roman Catholic, he encouraged the Roman Catholic Church to expand in the Congo. In the 1890's the Jesuits and the priests of the Sacred Heart of Jesus started mission work. 'The list of the additional Roman Catholic agencies which entered the Belgian Congo before 1914 is indicative of the attention the vast possession attracted and the devotion expended. In 1894 came the Trappists, in 1896 the Premonstratensians, in 1899 the Redemptorists, in 1905 the Mill Hill Fathers, in 1910 Benedictines and Capuchins, in 1911 Dominicans and Salesians, in 1909 the Brothers of Christian Schools, in 1910 the Brothers of Charity of Gand, in 1911 the Marists Brothers, in 1891 the Sisters of Charity of Gand, in 1895 the Sisters of Our Lady of Namur, in 1895 the White Sisters, in 1896 the Fransiscan Missionaries of Mary, in 1899 the Sisters of the Sacred Heart of Mary the Berlaer, and in 1911 the Daughters of the Cross of Liege. In 1914 more different Roman Catholic bodies were at work than in any political entity in Africa south of the Sahara.'[7] By 1914, it was estimated that the number of Congolese who had become Roman Catholics was more than 100,000.

In 1878 the first Protestant mission began working in the Congo. It was called the Livingstone Inland Mission. The goal of the L.I.M. was to establish a string of mission stations from the coast up the Congo River to Stanley Pool. By 1880 three mission stations had been established and staffed, although many of the early missionaries suffered from malaria and fever. The mission sent two steam powered launches to navigate the Congo River. By 1883 the L.I.M. had established ten mission stations, the furthest being 800 miles inland!

At about the same time that the L.I.M. was starting an evangelical witness in the Congo, the Baptist Missionary Society of England was also trying to begin work in the same area. The early Baptist missionaries finally found a route to the Upper Congo River, that part of the Congo River which is above the Stanley Pool and which can be used by boats for a thousand miles. 'Thanks to the generosity of Robert Arthington, who in 1880 had offered the Committee one thousand pounds Sterling to put a steamer, seventy feet in length and of less than twelve inches draught . . . The "Peace" was duly delivered and finally reached the Congo in 800 sections. Grenfell successfully built and launched her and in July 1884 took her on a maiden voyage.'[8] From this we see how ships were brought to Africa in the nineteenth century and how important they were for transportation and opening new stations in the pioneer days of the Church.

In the early 1880's the Livingstone Inland Mission decided to hand over its pioneer work in the Congo to the American Baptist Mission. This mission took over all the L.I.M. stations on the Congo River and then began developing new stations of their own. In 1886, the black American Baptist missionaries arrived in the Congo to further this work.

The success of the British Baptist and American Baptist missionary societies soon attracted other American missions. In 1886 the American Methodist Church began work in the Congo. In 1889 the first missionaries of the Christian and Missionary Alliance established a successful station in the Congo. The Belgian Congo covered a large geographical area and to meet the needs of the people to hear the Gospel additional missions were needed. In 1891 the Southern Presbyterian Church of the United States opened a mission station, then in 1895 the Disciples of Christ Church of America began to work. Other missions to begin work in Congo after 1895 include: the Plymouth Brethren, the Congo Inland Mission (Mennonites) and the American Southern Methodists. The reason for the large number of American mission societies working in Congo at this time (in comparison with the smaller proportion of West Africa) was that King Leopold was not afraid that the Americans would try to take his 'Congo Free State' away from him, like French or German nationals might try to do.

Toward the end of the period we are studying, i.e. 1878–1914, a new place of entry to work in the Congo was opened. Prior to 1910 most mission societies used the Congo River to enter the Belgian Congo. But in 1909 the General Director of the Africa Inland Mission, Mr C. E. Hurlbert, asked President Theodore Roosevelt of the United States to write to the Belgian Government for permission for the A.I.M. to enter the Belgian Congo from the eastern boundary and begin work. The Belgian Government agreed and the A.I.M. became the first organization to open a Christian work in the Congo from the east. In 1910 the A.I.M. sent a survey party to the eastern Congo to see about opening a station there. In 1912 the first permanent A.I.M. missionaries pitched their tents in the Congo and began the work.

In 1913 a new mission society was founded, called the Heart of Africa Mission. The famous missionary C.T. Studd, and a fellow worker travelled from the East African coast into eastern Congo and began to work fifty miles from the A.I.M.'s station at Dungu. 'When they reached Congo, however, they were informed that while permission had been given for the A.I.M. to start work there, no such entry could be granted to another Mission. It was therefore agreed that they should enter under the aegis of the A.I.M. and if they wanted to form a separate body they would be at liberty to do so.'[9]

As we come to the end of this brief survey of Christian work in the Congo, it is important to note the key role played by the Church in helping the people of the Congo. King

Leopold and later the Belgian government did not start any schools, and so any education that was available came only from mission schools. Then, too, most of the hospitals and dispensaries were operated by mission societies. Perhaps the greatest contribution of the Christians of this period was the movement to have the Congo Free State taken away from King Leopold. It was mainly the Protestant missionaries working in the Congo who saw and reported to the world the bad behaviour of Leopold's Congolese soldiers and the unfair taxes which Leopold demanded. The main desire of the Protestant missionaries was to help the Africans and so they loudly accused Leopold of mismanaging the Congo. Finally, in 1908 world opinion forced the Belgian government to take the Congo Free Estate away from King Leopold. After that, conditions in the Belgian Congo improved somewhat for the Africans.

ANGOLA

The last time we looked at Angola we saw that only the Roman Catholic Church had missionaries working in the territory. Most of the work was concentrated in three major towns on the coast. In 1879 the Holy Ghost Fathers were given permission by the Pope to begin work in southern Angola. The Holy Ghost Fathers displayed more initiative and drive than the Portuguese missionaries and soon they had established schools, orphanages, hospitals, a seminary for training African preists, and a novitiate for lay brothers. Most of these projects were carried out with money given by the Portuguese government to the Roman Catholic Church. 'By 1913 the Holy Ghost Fathers were counting in all Angola 29,200 native Roman Catholics in their care.'[10]

It was not until 1878 that Protestant missionaries entered Angola to preach the Gospel. The first mission was the English Baptists who established their headquarters at San Salvador. The American Board of Commissioners for Foreign Missions established a mission station in 1880 at Bihé, which was inland from Benguella. These missions were followed by the

Canadian Congregationalists (1886), the Plymouth Brethren (1889), the Angola Evangelical Mission (1897), the Christian and Missionary Alliance (1910) and the South Africa General Mission (1914). Progress was slow for these Protestant missions, because they did not receive money from the Portuguese government and they were developing a pioneer work. Nevertheless, by 1914 the foundation had been laid for further evangelization in the years to come.

Questions:

1. Why did the Cameroons Baptist Mission turn over their work to the Basel Mission in 1886?
2. Why did the American Presbyterians leave the work in Gabon? When did this happen?
3. What was the first Protestant Mission to begin work in the Belgian Congo (or Congo Free State as it was called then)? When did it begin?
4. When did the A.I.M. begin work in the Belgian Congo?
5. How did Protestant missionaries help the Africans living in the Congo before 1910?
6. What was the first Protestant mission society to begin work in Angola? Why did the Roman Catholic Church grow much faster in Angola than the Protestant churches?

[1] Groves, C.P., *The Planting of Christianity in Africa*, vol. III (Lutterworth Press, London, 1955), p. 57

[2] Ibid. p. 58

[3] Latourette, Kenneth S., *A History of the Expansion of Christianity: The Great Century*, vol. V (Harper & Bros., New York, 1943), p. 430

[4] Ibid. p. 431

[5] Ibid. p. 428

[6] Ibid. p. 429

[7] Ibid. p. 422

[8] Groves, C.P., *The Planting. . .*, vol. III, p. 113

[9] Richardsion, Kenneth, *Garden of Miracles: A History of the Africa Inland Mission* (Victory Press, London, 1968), p. 142

[10] Latourette, K.S., *A History. . .*, vol. V, p. 399

25

Continued growth in Southern Africa: 1878–1914

SOUTH-WEST AFRICA

The territory of South-west Africa became a German colony in 1885. Although South-west Africa seems like a rather large country on the map, it has a comparatively small population. Much of the land is either desert or semi-desert which will not support a large population. Around 1900 the population of the entire colony was thought to be only 200,000 people.

We have already noted the beginning of the Church in South-west Africa when we were studying the early mission development in South Africa. The first Christian work was opened in 1842 by the Rhenish Missionary Society which crossed the Orange River into Great Namaqualand. In the 1870's the Church was making good progress in its thrust of evangelism. During this period a new Protestant mission arrived; it was called the Finnish Missionary Society. Members of this mission began work in the northern part of the territory with the Ovambo tribe. In the 1880's there were numerous tribal wars which made Christian work difficult.

The German missionaries with the Rhenish Mission were glad at first that Germany had annexed South-west Africa. They thought that the Germans would bring peace to the tribes which were fighting each other and develop the colony by building railways, a postal system, etc. They soon realized, however, that the German colonialists were very strict administrators. At the same time German settlers were brought in to farm some of the land. The Protestant missionaries realized that the white settlers would take away all the good land from the Africans before long. They then forced the colonial administration to reserve certain land for Africans, so as to keep the Europeans away.

In 1903 the members of the Herero tribe revolted against the German colonialists. They killed many European administrators and German white settlers. The German government fought the Hereros using very harsh methods. Many innocent people died during the war. Soon the Hottentots in the region joined the war against the Germans. It was not until 1907 that the Germans defeated the Africans. The war had been so fierce that the tribal organization of the Hereros and the Hottentots had been destroyed.

This war brought great trouble for the Church. The colonialists and settlers accused some of the Protestant missionaries of helping the Africans in the war and of encouraging them to take back their land. Then, too, many Hereros came to hate all Europeans and so would no longer listen to missionaries who preached the Gospel.

After 1907 the Roman Catholic Church began to make greater progress in South-west Africa. Although they had begun their work in the colony in 1892, very few converts had been won.

By 1914 it was estimated that there were more than 10,000 members of the Protestant churches and about 5,000 members of the Roman Catholic Church.

BECHUANALAND (BOTSWANA)

We have already seen in chapter fourteen how the London Missionary Society under the direction of Robert Moffat opened up the territory of Bechuanaland to the Gospel. Bechuanaland was like South-west Africa in one way: most of it was desert or semi-desert. It, too, had a rather small population compared with the size of its territory. Therefore not as many missions or missionaries came to work in Bechuanaland as went, for example, to the Belgian Congo.

The L.M.S. remained the largest church organization in Bechuanaland during the period we are studying. During this time the L.M.S. was joined by the Wesleyan Methodist Mission, the Paris Evangelical Missionary Society and the Dutch Reformed Church. There was no settled Roman Catholic mission station before 1914.

During the period 1878 to 1914 many Africans received Jesus Christ as their Saviour and so the Church continued to grow. During that time the L.M.S. worked hard to help the Africans. Schools and hospitals were constructed. The L.M.S. also helped the Africans by protecting them from the greed of Cecil Rhodes. Great Britain had made Bechuanaland a protectorate in 1885 when Germany claimed South-west Africa. But in 1894 Cecil Rhodes tried to get the British government to give him part of the land of Bechuanaland to add to his new colony of Rhodesia. The chiefs of the local tribes were unhappy about this, and so in 1895 the L.M.S. arranged for three chiefs to visit England to tell the queen exactly what the problem was. The three chiefs were afraid that white settlers might try to take their land, that unfair white traders might cheat them and that the importation of liquor would increase. One African chief knew the danger of liquor and told the British Administrators: 'It were better for me that I should lose my country than that it should be flooded with drink. I fear Lobengula less than I fear brandy. . . I dread the white man's drink more than the assegais of the Matabele, which kill men's bodies. . . but drink puts devils into men, and destroys both their souls and their bodies for ever. Its wounds never heal. I pray your Honour never to ask me to open even a little door to the drink.'[1] Because of the words of these chiefs and the help of an L.M.S. missionary, Cecil Rhodes was kept out of Bechuanaland.

SOUTH AFRICA

By 1880 the Church in South Africa had made greater progress than in any other area on the continent. There was a large number of African clergy; many of the denominations were self-governing; and a large percentage of the total population was considered Christian. Although this picture of the Church looks quite good, the problems facing the church after 1880 soon dimmed the prospects for even greater growth. The big problem was that of friction between white settlers and Africans.

During the period 1878 to 1914 several new Protestant missions began work in South Africa. Many of the new missions came from Scandinavia and concentrated on reaching Zululand. Other new missions came from the United States. In 1889 the South Africa General Mission was formed. The work of this mission would soon spread out to other countries from South Africa. Today the S.A.G.M. is called the Africa Evangelical Fellowship (A.E.F.).

In 1892 a Wesleyan Methodist pastor called Mangena M. Mokone had a disagreement with the Wesleyan missionaries in the church in South Africa. Because Pastor Mokone did not think the Methodist Church was Africanizing fast enough, he decided to break away from that church. He then established his own independent church, which he called the Ethiopian Church. This event is important for us to note because it marks the establishment of one of the first African Separatist or African Independent Churches in modern times. Soon, two or three other African pastors in South Africa started break-away churches. We will note in later chapters the increase of break-away churches.

The Roman Catholic Church grew rather slowly in South Africa during this period. Only in Natal and the Cape Colony was a little progress made. 'In the Orange River Free State and the Bechuanaland Protectorate there were, in 1914, few native Roman Catholics. So, too, in the Transvaal, by 1914 only a small number of black Roman Catholics had been gathered, even in the congested mining city of Johannesburg.'[2]

We must end this section with a note on the political history of South Africa. In 1910 the British government helped the Europeans in South Africa to form the Union of South Africa, which became a self-governing country with full dominion status within the British Empire. We will see later that this granting of internal self-government to the Europeans in South

Africa would lead to increased problems between blacks and whites, so that we have the unhappiness of today as a result.

MOZAMBIQUE

Mozambique had been a Portuguese territory for several centuries. Yet, in 1878 the Roman Catholic Church was quite small. Only white officials in the coastal towns seemed to be members. The Portuguese had expelled all Roman Catholic missionaries some time around 1850. It was not until 1881 that some Jesuit missionaries re-entered Mozambique. By 1914 only 5,000 Roman Catholic converts could be numbered in the colony.

A Swiss Protestant Mission was the first Protestant agency to start work in Mozambique. Their first church was established by an African evangelist who had been trained at one of the Swiss mission stations in the Transvaal. In 1879 the American Board of Commissioners for Foreign Missions sent missionaries to the colony. Because of the bad climate a permanent station was not built until 1883. Other Protestant missions that came to Mozambique include the Free Methodist, the Methodist Episcopal and the Anglican churches.

SOUTHERN RHODESIA (ZIMBABWE)

The area which is now called Zimbabwe came under British protection in the latter part of the nineteenth century because of the work of Cecil Rhodes. Rhodes brought many white settlers into this region to develop farming and mining. In 1900 there were about two million Africans living in the territory.

Christianity first came to this area in the sixteenth century when early Portuguese missionaries tried to take Christianity to Zimbabwe. But this effort did not have any lasting results. It was not until 1859 when Robert Moffat led a party of missionaries into the territory, that a permanent mission station was again established. For thirty years the L.M.S. laboured in Rhodesia without very many people making decisions for Christ. 'With the coming of British rule a striking change

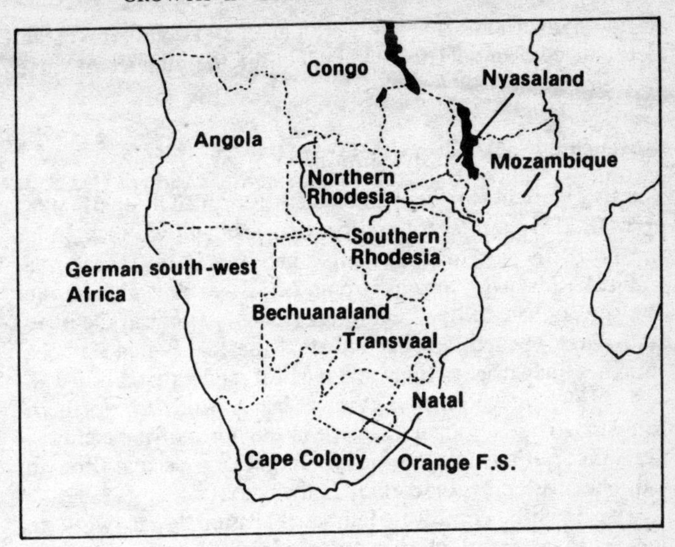

occurred. An eager demand for white teachers arose, presumably from the desire to achieve accommodation to the white man's regime. In the first decade of the twentieth century there was a rapid rise in schools and church members.'[3]

In 1891 the Church of England began work in Rhodesia. Through the hard labour of its early missionaries many new church members were gained, so that the Anglican Church soon became the largest church in the colony.

The opportunities for evangelism in Rhodesia soon attracted several other Protestant missions: the Wesleyan Methodists (1891) the Dutch Reformed Church (1891), the American Board of Commissioners for Foreign Missions (1893) the Seventh Day Adventists (1895), the American Methodist Episcopal Church (1896), The Brethren of Christ (1897), the South Africa General Mission (1897) and later the Presbyterian Church, the Salvation Army and the Church of Sweden.

In 1889 the Roman Catholics established a permanent work

in Southern Rhodesia. They were joined by two other Roman Catholic mission societies by 1914. But the number of their converts did not rise quickly.

NORTHERN RHODESIA (ZAMBIA)

The first work in Northern Rhodesia was opened by the L.M.S. in 1878. The permanent station that resulted was located in the northern part of the country between Lake Tanganyika and Lake Malawi. Although some L.M.S. stations along Lake Tanganyika had to be closed down, other stations in the highlands were opened, so that by 1914 the L.M.S. had schools, churches, industrial training and medical services established.

In 1891 the Roman Catholics began work in Northern Rhodesia. They also started work in the north of the country, near the stations of the L.M.S. In 1905 a second Roman Catholic mission began working in the colony.

The English Primitive Methodist Mission began work in the South-west part of the territory in the 1890's. The early missionaries spent time learning the language and soon wrote a grammar of the local language as well as translations of the New Testament and Christian hymns.

Other missions that established mission stations in Northern Rhodesia were the Paris Evangelical Missionary Society, the Dutch Reformed Church, the Seventh Day Adventists, the Baptists, the Brethren in Christ and the Anglican Church.

'The record of Rhodesia gives striking evidence of the energy and rapidity with which Christian agencies penetrated Africa in the third of a century preceding 1914. Until the last quarter of the nineteenth century only the London Missionary Society had established a continuing enterprise in that area. Beginning in the 1870's society after society, chiefly Protestant, but also Roman Catholic, entered, reduced languages to writing, began the preparation of Christian literature, pioneered in modern European medicine, multiplied schools, and gave rise to churches. By the year 1914 Christianity was making rapid headway. A little later, in the 1920's, Southern Rhodesia had about 59,000 Protestants and about 28,000 Roman Catholics, and the 1921 census reported in Northern Rhodesia 65,531 Protestants and 76,084 Roman Catholics.'[4]

NYASALAND (MALAWI)

Nyasaland covers a small amount of territory on the map, but has a large population for its size. This is due to the rich highlands which are healthy and fertile.

As we noted in a previous chapter, the Universities Mission to Central Africa was the first mission to establish work in Nyasaland. The early success of the mission was due in part to the work of a missionary called William P. Johnson. 'The son of a lawyer who died when the child was three years old, Johnson had been reared by his mother, at Oxford had a record about the average in scholarship and athletics, and was headed for the Indian Civil service. But while at Oxford he heard the call of the Universities Mission. He spent more than half a century as a missionary, preached, started schools, translated the entire Bible and the Book of Common Prayer into one of the tongues of Nyasaland and part of the Bible into another, and did some translating into three other tongues.'[5] The Universities Mission soon had a large number of schools, dispensaries, and teacher training schools. They also had a Bible school for training African pastors.

Another pioneer mission in Nyasaland was the Livingstonia Mission. Through the hard work of its early missionaries there had grown a sizable church of almost 10,000 members in 1914.

Other Protestant missions to begin work in Nyasaland include the Church of Scotland, the Australian Baptists, the South Africa General Mission and the Seventh Day Adventists.

The Roman Catholics did not establish a permanent mission station in the territory until 1901. There were few converts at first, and it was not until after 1914 that their church began to grow rapidly.

Questions:

1. What happened in South-west Africa at the beginning of the

twentieth century which made evangelism and church work difficult?

2. What was the largest and oldest mission society working in Bechuanaland? In what ways did it try to help the Africans?
3. What did the Rev. Mangena Mokone of South Africa do in 1891?
4. If Portugal is a Roman Catholic country, why was the Roman Catholic Church so small in Mozambique in 1914?
5. What was the first Protestant mission to begin work in Southern Rhodesia? What soon became the largest church?
6. In what part of Northern Rhodesia was the first mission station established? By what mission?
7. Briefly tell of the work of the Universities Mission in Nyasaland from 1878 to 1914.

[1]Groves, C.P., *The Planting of Christianity in Africa*, vol. III (Lutterworth Press, London, 1955), p. 150

[2]Latourette, Kenneth S., *A History of the Expansion of Christianity: The Great Century*, vol. V (Harper & Bros., New York, 1943), p. 373

[3]Ibid. p. 382

[4]Ibid. p. 390

[5]Ibid. pp. 381, 382

26

1878–1914: A period of rapid church growth in Africa

GERMAN EAST AFRICA (TANZANIA)

In chapter twenty we saw how Krapf and Rebmann were the first Protestant missionaries to take the Gospel to East Africa. In their travels they visited northern Tanzania, but it was not until the Roman Catholics arrived in the 1860's that a permanent mission station was established in what we now call Tanzania. In the late 1870's the C.M.S. and the L.M.S. established mission stations in northwestern and western Tanzania. The Universities Mission operated about three mission stations in southern Tanzania near Lake Malawi.

In 1885 Germany officially claimed the territory and named it German East Africa. Almost immediately the Protestants in Germany became interested in the colony and several German Protestant missions prepared to send missionaries to open Christian work. In 1886 a new mission society was formed in Berlin to work in German East Africa. It was called 'Berlin III'. It opened its first station in Dar es Salaam in 1887 and from there opened stations in Tanga and the surrounding area.

In 1891 the Berlin Missionary Society, which had been working in South Africa for many years, began work in German East Africa. Their first stations were opened in the south near Lake Malawi. 'By 1914 it had in all German East Africa 22 stations, 57 missionaries, and 2,308 communicants.'[1]

The Moravian Mission began work in German East Africa in 1891. They also worked in the south near Lake Malawi but later in 1898 took over an L.M.S. station south of Lake

Victoria. By 1914 the Moravians had 15 stations, 28 missionaries, and 1,780 baptized Christians.[2]

In the north, the Leipzig Missionary Society began work around Mount Kilimanjaro. A Christian witness had first been established in that area by the C.M.S. but after 1885 the English C.M.S. missionaries were not favoured by the German colonialists. So in 1893 the C.M.S. turned over its stations to the Leipzig Society and withdrew to the Kenya side of Mount Kilimanjaro, near Taveta. The Leipzig Society in turn gave up two stations in Ukambani where their missionaries had been working, and transferred to the Moshi area to take over the C.M.S. work.

The beginnings of the Africa Inland Church of Tanzania can be traced back to 1909 when Mr Hurlburt and Mr Stauffacher visited the territory south of Lake Victoria. The A.I.M. entered German East Africa at the request of the C.M.S. It happened in the following way. Bishop Tucker (of C.M.S. Uganda) and Mr Hurlburt '. . . had many conversations together, and the Bishop asked Mr Hurlburt whether the A.I.M. would be prepared to take over their work in what was then German East Africa. They had only one station, and that was at Nassa, on the east coast of Lake Victoria. It was difficult to administer it from Uganda, where the rest of their work was situated. Nassa had a history. Work had been commenced there in 1888. When Alexander Mackay had been driven from Uganda, he had found refuge there.'[3] So Mr Hulburt and Mr Stauffacher visited the territory and decided that the A.I.M. would accept Nassa station. Shortly afterwards the first A.I.M. missionaries arrived at Nassa.

The Roman Catholics were also active during this period 1878 to 1914. The Holy Ghost Fathers, who had begun the work at Bagamoyo, pushed inland. Soon they had many schools and a printing press. 'By 1914 two vicariates apostolic had come into being which together counted 25 stations, 43 priests, 29 brothers, 50 sisters, and nearly 20,000 Christians.'[4]

Other Roman Catholic agencies also began to work in German East Africa. The Benedictines worked in the southern part of the country. The eastern part of the colony was worked by the White Fathers. Soon the White Sisters and other women's societies joined the men in expanding the Roman Catholic work. 'In German East Africa, in contrast with most of the British possessions thus far surveyed, Roman Catholic Christianity was making greater progress than were the Protestant forms of the faith'.[5]

KENYA

The last time we surveyed Kenya, we noticed that the only Christian work being done was by Protestants in the territory near the coast. In 1878 the United Methodist Free Churches and the C.M.S. were the major missions. Most of the C.M.S. work was centred around the freed slave ministry at Frere-town. Hundreds of African slaves began to run away from their Arab masters at the coast and seek safety at Frere-town. Soon Christian Africans from Freretown began to establish other havens for run-away slaves. 'Missionaries were concerned about possible violence from Arab masters, and were worried concerning the legality of harbouring runaways; but African Christians were far less inhibited, hiding runaways by the hundreds. One Giriama Christian, David Koi, was invited to become teacher of a large settlement of these runaways at Fulodoyo. An Arab gang swept through the huts in 1883 and beheaded Koi, who thus became Kenya's first Christian martyr. Out of Freretown and other communities of ex-slaves came Kenya's first schools, the first African teachers and evangelists, and in 1885 the first ordained ministers. By 1890, there were about 2,000 baptised Anglicans and a few Methodists, Kenya's first form of organized and enduring Christianity.'[6]

In 1891 the Scottish Industrial Mission pushed inland from the coast to take the Gospel to the interior of Kenya. Their objective was to establish a station at Machakos, but the first party of African Christians and missionaries stopped at Kibwesi. The Scots tried to establish a church and industrial school at this location but within seven years decided that this was not the right place for such a mission station. In 1898 the station was moved to Kikuyu and was then taken over by the Church of Scotland.

In 1887 the German Neukirchener Mission started to work at Lamu, but later moved to Ngao on the Tana River. In the same area of Eastern Ukambani, the Bavaria Evangelical Lutheran Mission began work. The Bavaria Mission was taken over by the Leipzig Mission, which, in turn, turned over two stations to the A.I.M. in 1914.

After 1890 missionaries began to push inland more quickly. In 1893 'Independent missionary Stuart Watt, with his wife and family, walked from the coast to central Kenya, and finally settled at Ngelani in Ukambani.'[7] When the Watts were forced to leave Kenya because of ill health, they turned over their mission station to the A.I.M.

By 1894 portions of the Bible had been translated into Girima, Taita, Kikamba, Nyika, Fokomo and Gala.

In 1895 the Gospel witness was well established on the Kenya coast. As we have seen, missionaries were beginning to press inland. Yet the vast territory of interior Kenya remained unreached by the Good News of Jesus Christ. What was needed at that time was a new mission with a vision for the inland areas of Africa, a mission which could push forward into the unreached interior. For this job God called Peter Cameron Scott.

'Peter Cameron Scott was born in a humble dwelling with its door opening on to the street, near Glasgow, on March 7, 1867. His parents were earnest Christians.'[8] In November 1879, the Scott family emigrated to America and settled near Philadelphia. At the age of sixteen he began work as a printer, but because of ill health had to leave the job. After a visit to Scotland, he returned to America and later entered college. In November, 1890, he left America as a missionary headed for West Africa. In the Congo he laboured for some time with his brother John. John Scott soon died from fever and Peter became so sick that he had to return to America.

After Peter Scott returned to the United States he told friends of the need for a mission to reach inland East Africa. 'In August, 1895, at a meeting of farewell and dedication,

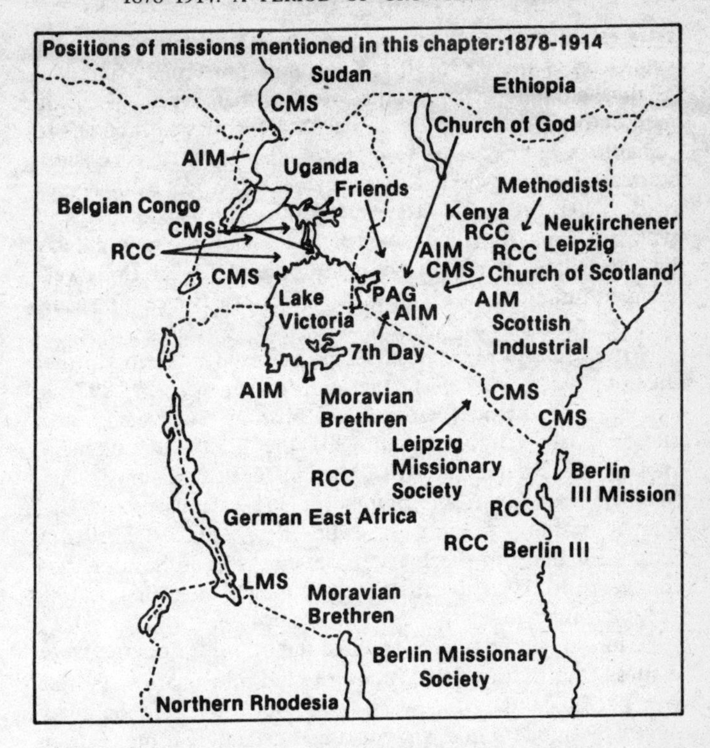

a little company of seven – four men and three women, Peter's own sister, Margaret, among them – were set apart for this venture. Later, in Scotland, they were to be joined by one more. Peter was unanimously elected leader, and they sailed the next day from New York. On October 17, they arrived at Mombasa, where, after prayer and consultation, it was decided to leave the ladies, . . . while the men, . . . began the inland trck."[9] On December 12, 1895, the party reached Nzawi and it was here that Scott and his companions decided to establish the first mission station of the A.I.M. and the first church of the Africa Inland Church. The ladies were then brought up from Mombasa. After Nzawi these first missionaries established a mission station at Sakai and then Kilungu. On October 3, 1896, the Kangundo mission station was established. Peter Scott worked for less than a year in Ukambani before he died on December 4, 1896. It was then left to the others in the party to carry on the work that had been started by a man who had been obedient to God's call.

In 1903 the A.I.M. transferred the main headquarters of its work from Kangundo, which was not on the new railway line, to Kijabe. After Kijabe, many other A.I.M. stations were opened, but since this is just a survey course, we cannot name them all here.

After the A.I.M. started its push inland in Kenya, other missions began to move further and further west. In 1897 the Church of Scotland (Presbyterian) Mission established a new station near Nairobi and in 1901 the C.M.S. did likewise. In 1902 the Friends Industrial Mission began at Kaimosi. Then in 1905 the American Church of God established its first mission station at Kima. In 1906 the C.M.S. established a school for the sons of chiefs at Maseno while in South Nyaza the Seventh Day Adventists were building their first station at Kendo Bay.

'Interestingly enough, not all of the early missionaries were whites. One of the first Church of God missionaries at Kima was Yohana Mbila, a Shangaan from South Africa. Mbila introduced the modern hoe, and was the outstanding Kima evangelist in the early days. As a result of his example, Mbila's first convert, Yohana Owenga, journeyed into Congo with a missionary party in 1914. Owenga and a number of white missionaries perished on a further journey in 1915, when Kima itself was only nine years old. Another African, Shadrack Mliwa from Taveta, accompanied the first C.M.S. missionaries into Central Kenya, settled at Kerugoya, lived out his years there, and died in the early 1960's surrounded by a large and flourishing Kikuyu church. Many of the first African Christians were spiritual giants.'[10] In 1909 Molonket ole Sempele, a Masai Christian and member of the A.I.M. church, sold his cows so that he could travel to the United States to study for three years at Bible college to find out more about God's Word.[11]

After 1910 the Gospel message was taken to many more new places in Kenya and some new missions entered the country. For example, in 1911 the A.I.M. opened the Nyakach station near Lake Victoria. In 1912 the first Methodist minister in Kenya, Rev. Joseph Jara, a Pokomo, walked to Meru from Mombasa to establish the first Methodist mission station in that area. Also in 1912 the Pentecostal Assemblies of God's first mission station was opened at Nyangori.[12]

In 1914 the first independent or splinter church was founded in Kenya, when Johana Owalo formed the Nomiya Luo Mission in western Kenya. The Nomiya Luo Church no longer exists in Kenya.

The first permanent modern Roman Catholic mission station in Kenya was established at Mombasa in 1890 by the Holy Ghost Fathers. 'In 1891 the Holy Ghost Mission opened a station at Bura, near Voi, and by 1899 they had reached Limuru, west of Nairobi. Ukamba country was explored in 1907, and the construction of the Kabaa station and school in Machakos district was initiated in 1913. By the beginning of World War One in 1914, there were Holy Ghost missions among the Kikuyu, in Ukambani, at Bura and Mwanda in Taita, and at several points along the coast.'[13]

UGANDA

As we have seen, Christianity was first brought to Uganda by Dallington Muftaa and Henry Stanley. In 1877 the first C.M.S. missionaries established a mission station at King Mutesa's capital. Then in 1879 a Roman Catholic missionary arrived at King Mutesa's palace and asked for permission to start work. The C.M.S. missionary, Alexander Mackay, asked the Roman Catholics to start work in one of the other kingdoms that had no Christian witness. The Roman Catholics refused and King Mutesa allowed them to settle. It was not long before King Mutesa and the people of Buganda were confused by the two sets of doctrine. Instead of helping the progress of the Gospel message, the arrival of the Roman Catholics only hindered it by bringing confusion and hatred. 'In December, 1879, Mutesa and his chiefs publicly rejected both

Christianity and Islam, declared their loyalty to the ancestral faith, and forbade the missionaries to teach or the people to visit them. By July, 1880, however, the Arab traders were in the ascendant, with Mutesa once more declaring himself a Muslim. Too level-headed, nevertheless, to be duped by the Arab slanders against the missionaries, he once more gave liberty to teach and even encouraged pupils to attend Mackay for industrial instruction. For Mackay he retained a high regard.'[14]

When the missionaries were allowed to teach and preach among the people again in 1880, they once more began to reach out. 'On March 18, 1882, five young men were baptized – the first baptisms in the Anglican mission. Between this date and November, 1884, eighty-eight persons had received the rite. The Roman Catholics claimed an even larger number, and on the ground that this exposed them more to Arab hostility, retired to the south of the lake from October, 1882, to July, 1885.[15]

In 1884 the Archbishop of Canterbury consecrated James Hannington the bishop of the new church district of 'Eastern Equatorial Africa' to be centred in Buganda. He arrived in Mombasa in January, 1885, and set off for Buganda by the direct route across Kenya, instead of going through Tanganyika as the other C.M.S. missionaries had done. As Bishop Hannington approached the Buganda border from the eastern side, the new king, Mwanga, became frightened and ordered that the Bishop be killed. Shortly after this incident King Mwanga began a persecution of Christians in Buganda. King Mwanga then ordered the death of three C.M.S. Christians. 'Seruwang, Kakumba and Lugalama, after being maimed with knives, were cast on to a framework over a slow fire, and so became the first Christian martyrs of Uganda, January 30, 1885.'[16]

In May and June, 1886, King Mwanga ordered the severest persecution of his rule. Both Protestants and Roman Catholics were captured and burned at the stake. Mackay described the persecution with these words: 'Those who were at the capital. . . were first arrested. About a dozen were butchered at once . . . many were speared or otherwise killed in the endeavour to capture them in various parts of the country, while thirty-two were burnt alive in one huge pyre...'[17] These men who gave their lives because of their faith in Jesus Christ are called the 'Uganda Martyrs'.

In July, 1887, Mackay was forced to leave Buganda because King Mwanga threatened to kill him. He established a C.M.S. mission station at Nassa in northern Tanganyika but in 1890 he died from fever.

From 1887 to 1890 there were great political changes in Buganda. Mwanga and his brothers fought among themselves to keep control of the government. Each brother was supported by a different group. The Muslims favoured one man, the Protestants and Roman Catholics another. Then the Imperial British East Africa Company under Captain Lugard appeared in Buganda and a new power factor had to be considered. Finally in June, 1894, Great Britain declared Uganda a Protectorate. This caused the political fighting to come to an end and with peace once more restored in Buganda, the work of the Gospel could go on.

'Meanwhile the Protestant Mission, with quiet at least on the political front, reported in March, 1896, the number of baptized Christians as 6,905 of whom 1,335 were communicant members, a catechumenate numbering 2,591, and an estimated army of "readers" (including all who were seeking to become literate, whether with a view to baptism or not) of 57,380.'[18]

The result of the faithful work done by the C.M.S. was the establishment of the Church of Uganda. Almost from the start the Church of Uganda was a self-supporting and self-propagating church. 'The Baganda churches were largely self-supporting, erecting their own structures and paying the stipends of the native staff. A diocesan organization, heading up in a synod, was gradually developed with the African Christians having a large share in it. The Baganda proved eager missionaries. More than once their enterprise led to the introduction of the faith to neighbouring tribes. Europeans joined in the extension of the Christian message to other peoples. Group conversions to Christianity were witnessed. . . Within less than a generation Protestant Christianity, through the agency of the Church Missionary Society, had made amazing headway. In 1914 the number of baptized Christians was 98,447.'[19]

After 1894 the Roman Catholic mission also grew rapidly. The White Fathers Society was joined by the Mill Hill Fathers from England and together they established many mission stations in Uganda. Like the C.M.S. they established schools, but by 1914 they only had one third as many students in their schools as the C.M.S. had. Nevertheless, by 1914 the Roman Catholics could claim more than 135,000 converts in Uganda. In 1914 Uganda was the strongest and largest Roman Catholic Church district in Africa.

ETHIOPIA

Ethiopia remained a difficult land for the Gospel message during the period 1878 to 1914. The Roman Catholic mission which had been in the country prior to 1878 continued its work, but with few converts as a result.

'Two non-Roman missions to Abyssinia that were attempted in the 'eighties came to nothing. In 1881–2 a Swedish mission to the Gallas sought entry to the country by way of the Sudan. They succeeded in reaching Famaka on the Blue Nile, some 360 miles south of Khartoum – they were then on the Sudan-Abyssinia frontier – but found the country so disturbed that they fell back on Khartoum.'[20] Later a Russian Orthodox Mission tried to establish work in Ethiopia but failed to come to agreement with the Coptic Church.

By 1914 the Coptic Church was still the dominant religion in Ethiopia. The Protestant and Roman Catholic witnesses were still very weak in that land.

SUDAN

In 1873 a Catholic mission had been opened in southern-central Sudan by Daniel Comboni. But in 1883 Muhammad Ahmed proclaimed himself the Muslim Messiah of Sudan and led a revolt against all foreigners. The Catholic missionaries were captured and three died during their imprisonment by the Mahdi (Muhammad Ahmed). From 1883 to 1896 the Mahdi ruled Sudan and urged all his followers to live strict lives according to the laws of Islam. In 1896 the Egyptian-

British army defeated the armies of the Mahdi and a colonial government was set up in Khartoum.

The new colonial government forbade Christian missions from working among the Arabs in the north of Sudan, so as to keep the Muslims from becoming angry. The Christians were free to work among the Africans in the south of the country. In 1900 the American Presbyterians established their work in Sudan. In 1906 the first C.M.S. missionaries arrived in southern Sudan, entering from the Uganda border. By 1914 the C.M.S. had five mission stations in southern Sudan.

Questions:

1. Name three German mission societies that worked in German East Africa, and name the general part of the country in which they worked.
2. When did the African Inland Mission begin work in Tanganyika? How did this happen?
3. Who was the first Kenyan Christian martyr? Why was he killed and by whom?
4. Briefly tell of the early life of Peter Cameron Scott.
5. Who were the 'Uganda Martyrs.? Why were they killed?
6. Briefly tell of the growth of the Church of Uganda.
7. Why did missions develop very slowly in Ethiopia?
8. In what part of Sudan did the Protestant missions begin to work?

[1]Latourette, Kenneth S., *A History of the Expansion of Christianity: The Great Century,* vol. V (Harpers & Bros., New York, 1943), p. 406
[2]Ibid. p. 407
[3]Richardson, Kenneth, *Garden of Miracles: A History of the Africa Inland Mission* (Victory Press, London, 1968), pp. 101, 102
[4]Latourette, K. S., *A History*..., p.407
[5]Ibid. p. 409
[6]Barrett, D. B. & Others Ed., *Kenya Churches Handbook: The Development of Kenyan Christianity, 1498–1973* (Evangel Publishing House, Kisumu, Kenya, 1973), p. 31
[7]Ibid. p. 22
[8]Miller, Catherine S., Peter Cameron Scott: *The Unlocked Door* (Parry Jackman Limited, London, 1955), p. 15
[9]Ibid. pp. 29, 30
[10]Barrett, D. B. & Others, Ed., *Kenya Churches*..., p. 34

[11]Ibid. p. 23
[12]Ibid. p. 23
[13]Ibid. p. 31
[14]Groves, C. P., *The Planting of Christianity in Africa, Vol.III* (Lutterworth Press, London, 1955), p.89
[15]Ibid. p. 89
[16]Ibid. p. 92
[17]Ibid. p. 93
[18]Ibid. p. 97
[19]Latourette, I. S., *A History...*, p.417 & 418
[20]Groves, C. P., *The Planting... Vol. III*, p.173

27

Evaluation of the period 1878–1914

If you look back to page 147 you will note that at the beginning of this period of African history, the areas that had heard the Gospel message in Africa were quite limited. However, by 1914 the territory in Africa which had been exposed to the light of the Christian witness had more than doubled. At the same time the continent of Africa was entering the modern twentieth century. The Church was making great contributions to this advance in Africa. In this chapter we want to find the answers to three questions: (1) What contributions did the Church make to Africa from 1878 to 1914? (2) Why did the Church grow so rapidly during this period? and (3) How did European colonialisation affect the growth of Christianity?

CONTRIBUTIONS OF CHRISTIANITY

As you read the past four chapters you no doubt noted many things that Christianity contributed to Africa. The greatest contribution of the missionaries and African church workers during this period was the announcement of the Good News of Jesus Christ which brought the most wonderful change in people's lives. In many places in Africa Satan held the people in the bondage of fear. But when the Gospel was brought to a new place, its light made the darkness of fear disappear and brought a new life of joy and freedom to people. The Good News made a great transformation in the lives of families and the day to day living of whole communities.

Another great contribution was the reducing of the spoken

languages of Africa to writing. Before 1878 very few languages in Africa south of the Sahara had an alphabet and a means of writing. The early missionaries made an alphabet with letters to meet the needs of each local language. As a result, many tribes in Africa were able to keep written records for the first time in their history. But the Church did not only give the people a way of writing; they also provided books for the people to read, the most important of which was the Bible which could guide people in their Christian life.

Closely related to linguistic work was the establishment of schools to teach reading, writing and other skills. Without the work of the Church in Africa in establishing schools, the development of the continent might have been delayed twenty, thirty or more years. Certainly, the colonial governments would not have been able (or perhaps willing) to build all the schools which the missions built between 1878 and 1914. The educational system of Africa owes a great debt to the churches for this great service. Satan wants people to remain in ignorance and darkness, but it is God's will that people be given education and light.

The missionaries were usually the first people in each new territory to establish hospitals. Through the efforts of these people new treatment was given to ancient diseases. The result was that fewer and fewer people died in childhood and people could live more healthy and useful lives than ever before. The Christian message also included the 'Law of Love'. Early missionaries and then those in the twentieth century brought love and knowledge for such dreaded illnesses as leprosy so that the people who suffered from such diseases no longer had to suffer as outcasts from their own tribes.

Many early missionaries and church workers helped people with new knowledge about farming. New crops were introduced and better methods of production were taught. As a result the amount of food grown by people increased rapidly.

Finally, the early church workers also taught technical and practical subjects such as tailoring and blacksmithing to the people. With this new knowledge Africans were able to increase their standard of living.

RAPID CHURCH GROWTH

The second question is more difficult to answer. There does not seem to be any one reason why the Church in Africa began to grow so much more rapidly from 1878 to 1914 than ever before. However, there do seem to be some factors which together may have contributed to this rapid growth.

First of all there was the 'Great Revival' of the nineteenth century in Europe and America. 'Among revival movements in Great Britain and America in the latter part of the nineteenth century, which rekindled the fires of devotion in many lukewarm Christians and brought many thousands of others to the point of personal commitment as believers, none was of more significance than that under the leadership of D. L. Moody.'[1] Mr Moody held meetings in Great Britain and America that attracted thousands to Jesus Christ. But Mr Moody was not just an evangelist who led people to Christ and left them. Instead he encouraged them to reach out to other people. Mr Moody was especially interested in students and as a result of his encouragement the Student Volunteer Movement was started in 1891 in the United States and in Great Britain the Student Volunteer Missionary Union was founded in 1892. As a result of the work of these movements and others, hundreds upon hundreds of young men and women in Great Britain and America dedicated themselves to taking the Gospel to the unreached areas of the world. With so many people willing to go anywhere in the world, the mission societies had enough people to enter new areas of Africa and start new mission stations.

A second influence was new discoveries in medicine. In 1897 Ronald Ross discovered that malaria was carried by the Anopheles mosquito and then he suggested that if mosquitoes could be controlled or kept from coming into contact with men, malaria could be wiped out. With the help of new drugs, malaria no longer could kill such large numbers of missionaries.

With this new knowledge fewer missionaries died in the twentieth century than in the nineteenth from malaria, yellow fever, etc.

A third factor was the improved communication and transport system after 1878. By 1910 there were railways in more than half the colonies in Africa. The building of the Uganda Railway, for example, had a great influence on the inland push of missions in Kenya. Then, too, river and lake steamers made transport easier for missionaries and church workers in the interior. The colonial governments began to build and maintain roads. Later a postal system was established and telegraph offices were built in major towns.

EFFECTS OF COLONIALISM

Finally, we should evaluate the effects that the arrival of the colonial governments had on the development of the Church.

On the positive side, the European colonialists brought to an end the remaining pockets of slavery in Africa. Until 1900 there were still some Arabs practising slavery in East Africa but because of colonial laws this practice was soon wiped out. In the interior slave raids between warring tribes was also ended and the people of Africa no longer had to fear being taken away from their homes to a life of slavery.

The colonial governments reduced the large number of inter-tribal wars that had weakened Africa for many centuries. Boundaries were established for each tribe and the colonialists tried to solve arguments which arose between tribes.

The colonial governments also brought improved communications, as we noted above. Railways were built and a postal and tele-communications service established. All of these items made it easier for missionaries and church workers to travel. The improved communications made it easier for the local churches to communicate with each other. However, we should note that while these improved systems of travel and communication helped the cause of the Gospel, it also assisted the ungodly as well, such as the European tobacco companies, the liquor traders, etc.

In these three areas, the arrival of colonialism benefited the growth of the Church, but in many more areas, the arrival of colonialism hindered Church growth.

First, the colonial governments dictated to the missionaries and churches in many instances where they could and could not work. This was particularly true in the colonies that had Muslim populations. For example, while the independent Empire of Ethiopia allowed missionaries to evangelize among the Muslims, such colonial powers as France, Germany and Great Britain often prohibited missionaries from starting work in areas where there was a large population of Muslims.

Colonialism hurt the missionary effort in Africa because of European rivalries. The Germans did not wish French or English missionaries to work in their colonies, while the French did not want German and English missionaries in their colonies, etc. As we have seen this caused many missions to close down their mission stations in different colonies between 1885 and 1914.

When the colonial officials began to organize their African colonies, they naturally attracted traders. Of course, the traders had come to Africa before the colonialists and it was often the European traders in Africa who had begged their home countries to take African colonies. Nevertheless, once the colonialists established their governments, the number of traders increased. These European traders and businessmen brought many evils and vices from Europe and introduced them to Africa. Among these are materialism, the destructive habit of tobacco smoking, and strong liquor. Once these vices got control of men's lives, it was even more difficult to win them to Christ.

Colonialism also encouraged the migration of large numbers of Europeans to come to Africa and settle. These settlers in many different ways began to take land that would be needed later by Africans when tribes got large. Generally these 'settlers' opposed the Church and missionary work among Africans because most settlers did not want to see Africans come to a place of power and responsibility in government. As we have seen in our study of Bechuanaland, white settlers even used force to destroy and break down some L.M.S. mission stations. These settlers and European businessmen also led to the break-down of the tribe. In his book *Cry The Beloved Country*, Alan Paton has one of his characters, a Zulu pastor, say: 'My friend, I am a Christian. It is not in my heart to hate a white man. It was a white man who brought my father out of darkness. But you will pardon me if I talk frankly to you. The tragedy is not that things are broken. The tragedy is that they are not mended again. The white man has broken the tribe. And it is my belief – and again I ask your pardon – that it cannot be mended again. But the house that is broken, and the man that falls apart when the house is broken, these are the tragic things.[2] The colonialists helped the settlers and businessmen break up the tribe by 'forced labour' laws and other regulations which forced Africans to work for these foreigners. Once Africans left their tribal areas it became very difficult for Christian workers to bring them to salvation. Of course, this did not happen in all African colonies, but the force was particularly strong in South Africa, Mozambique, Rhodesia (North and South), the German Colonies and the Belgian Congo.

This chapter has been a brief evaluation of the period 1878 to 1914. There are other important points that could be mentioned here, but these brief entries should provide you with enough background so that you can better understand the time.

Questions:

1. Name four contributions that the Church made to Africa between 1878 and 1914.
2. Why did the Church develop so much more rapidly from 1878 to 1914 than it did from 1840 to 1878? Give as many reasons as you can.
3. How did colonialism hinder the development of the Church in Africa?

[1]Groves, C.P., *The Planting of Christianity in Africa*, vol. III (Lutterworth Press, London, 1948), p. 202

[2]Paton, Alan, *Cry, The Beloved Country* (Charles Scribner's Sons, New York, 1948), p. 25

28

West Africa 1914–1960: Movement toward full church autonomy

INTRODUCTION TO THIS PERIOD OF HISTORY

In the past five chapters we read about the rapid development of the African Church during the period 1878 to 1914. As we saw, it was during this period that most of the inland areas of Africa received their first Christian witness. It was, of course, impossible to mention all the church and missionary organizations that began work during that time, and so we only looked at the outstanding ones. It is now time for us to move into a new period of history: 1914 to 1960. During this time the number of church and mission organizations continued to increase as well as the number of pastors, church workers and missionaries. It is impossible for us in this survey to write about all of these additional groups. In fact, there really is not space to review the development of each of the churches that we mentioned in the last section. So for this section of history we must adopt a slightly different method of study.

We will continue to use four main sections of Africa south of the Sahara that we have been using. But, instead of making a detailed study of how the different churches in each colony continued to grow, we will just survey the general development of the church in that area of Africa. The next four chapters will contain general observations concerning African Church history, which, it is hoped, will give you a good picture of the Church during this period.

WEST AFRICA AND THE FIRST WORLD WAR

In August, 1914, the largest countries of Europe divided into two groups and began the most destructive war in the history of the world up to that time. One side, called the Allied Powers, consisted of Great Britain, France, Belgium, Italy and Russia. On the other side, named the Central Powers, were Germany, Austria and Hungary. For almost three years the two sides fought, but neither side was strong enough to win a complete victory. Finally in April, 1917, the Allied Powers persuaded the United States to join their side and within a year and a half the Allies were able to defeat the Central Powers.

This European War brought many troubles for Africa. Since this is not a political history, we will not study these problems. World War One also caused delays and setbacks for the development of the Church, and these we must look at. First of all, as you remember in our last section, we observed that there were German missionaries working in the Gold Coast (Ghana). Most of these people were German citizens who were members of the Basel Misson, which is a Swiss Mission and the Bremen Mission, which is a German one. At the beginning of the First World War, the British government allowed Germans to continue their church work in the Gold Coast. 'For two years the missionaries remained at work, but the strain of the war told, and these German nationals, human as they were, allowed expression to their national sympathies which were found to intrude, so it was alleged, into their missionary and educational work. In consequence the Bremen workers were deported in 1916 and those of the Basel Mission in the following year.'[1] The Protestant Church in the Gold Coast lost many good teachers and missionaries just because they were German citizens.

The other territory in West Africa where there were many German missionaries was Togo. The British and French armies drove the German colonialists out of Togo and for two years allowed the German missionaries working in that colony to remain. But in 1916 the Allies felt that the German missionaries might cause trouble, and so they were forced to leave.

The Christian work done by the German missionaries did not die when these people were forced to leave. In the Gold Coast the United Free Church of Scotland took over the work of the Basel Mission. The Basel Mission and the Free Church were similar in theology and church government as both come from the Reformed Tradition. In the area run by the Bremen Mission there was no immediate help from a British mission. Fortunately the Bremen Mission had many trained pastors and had established a good church government. When the missionaries left, the African pastors took on the extra work and responsibility so that the church could continue. One such pastor was Rev. R. D. Baeta who played an outstanding part in the history of that church at the time.

In the other colonies of West Africa the progress of the Church was not upset as much as in the Gold Coast and Togo. There were problems, though, such as no new missionaries being able to come to help, shortage of supplies from Europe and increasing cost for medical supplies, printing supplies, etc. In spite of these problems, the Church in West Africa did continue to grow. For example, consider only the Anglican Church working in Nigeria '. . . the Christian community rose from 51,750 in 1914 to 78,189 in 1918, while the total number of adherents increased from 74,686 to 122,238. In this case the African lay agency (pastors, evangelists and teachers) grew from 784 to 1,432 in the same period.'[2]

THE CHURCH IN WEST AFRICA FROM 1918–1939

In 1918 World War One ended and for twenty years there was relative peace in the world. At the end of the war the British, French and Belgian governments decided that German missionaries should not be allowed to return to work in Africa. This was a very sad thing for the German mission societies, but then in 1924 the British changed their minds and Germans were allowed once more to do mission work in British colonies. Shortly after this the Bremen and Basel Missions returned to their work in the Gold Coast and Togo. However, two Scottish missions had been carrying on the church work for these missions, and so some adjustments had to be made. It was finally decided that there would be one 'Reformed' type African church for which the three missionary organizations would work. This was a very good solution. Once the war ended, there was not a sudden flood of new missionaries coming to Africa to assist the Church. It took about three years from 1918 to 1921 for the movement of missionaries to get back to the pre-war level. At the same time, the shortages of equipment during the war were overcome slowly after 1918.

In chapter twenty-three we studied the impact of William Wadé Harris on the history of the Church in West Africa. As noted in that chapter, the Methodist Church tried to help the people who had repented as a result of Prophet Harris's preaching, but was hampered by French colonial restrictions. It must be remembered that Prophet Harris also visited the Gold Coast for three months during his preaching tour in Ivory Coast. From 1915 until 1925 the Methodist Church of the Gold Coast tried to help those people of the Nzima District who had turned from their idols.

'Being a self-supporting and self-propagating church pledged to school work, the Methodists needed the financial collaboration of the population; this was resented as "money-making". But the main reasons for the failure of the Methodist Church to become the national church of Nzima were three: lack of staff, vigorous competition from the Roman Catholics, and the appeal of the faith-healing churches. Nevertheless, the Methodists remain the strongest denomination in Nzima.'[3]

Four indigenous independent churches sprang up in the Nzima district as a result of Prophet Harris' visit. Two of these churches were established by former fetish priests who had been converted by Harris. These indigenous churches continue to work in the Nzima District today.

In the area of education, for the period 1918 to 1939 quite a few changes were made. By 1920 the colonial governments were well established throughout West Africa. They began to wonder about the quality and type of education being offered by the thousands of mission schools. After World War One several different surveys were made, particularly in British colonies, concerning education. The Phelps-Stokes Commission was one research project which tried to assess the progress of mission school education and make suggestions to the missions for future development. The report found that some missions did not supervise their schools closely and most schools were located in heavily populated areas, leaving rural areas with few schools.

After World War One the churches and mission societies worked at up-grading their schools by establishing more elite schools for giving higher education. 'The most oustanding event in the education drive of the 1920's (in Ghana), however, was the foundation of Achimota.'[4] Achimota was established in 1924 as a model school for Ghana. There were classes from kindergarten through to secondary school and teacher training. The first Vice-Principal of the school was Dr. J.E.K. Aggrey. Dr. Aggrey had gone to the United States to train for the ministry of the A.M.E. Zion Church. Following the completion of those studies he attended Columbia University in New York where he graduated. He served the A.M.E. Zion Church upon his return to Ghana and was also on the Phelps-Stokes Commission. Much of the success of Achimota has been credited to the work of Dr. Aggrey. Christians such as Dr. Aggrey helped the Church make great contributions to the development of education in Ghana and other countries of West Africa during this period of history.

During this period many mission societies continued in their efforts to establish 'indigenous' churches. By this is meant that they wanted to develop an African church which had its own church government and was self-supporting, self-governing and self-propagating. To this end, the missions continued to raise the standard of theological education being given to West African pastors and evangelists. Several West Africans were sent overseas for theological education. By 1938 many churches in West Africa were well on their way to complete autonomy from the mission organizations that had begun the work. An example of this is the growth of the

Presbyterian Church of the Gold Coast. 'By 1918 the Church was self-governing and by 1950 had reached complete independence. Although for some years the Scottish Mission held the right to veto any decision of a Church Court which was considered not to be in the best interests of the Church, this veto was never used.'[5]

This period also saw the appearance of more African separatist churches in West Africa. As we noted in chapter twenty-five, the first African separatist church occurred in South Africa in 1892. As the years went by more Africans decided that they wanted to establish their own denominations. The most successful of these split-off churches found that it was important to be different in one or more ways from the major churches around them. Some splinter churches had special clothing for members, others laid down special laws such as not taking medicine, while others paid special attention to dreams and healing. An example of one such separatist movement was the 'Elijah the Second' group that appeared in southern Nigeria during World War One. 'Garrick Sokari Braid, (the founder), had been a well accredited member of St. Andrew's Church in the New Calabar district and a trusted evangelist. He had by degrees become noted for dreams and visions of future happenings which the event confirmed, so it was alleged. He also had much success, it was said, in the healing of the sick by his prayers. On declaring himself to be Elijah II he rapidly acquired a remarkable influence in the Delta region among Christians and non-Christians alike. Three quarters of the congregation of St. Stephen's, the cathedral church at Bonny, declared for him; chiefs and headmen would acknowledge deep obeisance. He issued two emphatic prohibitions: no medicines should be used or medical help sought from either African or European doctors, and no alcoholic liquor must be taken.'[6] In time, some of the more active members of the sect began to break some government laws, and so the administration had to put some limitation on the group. Later people lost interest in the group and it began to shrink in size.

With regard to evangelism and church growth, the period

of 1918 to 1939 saw continued growth within the coastal colonies of West Africa. During this same time, church planting and growth was very slow in the interior colonies of French West Africa, as the Muslim population remained resistant to the Gospel message. In non-Muslim areas, great numbers of people were turning to Jesus Christ. For example, in the interior of Nigeria, quite near the Muslim area of the north, these results occurred: 'In the central belt of Nigeria . . . there were long periods of preparing the ground and planting the seed and very little sprouting before 1930. However, the winds of change have brought about a different situation from those early years. . . In 1930 attendance at Christian worship began to increase significantly. Between 1935 and 1940 attendance at Sunday morning services more than doubled in the Sudan United Mission areas. This increase is partly due to two factors: (1) increased responsibility being taken by Nigerian evangelists in preaching, and (2) the resultant forming of many small worshipping groups far from mission stations. In 1935, in the Sudan United Mission area, 55% of the Sunday attendance was at mission stations and 45% at preaching points. In the Plateau Church the average Sunday morning attendance in 1925, after twenty-one years of preaching, was only about 1,000 and in 1930 it had risen to over 2,000, but by 1942 it had passed the 10,000 mark.'[7] Similar church growth was experienced in many other places in West Africa during this period.

Another important development was the establishment of joint missionary councils. In countries like Nigeria, Gold Coast and Sierra Leone there were as many as fifteen different missionary societies working. Many missionary leaders thought a committee or council should be formed to which all the missions could belong, so that they could co-operate in their work a little more. In 1929 the Gold Coast Christian Council was formed with four member denominations. Shortly the Christian Council of Nigeria was formed with nine members. These councils helped the missions to speak with 'one voice' to the colonial governments. They also fostered a spirit of cooperation. Later these National Councils would become

National Church Councils. Although these councils were originally formed to promote evangelism and church growth, in the period following World War Two many liberal European mission leaders tried to push these councils into the ecumenical movement, so that the councils would be political and social forces in their own countries.

WORLD WAR TWO

In September, 1939, major war broke out again in Europe. Once again war hindered the fast moving development of the African Church. Although the Word was hindered, it was not halted and Christianity continued to make progress.

Once again German missionaries were arrested and prevented from carrying on their work. Since the Bremen and Basel missions had been working with Scottish missions in both Togo and the Gold Coast, the departure of the Germans did not cause as much difficulty as in 1916 and 1917. In 1939 the African Church had even more well trained Church leaders and even more experience in church government than in 1916, and so church growth continued.

Once again the missionaries in Africa faced similar difficulties to those they had in 1914. But, 'Such statistics as became available showed a continuing increase in full (church) membership and in the catechumenate, while African leaders were drawn into new positions of responsibility in the emergency and acquitted themselves with a devotion and an efficiency for which their missionary mentors often enough were scarcely prepared.'[8]

During the World War Two years the pressure for mission schools continued. Both the government and the people asked for more and more teachers and schools. 'The missions, already deeply committed to the cause of education, therefore continued to play their part in increasing measure. Nigeria was a case in point. Here the Southern Provinces experienced a growth of primary education in the decade 1937–1947 in respect of voluntary assisted schools (almost entirely a mission category) from 339 to 473 with an enrolment of 69,464 in 1937 and of 153,759 in 1946.'[9]

THE CHURCH PREPARES FOR INDEPENDENCE

With the end of World War Two a new anticipation swept Africa. In many countries African politicians began to alert people to the need for political independence. After 1955 political independence was acquired by one after another of the colonies of Africa. The Church of Africa had a new obligation: to contribute to the spiritual development and growth of the new nations. In the period following 1945 the many Protestant churches of Africa had to prepare themselves for their own independence or autonomy and assume the rightful position of leadership in the all important work of evangelism and discipleship.

In the period following World War Two the participation of mission and church organizations in education began to decrease. By this is meant that while missions and churches continued to maintain primary schools and in some places even opened new ones, more and more primary schools were being established by non-religious groups such as provincial governments and local county councils. In some colonies there were people who had developed a strong anti-Christian, anti-missionary feeling. They suggested to the colonial government that all the schools be taken away from religious organisations. After 1950 the colonial governments tightened their hold on education. They made regulations which limited the number of periods of religious instruction each week and even drew up the syllabus of what could be taught. The period in which the Church had been the most important contributor in education was rapidly drawing to a close in West Africa.

Literature work after 1945 took on a more important role than ever before. In 1900 very few Africans could read, but by 1945 there was a great literate public. Early missionaries had given Christians Bibles to read, but now additional Christian literature was needed. After World World Two more and more African Churches took an interest in publishing and the amount of Christian literature increased rapidly. A new approach to literature work was taken by the S.I.M. in West Africa. 'That a Christian magazine with plentiful illustration, articles on topics of current interest and pleasing format would be eagerly bought and read was shown by the Sudan Interior Mission's publication in Nigeria, *African Challenge*, which secured a curculation exceeding 100,000 (by 1954).'[10]

Another new means of evangelism presented itself during this period of history. In 1954 three young missionaries with the S.I.M. established the first Christian radio station in West Africa. Most countries in Africa only allow one radio station to transmit within their territories. This radio station is usually owned by the government. However, there are some countries, among them Liberia, Ethiopia, Burundi and Mozambique, which license commercial or private radio stations to operate within their borders. So it was that in 1954 evangelism in Africa took another step forward by way of radio when the S.I.M. opened 'Radio Village' near Monrovia in Liberia. At first the number of broadcasts was small, but today the station broadcasts to many places in West Africa and beyond in a large variety of languages.

In 1957 political independence came to the first West African colony. Soon Ghana, formerly the Gold Coast, would be joined by many more former colonies in West Africa. The African Church was prepared to meet the new day of political independence. In most cases, the major missions had already granted 'independence' or autonomy to their African churches by the time political independence arrived. When the mission societies had come to West Africa many years before their goal was not to establish churches which would be run from overseas for years and years to come, but rather to establish autonomous, national churches which would be maintained and governed by the Christians of each particular country. In addition to helping the African churches develop a form of church government and administration, the mission societies (particularly after 1945) began to hand over to the African denominations the 'tools' or mission property, i.e. printing presses, mission stations, hospitals, etc., needed by the churches fully to meet their obligations for evangelism and church growth. The example of the S.I.M. in Nigeria will illustrate what happened in many similar situations in the different countries in West Africa. 'The Association of Evangelical Churches of West Africa is the indigenous Church which has resulted from the witness of the Sudan Interior Mission. Meeting each year from 1950 to 1954 it prepared a constitution. At a meeting in Kagoro in 1954 the constitution was accepted by the leaders of the Church and at Egbe on May 18, 1954, the Church of ECWA was founded. The Sudan Interior Mission is gradually turning mission property over to the Church. By the end of 1962 ECWA had received nine mission stations and nine more were in the process of being turned over. . . A very important part of the Church is its evangelistic thrust through its 'African Missionary Society', which has sent out 140 of its own missionaries. (There were about 85 actually in missionary service as of July, 1963.). . . In ECWA there are about 700 (1962) organized churches, an increase of 140 since 1960.'[11]

By 1960, then, the Church of Jesus Christ in West Africa had assumed an important position in the development of the newly emerging nations. The period of political independence held unlimited opportunities for the African Church to meet the needs of the people of West Africa.

Questions:

1. How did World War One hinder the progress of the Church?
2. What mission society went to help the people of the Ivory Coast who had been baptized by William Harris?
3. What happened to German missionaries during World War Two?
4. What new type of literature work did the SIM try after World War Two?
5. What is an autonomous church? What are its obligations?

[1]Groves, C.P., *The Planting of Christianity in Africa* vol. IV (Lutterworth Press, London, 1958), p. 18
[2]Ibid. p. 56

[3]Ibid. p. 275
[4]Ibid. p. 300
[5]Smith, Noel, *The Presbyterian Church in Ghana 1835 – 1960* (Ghana Universities Press, Accra, 1966)
[6]Groves, C.P., *The Planting. . .*, vol. IV, p. 126
[7]Grimley, J. B. & Robinson, G. E., *Church Growth in Central and Southern Nigeria* (Wm B. Eerdmans Pub. Co., Grand Rapids, Mi., 1966), p. 80
[8]Groves, C. P., *The Planting. . .*, vol. IV, p. 245
[9]Ibid. p. 246
[10]Ibid. p. 294
[11]Grimley & Robinson, *Church Growth. . .*, pp. 83, 84, 85

29

West-Central Africa – Moving forward 1914–1960

WORLD WAR ONE

As we move on in our survey of the period 1914 to 1960, our study takes us to West-Central Africa and the beginning of World War One. The only German colony in this section of Africa was the Cameroons. As we have seen, there were three major Protestant denominations working here: the Basel Mission, the German Baptists and the American Presbyterians. The first two groups were mainly made up of German missionaries. In January, 1914, another German mission began work in the Cameroons, but had not made much progress by August when the war broke out. The Roman Catholic work was mainly carried out by German missionaries.

By 1915 the Germans gave up trying to defend the Cameroons and the French government took over the major portion of the colony and established a government which lasted until 1960. A small portion of the territory in the north-west was given over to Britain to govern. The French wanted the German missionaries removed from their work as soon as possible. So it was decided that the Paris Missionary Society would take over the leadership of the Protestant work while the French Fathers of the Holy Ghost would replace the German Roman Catholic missionaries. The American Presbyterians in the south of the country continued their work unhindered.

At the end of World War One the French government decided not to allow any German missionaries to return to the Cameroons and so the special arrangements that had been made during the war became more or less permanent after 1918.

As in West Africa, so also in this part of Africa, the development of the Church suffered because of the war. Nevertheless, in some areas progress was made even during this difficult time. In eastern Congo, where the A.I.M. had just started its work before the war, several new stations were opened from 1914 to 1918.

1918–1939 PERIOD OF RAPID GROWTH

After the war there was a new push by Protestant mission organizations to enter West-Central Africa. In 1918 the Lutheran Brethren arrived in Cameroons to help the Paris Mission in the development of the work. They were joined in 1920 by the Brethren Church Mission from the United States. In the deep inland area of Ugangi-Shari (C.A.E.) the Council of Baptist Missions of North America began work in 1920. As you may remember from our last study of this area, there was hardly any Protestant witness in this part of Africa before 1914. The A.I.M. opened work in this French colony in 1924 when Mr John Buyse from an A.I.M. station in the Congo built a small hut at Zemio. Within the year a French and an American missionary couple joined him there to help build up the A.I.M. work in eastern Ubangi-Shari. And so the A.I.M. took another step toward Lake Chad, which was the goal Peter C. Scott had set for a string of mission stations that would start in Mombasa and stretch westwards. In the same year two other stations were established: one at Obo and the other Djema. By 1925 the A.I.M. had eleven missionaries working in that colony, but within eight years, the number was reduced to one because of disease and furlough trips. Later, other missionaries volunteered to go to Ubangi-Shari to help with the work.

In the Belgian Congo the number of missionaries increased as well, as did the number of new Protestant mission societies. 'In the two decades between the wars the number of Protestant missions was more than doubled (in Congo). In 1919 the

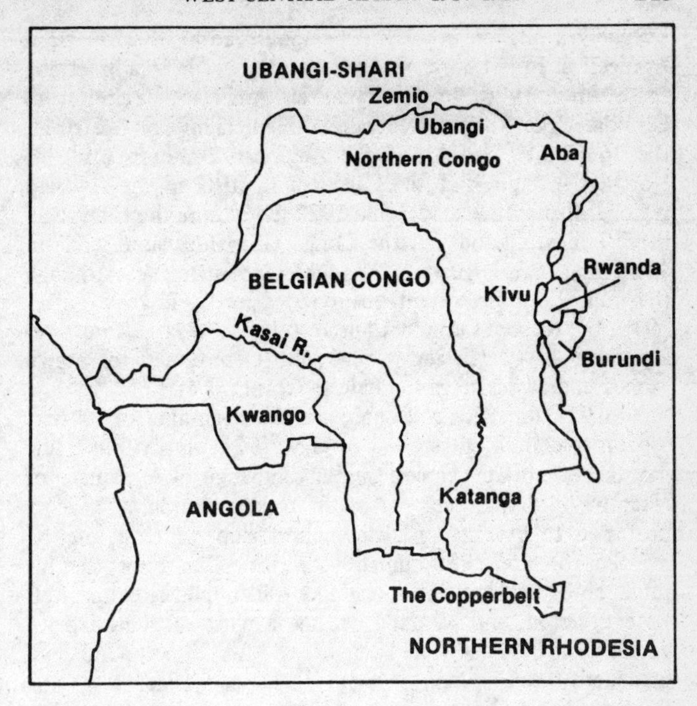

Norwegian Baptists entered northern Congo; in 1920 the American Mennonite Baptists entered northern Congo; in 1920 the American Mennonite Brethren came to the Kwango area. The Seventh Day Adventists, already established in a dozen African territories, arrived in Congo in 1921, which is the same year the Belgian Protestants entered Ruanda, the Swedish Evangelical Free Church of North America came to the Kivu area, and the Assemblies of God Mission started in northern Congo. In 1922 the Kivu region saw three new arrivals: Norway's Free Evangelical Mission to the Heathen, the Evangelization Society, Africa Mission, and the British Pentecostal Union Mission. After the coming of the Ubangi

Evangelical Mission in 1923 (first sponsored by the American Evangelical Free Church) there seems to have been a breathing space until 1926. In that year an Anglican mission from Uganda – the Ruanda General and Medical mission – arrived, the Immanuel Mission of the American Brethren came to Northern Congo, and the Canadian Baptists to the Kwango region. Also to the Kwango in 1927 there came the Unevangelized Tribes Mission and the Congo Gospel Mission, while in 1928 the Danish Baptists also entered Ruanda.'[1] Although the number of Protestant missionaries greatly increased after 1918, the Roman Catholic Church still had the largest missionary force in the Belgian Congo and it continued to receive money and advice from the Belgian Government.

In 1921 the Belgian Congo saw the beginning of its first separatist church. 'It started in May, 1921, and within a few months was in full career. Simon Kimbangu of the village of Nkamba, himself a member of the Baptist church at Wathen, professed to have had a Divine commission, which at first he resisted, to undertake a ministry of healing. The report that his touch could heal the sick spread like wildfire, mission hospitals were deserted, and Nkamba became a place of pilgrimage to which even the dead were brought.'[2] At first Simon Kimbangu preached the Christian message as he had heard it at the Baptist Church; he was particularly strict in demanding that men should not practise polygamy. However, within a short time the people who gathered around Simon Kimbangu began to introduce superstitions and practices from their traditional religion until the Kimbanguiste Church became a mixture of Christianity and traditional religions. The Belgian government arrested Simon Kimbangu and was going to have him put to death, but a group of missionaries wrote to King Albert of Belgium and claimed that Kimbangu had done nothing that deserved death, and so the king reversed the sentence. After 1923 the Kimbanguiste Church continued to grow because it allowed its members to keep many of their traditional beliefs, while at the same time it had the appearance of being a type of Christianity. Today the Kimbanguiste Church is quite large. In Zaire the government only recognizes three churches: The

Church of Christ of Zaire (Protestant), the Roman Catholic Church and the Kimbanguiste Church.

In the area of education, the churches continued to be quite active, In French Equatorial Africa (Cameroons, Gabon, C.A.E. French Congo, and Chad) the colonial government had rather strict standards of education. The schools were to be used to teach the pupils the 'greatness' of France. Since this was so, the French colonialists preferred to have only Frenchmen teaching in their schools. This made the work of mission schools difficult.

In the Belgian Congo the colonialists continued to give money to Roman Catholic missions for schools between 1914 and 1926. Then the Roman Catholic Church wanted to be sure that no money was given to Protestant missions and so a new arrangement was made '. . . in 1926 an agreement was made between the (Belgian) State and the Vatican that all subsidies for education should be given to Roman Catholic Missions. The generous grants made it possible for thousands of Congolese to be given primary education in Catholic schools and for large establishments of higher education to be erected. Protestant Missions did their best, but funds were insufficient.'[3] So for the period 1926 until 1948 (when the law was changed to allow some Protestant missions to receive government money), all the government subsidized education was in the hands of the Roman Catholics. Nevertheless, many Protestant churches in the Congo established private schools, but these were very expensive to run.

In Angola, the Portuguese government made a law which forbade any school in the colony to teach African languages or to print books in them. Everything was to be done in Portuguese. This, of course, made primary school education very difficult and hindered those Protestant missions which desired to print the Scriptures in the local languages.

The churches continued to contribute in the area of medical services. More hospitals and clinics were established during this period. Much was done by the A.I.M. in the Congo through medical work. 'The first hospital was opened at Aba by Dr Elizabeth Hurlburt. When she passed away in 1922, it was left without a resident doctor until 1926, when Dr and Mrs Ralph Kleinschmidt, who had served in Congo since 1923 under another mission, transferred to the A.I.M.'[4]

Theological education was also established by the many different missions to train pastors and evangelists. An example of this work is the start made by the A.I.M. in the Congo: 'The first Evangelists School was opened at Aba in 1924 in the care of Mr and Mrs Harry Stam. Candidates from all over the Congo field gathered there. Many of those who were in the first class are now leaders in the church. After many years at Aba, this school was transferred to Adi, and a Pastors' Course was added to its curriculum.'[5]

During this period many of the Protestant churches in the Congo felt the need for a central organization to represent their position and views to the colonial government. The Congo Protestant Council had been organized to meet this need, but not all the Protestant Missions belonged to it. There were many ecumenically minded people in the Congo Protestant Council who wanted to form one giant Protestant Church in the Congo. In 1934 some of the missions began discussions for forming such a church. In 1935 the great missionary leader Dr Mott visited the Belgian Congo and met with mission leaders. 'There, valuable plans were laid for co-operation in the educational field, and it was on this occasion that the proposal to adopt a common name for all churches connected with Protestant missions in Congo was submitted – L'Eglise du Christ au Congo – (The Church of Christ in Congo) a name that was agreed to in 1935.'[1] In the beginning only ten Protestant missions cooperated in the Church of Christ in Congo, but over the years other groups affiliated with it, until 1972 when the Zaire Government announced that all Protestant Churches should either join the Church of Christ in Zaire or disband.

WORLD WAR TWO

Once again war brought difficulties for the Church. However, as in West Africa at this time, so, too, in this area of Africa, the national church was better prepared to cope with the difficulties brought about by the global conflict.

In French Equatorial Africa the Federation of Evangelical Missions of the Cameroons and Equatorial Africa was formed in 1941 to aid Protestant missionary co-operation in a region where the Roman Catholic Church was quite strong.

During the war large numbers of Africans from French Equatorial Africa and the Belgian Congo were recruited to serve as soldiers and helpers. This meant that many local churches had a drop of men in their membership during this time.

THE ROAD TO INDEPENDENCE

In 1945 many people in West-Central Africa began to take a new interest in politics. For the most part the desire for political independence did not seem to be as advanced as in West or East Africa at the same period. The well educated Africans in French Equatorial Africa were for the most part willing to work within the French colonial system. In the Belgian Congo there were so many small tribes that there was no single strong nationalist voice. In Angola the Portuguese colonialists tried to prevent the Africans from gaining a political consciousness which would make them seek political independence.

In the area of education in the Belgian Congo, the restrictions against Protestant churches were lifted somewhat in 1948 when the Belgian Government agreed to give subsidies to Protestant schools. However, there were many conditions, including a special year of study in Belgium for those who would be running each school.

Just as West Africa was ahead of West-Central Africa in political development, so too the West African Protestant churches were further ahead of the West-Central churches in church government and autonomy. We must remember that this area of Africa was ruled by the French, Belgian or Portuguese colonialists and that the European countries from which they came were mainly Roman Catholic in religion. As we have seen, these colonial governments favoured Roman Catholic missionaries by giving them financial assistance and making laws which helped the Roman Catholic work. The result was that in this whole area of Africa the Roman Catholic Church was quite strong by 1960 and its membership was very large. On the other hand, the Protestant missions had had a more difficult time building up their churches. Thus by 1960 the Protestant churches in this area were not in as favourable position as the churches of West Africa with regard to full church autonomy. However, after 1960 things began to change more rapidly.

Questions:

1. What happened to the German missionaries in the Cameroons in 1915?
2. Who was Simon Kimbangu? What did he do?
3. How did the Belgian colonialists help the Roman Catholics in the area of education?
4. When was the Church of Christ in Congo organized? Why was it formed?
5. How did the Belgian government change its educational policy in 1948?

[1]Groves, C.P., *The Planting of Christianity in Africa*, vol. IV (Lutterworth Press, London, 1958), p. 122
[2]Ibid. p. 127
[3]Richardson, Kenneth, *Garden of Miracles: A History of the Africa Inland Mission* (Victory Press, London, 1968), p. 161
[4]Ibid. p. 167
[5]Ibid. p. 173
[6]Groves, C.P., *The Planting. . .*, vol. IV p. 228

30

South Africa 1914–1960: More church autonomy

WORLD WAR ONE

In southern Africa the German occupied territory was German South-West Africa. As in the other German territories, the war brought much hardship to the Church in that colony. In 1916 the South African army defeated the Germans in South-West Africa and the South Africans took control of the country. Many German missionaries were imprisoned for a little while, but some were allowed to return to their mission stations and continue their work. The biggest problem that the German missionaries had after they returned to their work was how to meet expenses. Because of the war, no money was coming from Germany, and so the missionaries had to raise funds through their own efforts in South-West Africa.

Elsewhere in southern Africa, the war brought the same hardships to the growth of the Church, as were felt in West Africa and West-Central Africa.

During the war there was one important rebellion which should be noted in our history, since it claimed to be a Christian revolt. The Chilembwe Rising can actually be traced back to 1892 when an independent missionary called Joseph Booth began a mission station near Blantyre, Nyasaland (Malawi). In addition to presenting Christianity, Joseph Booth taught racial intolerance. He taught those Africans who joined his mission church that white people could not be trusted and were generally bad. His teachings caused so much bad feeling around Blantyre that the Government deported him. However, before he left, he sent one of his converts,

John Chilembwe, to the United States where he studied at a black American college for three years. Chilembwe was ordained a pastor in the United States and then returned to Nyasaland where he established the 'African Baptist Church and Provident Industrial Mission'. John Chilembwe's main message was the same as that of Joseph Booth. Now although John Chilembwe claimed to be a Christian, he soon began to urge his followers to do exactly what the Bible forbids, that is, to kill 'your enemies'. Chilembwe tried to change the social conditions in Nyasaland by force rather than following Christ's injunction to love one's enemies and do good to those who hate. On January 23, 1915, John Chilembwe led a group of two hundred followers in an attack against a white farmer's house. Three Europeans were killed and another wounded. A second attack was made on Blantyre. Large numbers of Africans refused to join Chilembwe's revolt, and so he tried to run away to Mozambique when the revolt became a failure. He was trapped by the army before he could leave the colony and died in the battle which followed.

1918–1939

The war had brought more economic development to South Africa and Northern Rhodesia, than they had experienced before 1918. The war had caused demand for gold and industrial things which could be made in South Africa, while the demand for copper expanded the Northern Rhodesia mining industry. The result was that after 1918 these industries continued to grow, and, as they did, they drew more and more Africans from the rural areas to work in the mines and industry. The introduction of a 'money' economy and a situation where men left their wives and children in the reserves for long periods of time led to the breakdown of the tribe. This meant that people no longer followed tribal customs of courtesy and respect. The result was that lawlessness increased and moral standards dropped. This was particularly true in the case of South Africa, but also applied to Northern and

Southern Rhodesia and Nyasaland, where Africans were recruited to work in the mines.

Such a situation was an ideal time for the Church to try to show the people their need for the real meaning to life that Jesus Christ gives. But there were not enough church workers or missionaries to work in the cities and mining areas. In addition, many mining companies and company owners did not want missionaries to work with their employees, since they thought the missionaries might make the employees restless. Some progress was made, but not as much as should have been.

The period 1918 to 1939 was an important time for church autonomy in South Africa. As you remember, the Church grew faster in South Africa during the nineteenth century than anywhere else in Africa. By 1918 the major churches in South Africa had been in existence for about one hundred years. As you might expect, the time was right for Africans to take over the leadership of these churches. Not all the churches can be mentioned, but there are a few examples which we can observe.

In 1897 the Presbyterian Church of South Africa was formed, which included some Presbyterians churches made up of white people and other Presbyterian churches with African members. However, there was some confusion as to whether the white Presbyterians in South Africa should run the church government of the Africans. In 1923 the Bantu Presbyterian Church of South Africa was formed in which Africans would hold the positions of power. 'The new Church comprised some forty-five congregations organized in seven Presbyteries with communicant membership of over 22,000 and 7,000 candidates in preparation for membership, these all being confided to the pastoral care of forty-eight ordained European and African ministers, for the missionaries accompanied their congregations into the new Church with full powers as the African ministers. . .'[1] In 1927 the Bantu Baptist Church was organized so that the African Baptist pastors could take over the administration and running of the Baptist churches.

In Basutoland (Lesotho) the Paris Missionary Society had

begun preparing its African Church for independence in 1872. Finally in 1898 a Central Church Council or Assembly was formed for the Church of Basutoland. 'The Seboka, or Assembly, was to be composed of European missionaries and the Basuto ordained pastors, on terms of equality, with various lay representatives, and was to have jurisdiction in all affairs of the Church – discipline, finance, the creation of parishes, the primary, Bible and Theological Schools. All business was to be conducted in Sesuto. The year 1898 may therefore be regarded as the date of birth of the Church of Basutoland. The Constitution, Rules and Regulations as eventually adopted and revised were issued in 1927 in a series of nineteen chapters covering all aspects of the life and work of the Church'[2]

After World War One a new religion appeared in Africa. It was brought by missionaries from America who called themselves Jehovah's Witnesses. They are not Christian, because they do not believe that Jesus is the Son of God. They first began working in South Africa, and then moved up to the 'copperbelt' area of Northern Rhodesia. They gained most of their converts in urban areas. Their message claimed that a new age was coming in which all the present governments would be torn down and people belonging to their church would rule the world. They said both Protestant and Roman Catholic churches were tools of Satan. This group caused so much trouble that it was soon banned in Northern Rhodesia and Nyasaland. (Because Jehovah's Witnesses are 'anti-government' they will not even co-operate with independent governments in Africa. Shortly after independence, the Government of Malawi announced that the Jehovah's Witnesses were still a banned religious organization and were not allowed to work in Malawi. There are many countries in Africa where the Jehovah's Witnesses are banned.)

By 1918 there were about 120 African separatist churches in the Union of South Africa and each year their number increased. For the purpose of African Church history, these South African separatist churches are put into two categories. The one group is called the 'Zionist churches'. These separatist churches '. . . were characterized by prophets and a claim to the Bible as chief authority but with little concern for education. . .'[3] In many of these churches there is a major emphasis on the Old Testament and the religion of the Jews; in fact there are some Zionist type churches in South Africa which reject the New Testament altogether. Other denominations in this group practice faith-healing and other 'Pentecostal gifts'. The other type of church is called the 'Ethiopian type'. Churches in this group are closely patterned after the major denominations in South Africa. They conduct their services in the same way and are very interested in education and improvement of the church. Their major difference with the main denominations is their rejection of European missionaries.

As the years went by both types of separatist churches continued to grow in South Africa. In 1932 there were 292 such denominations registered with the Government, but just one year later there were 322 such churches. By 1948 there were more than 900 separatist denominations in South Africa! We may ask the question as to why there are so many of these denominations in South Africa. While it is hard to find a single exact answer, it is generally believed that because the South African government has established a colour bar between black and white people in the country, many Africans do not want to have anything to do with churches that have any history of contact or co-operation with the whites in South Africa.

WORLD WAR TWO: 1939–1945

There was not very much difficulty for the Church in southern Africa during World War Two. Only five Protestant missionaries had to be put into detention during the war because they were Germans in South-West Africa. The few German missionaries in South Africa were allowed to continue with their work.

During the war the Christian Council of South Africa strengthened its position. The Christian Council of S.A. was formed in 1936 with nine major denominations as members. In 1941 the Dutch Reformed Church of South Africa withdrew from the organization because it did not agree with the racial outlook of the Council. Like the other Christian Councils we have studied, the original purpose of this Council was to give the Protestant churches one voice with which to speak to the government.

THE POST-WAR PERIOD: 1945–1960

Unlike the other areas of Africa, for most of the territory in southern Africa, the period 1945 to 1960 was not a preparation for independence. In fact, in many cases the small populations of white settlers made even greater efforts to take away rights and liberties from Africans. During this period the Church continued to stand for justice and brotherhood, but laws in South Africa, South-West Africa, Mozambique and Rhodesia made the work of the Church more and more difficult.

In 1948 the Nationalist Party was elected in South Africa. The official programme of that party was the policy of 'Apartheid' or 'racial separateness'. Year after year they passed laws in South Africa which would keep Africans from mixing with Europeans. 'One of the most far-reaching "apartheid" measures was the Bantu Education Act of 1953, which took African education out of missionary control, and made it an instrument of government policy in reshaping men's minds. . . Africans, therefore, were to be given an inferior kind of education, to fit them for their chief function in South Africa, that of labourers.'[4] For more than a hundred years church leaders and missionaries had sought to give the best and most helpful education to the Africans in South Africa, but after 1953 the South African government no longer allowed them to help Africans in this way.

In 1954 a Federation of Northern and Southern Rhodesia and Nyasaland was arranged by the British government. The federation worked against the interests of the Africans and within ten years it was dissolved, so that Zambia and Malawi could become recognized independent states. Meanwhile the churches in Northern Rhodesia and Nyasaland continued to make progress toward full autonomy.

In Bechuanaland (Botswana) a self-governing church made up of the churches established by the London Missionary Society began to function in 1943. At first it was composed of both African and European leaders but in time the leadership passed fully into the hands of the Africans.

In Mozambique work by Protestant missions continued to meet with continued problems after 1945. In 1940 the Portuguese had attempted to stop the entrance of Protestant missionaries into Mozambique. However, in 1945 this ban was lifted, and some Protestants were allowed to enter. In the years that followed, official laws and trouble with entry permits (visas) made development of the Protestant church in Mozambique difficult.

By 1960 the Church in Southern Africa was quite strong. Yet, in the lands which had white-minority governments, the growth of the Church suffered because of hatred caused by the colour-bar, 'apartheid' and laws enacted by the white people in those territories to limit the work of the churches. Although most of the Protestant churches in South Africa, South-West Africa and Rhodesia are autonomous, the lands in which they work are not really free, since they have not yet gained 'majority rule'.

Questions

1. What was the Chilembwe Rising? Why was it not a 'Christian' revolt?
2. What is a 'Zionist Type' of church?
3. What is an 'Ethiopian Type' of church?

[1]Groves, C. P., *The Planting of Christianity in Africa*, vol. IV. (Lutterworth Press, London, 1958), pp. 189, 190
[2]Ibid. p. 200
[3]Ibid. p. 129
[4]Oliver, Roland, Atmore, Anthony, *Africa Since 1800* (Cambridge University Press, 1967), pp. 259, 260

31

East Africa 1914–1960 Development of the autonomous church

WORLD WAR ONE

The years 1914–1918 are generally considered to be dim years for the Church because the advance of evangelism was hindered. Just as the war started though, there was one bright spot in Uganda that we should note. On August 8, 1914, Daudi Chwa became eighteen and as such reached the legal age to become the Kabaka Buganda. 'On November 7, the formal investiture took place at the traditional site on Budo hill, some eight miles from the capital. As a Christian the Kabaka broke away from all precedent by having as the coronation ceremony a Christian service conducted by the Bishop of Uganda. He had the previous September taken as wife an educated Christian girl who received recognition as his queen consort. . .'[1]

German East Africa (Tanganyika) was Germany's most valuable colony. When the war started in 1914 the Germans made a great effort to keep Tanganyika as long as possible. As we have already seen, the Germans were easily displaced from Togo, Cameroons and South-West Africa. But in East Africa, the German forces, under the leadership of von Lettow-Vorbeck, were able to occupy and continue fighting until 1918. This long fight was very costly to East Africa, as it meant that more soldiers died over a period of four years.

Quite early in the war the British and Belgian forces captured the border areas of Tanganyika, so that those German missions around Mount Kilimanjaro and Lake Malawi fell into British hands almost from the start. The British army allowed the German missionaries to continue working on those stations for much of the war. At the beginning of the fighting there were one hundred and fifty German Protestant missionary men working in Tanganyika and a large number of German Roman Catholics. By 1916 the British army was not allowing Germans to remain on all mission stations, and so some missionaries were detained until the end of the war. 'Because the Church was still at an early stage of its growth, the loss sustained was very great. Missionary personnel were still needed and other Protestant missions, whose members were non-German, tried to help: the C.M.S. at Bukoba and the U.M.C.A. (Universities Mission to Central Africa) and two Scottish societies in the south. In 1922, some American Lutherans came to work in the Kilimanjaro area and, in 1925, the German societies began to return to their former areas. However, the war and the prolonged absence of German missionaries severely affected a young church which was not yet strong enough to stand on its own.'[2]

1918–1939

After World War One German East Africa was given to Great Britain as a mandated territory; thus the three territories of East Africa – Uganda, Kenya and Tanganyika – were all under British colonial rule. Unlike the French, Portuguese and Belgians, the British did not favour their own national church (the Anglican) with special subsidies for schools and other work. Instead, the British government usually offered equal financial assistance and advice to all recognized missions. While the Protestant churches suffered in French, Belgian and Portuguese Africa because of opposition and lack of support, the Roman Catholic Church in British Africa got the same subsidies as the Protestants.

Education in East Africa during this period of 1918 to 1939 followed a plan of development similar to that in British West Africa. In 1923 the British government held a meeting in England at which they formed a commission to supervise education in the colonies. The commission had representatives of both Protestant and Roman Catholic missions on it as well as government officials. After 1923 the colonial governments offered more money to mission schools and at the same time began to raise the required standards of education. Most Protestant missions co-operated with the government in education and so received financial assistance. The Roman Catholics were very happy to receive the British government money. In fact the Education Advisor for Roman Catholic Missions in British colonies told Roman Catholic missionaries in 1928 in Dar es Salaam: 'Co-operate with all your power; and where it is impossible for you to carry on both the immediate task of evangelization and your educational work, neglect your churches in order to perfect your schools.'[3] The Roman Catholics realized that schools were an important way to bring converts into their church.

Realizing the need for higher education after primary school the missions in East Africa established secondary schools. 'The first of these was one of the outcomes of Protestant efforts in Kenya toward church unity. In 1926, the Alliance of Protestant Missions founded Alliance High School. Situated at Kikuyu, it became a great centre of Christian education.'[4] The Roman Catholics founded Kabaa High School in 1930 which moved to Mangu in Central Province in 1940. Secondary schools were also built in Tanganyika and Uganda by mission societies.

From 1918 to 1923 the settlers in Kenya tried to make the British government pass laws which would benefit them. In 1919 the Governor General of Kenya issued a circular in which he told his officials to use force if necessary to make African men work on farms owned by settlers. Missionaries in several missions protested against this announcement and through the Alliance of Protestant Missions made a formal protest to Britain. Through the work of mission leaders in England, the colonial government circular was cancelled. Later in 1923, because of the interest shown by mission leaders and other people in Kenya, the British government issued the Devonshire White Paper which said that African interests in Kenya would always come first, not the interests of the settlers.

In the period 1918 to 1938 several new mission societies came to East Africa. As we have just seen, the American Lutherans started work in Tanganyika in 1922. The A.I.M. began work in Uganda for the first time in 1922. Under an agreement with the C.M.S., the A.I.M. worked in the West-Nile District, and the churches that were established became part of the Church of Uganda. In Kenya the Salvation Army began work in Nairobi, Thika, Malakisi and Embu in 1921. These are just three examples of the many new groups that entered East Africa after the war.

Mission societies continued to make their contributions in the area of medical work. In Tanganyika in many regions the mission hospital was the only hospital. The C.M.S., the U.M.C.A., the Lutherans, the A.I.M., and the Roman Catholics all operated hospitals there. In Uganda the C.M.S. and Roman Catholic missionaries had established medical work late in the nineteenth century. In 1918 the C.M.S. established a school for training midwives. 'By the end of 1971 just over 50 per cent of the 16,400 hospital beds in Uganda were still being provided by church or voluntary organizations.'[5] In Kenya the East African Scottish Mission built the first hospital in Central Province in 1908. The Roman Catholic Church and other missions were also active in the establishment of medical work. 'From its start, whenever possible, the Africa Inland Mission undertook medical work, most stations having dispensaries. The present work of the Africa Inland Church in Kenya includes three hospitals – at Kijabe, Kapsowar and Lokori – and twelve dispensaries.'[6]

The period 1918 to 1939 saw the growth of councils of co-operation in two of the East African territories. In Kenya the movement toward a joint missionary council was predated by an attempt to form a single Protestant church which would be built up by Protestant missions. In 1908 a meeting was held at Maseno with the major Protestant missions working in Kenya to discuss the idea of having a United Christian Church in Kenya. Then in 1913 a conference was called at Kikuyu to discuss the matter. 'The conference met at the C.M.S., Thogoto, and delegations were present from the

C.M.S., the C.S.M. (Church of Scotland Mission), the A.I.M., the U.M.M. (United Methodist Mission), the Nilotic Independent Mission, the Lutherans, the F.A.M. (Friends Africa Mission), the S.D.A. and the G.M.S. (Gospel Missionary Society).'[7] A constitution was drawn up which held to an evangelical statement of faith. The representatives of the A.I.M. stated that they would only join such a united church if the constitution made it clear that the church would remain true to the inerrant Scriptures and the Gospel of salvation in Jesus Christ. 'The only difficulties which arose during discussion were concerning baptism (Baptists) and confirmation (Anglicans), and so amid scenes of great enthusiasm the Constitution was signed by representatives of the A.I.M., and the C.M.S., the U.M.M. and the Independent Nilotic Mission (shortly to be merged with the A.I.M.).'[8] What followed was a joint communion service at which the representatives of the proposed United Church in Kenya took part. After the communion service members of the Anglican Church objected to the fact that members of the A.I.M. and other non-Anglican missions had taken part in the communion service. Local Anglicans wrote a letter to the Archbishop of Canterbury, who then told the C.M.S. in Kenya it could not hold joint communion services in future. So it was, that the C.M.S. and the Anglican Church thwarted the first attempt at having a united Church in Kenya. In 1918 another meeting was held to form an Alliance of Protestant Missions in Kenya. However, no united church was formed because the C.M.S. differed with the A.I.M., C.S.M. and U.M.M. on the issue of communion. In 1923 the Anglicans once again hindered church co-operation: 'The Alliance of Protestant Missions was badly shaken when the C.M.S. which had suffered a split in Britain in 1922 during the controversy over modernism, split in Kenya too with the appearance of a new Anglican body, the Bible Churchmen's Missionary Society (B.C.M.S.).'[9] In 1924 some Anglicans and others began to bring new ideas about doctrine and other matters into the Alliance. The A.I.M. pointed out that this was against the spirit of the original agreements of 1913 and 1918 and so withdrew from the Alliance. The A.I.M. rejoined the Alliance when the theological issues had been clarified but after 1932 no longer took part in any discussions. The other members kept trying to form one united church. In 1961 they began six years of meetings among Anglicans, Presbyterians, Methodists, Lutherans and Moravians in Kenya and Tanzania, yet they were unable to form a united church. This seems to indicate that the establishment of a single 'super' church in East Africa (ecumenism) is not possible at this time.

In 1924 the Kenya Missionary Council was formed to represent all Protestant missions, whether they were in the Alliance or not. In 1944 the Christian Council of Kenya was formed in place of the Kenya Missionary Council. The A.I.M./A.I.C. were charter members of the C.C.K. Many members of the new council made it quite clear that the C.C.K. was not to join any international organization so that it would be free from getting tied up with the ecumenical movement.

In Uganda there was nothing like the Kenya Missionary Council or the C.C.K. because the C.M.S. was the only major Protestant mission in the country for a long period.

In Tanganyika the Tanganyika Missionary Council was established in 1937. In 1948 it became the Tanganyika Christian Council and later it changed its name to the Christian Council of Tanzania. It is very similar to the C.C.K. in its work and objectives.

Turning to another aspect of Church history, in 1929 and 1930 there developed the 'circumcision crisis' in the central part of Kenya. The question was whether girls should be forced by the elders of the tribe to undergo circumcision. The question had been raised long before 1929. 'From the earliest days missionaries of the Church of Scotland Mission taught against female circumcision. The reasons given were medical, arising from the nature and after-effects of the operation. By 1912, this teaching had begun to have effect on the younger girls in mission boarding schools. Then in June, 1914, two girls expressed their wish to abandon the operation. However, both the missionaries and the leaders of the small baptized community felt that the time had not yet come for outright rejection of the rite in public. So it was agreed by the girls, their parents and the circumcisers that the operation should be performed in Kikuyu Hospital by the usual circumcisers and with Christian sponsors. The same procedure was adopted in 1915, but on this occasion one of the girls lost her nerve and underwent the operation with great reluctance. She was extensively cut as a result and so the experiment was not repeated. A similar experiment was made in Tumutumu, and in 1915, three girls were operated on by tribal circumcisers Dr. Philip who witnessed the operation found it so brutal that he refused to sanction its being repeated and therefore subsequently opposed the custom by every means in his power. This led to reviews of policy by the churches, and in March, 1916, the church committees at Kikuyu and Tumutumu recommended that circumcision of baptized girls or girls of Christian parents, or girls in mission schools, be made a matter of church discipline. It would seem that at the Gospel Mission station at Kambui, the A.I.M. station at Kijabe and the C.M.S. station at Kabete, teaching proceeded along much the same line.'[10]

From 1916 until 1929 the churches continued to teach against female circumcision. In March, 1929, the members of several denominations in Central Province met at Tumutumu to discuss the problem. It was agreed that the rite was evil and should no longer be practised by Christians. Then in June, 1929, a girl at Kambui school was kidnapped on a public road and circumcised by force. The matter was taken to court, but the magistrate ruled against the Christians, which in effect said that the elders of the tribe could kidnap any girl they wanted to in future and have her circumcised. The Kikuyu Central Association took up the side of the traditional rite of circumcision while members of the church argued against them. The result was that the whole countryside was upset by the controversy. 'The immediate result was serious disturbance and disruption of mission work with a drop in school and church attendance. The long-term effects were far-reaching, an obvious one being that it was then (1929) that the seeds of widespread separatism were sown in Kikuyuland, to result in the formation of African independent churches.'[11]

The 'circumcision crisis' was limited to one small part of

East Africa, but in 1929 a movement began in the far western part of East Africa which was soon to move widely through the whole territory. From around 1910 to 1930 there had been 'mass movements' to Christianity in many parts of East Africa. By this is meant that large numbers of people decided together to become Christians. They went to the C.M.S. or other missions and presented themselves for baptism. Although the missionaries and pastors tried to impress upon the people the importance of knowing Jesus Christ as Saviour, there soon appeared a large body of people who were members of churches, but who were not really saved. In 1928 two Uganda churchmen working at an Anglican mission in Rwanda, came under the conviction of the Holy Spirit and realized their need for full salvation through Jesus Christ. Under the leadership of a missionary, Dr. Joe Church, they found true peace with God. They then set about confessing their past sins and wrong-doings publicly. People could see the changes in their lives. 'The first mass movement of the Revival took place in Rukinga, in March, 1928. But this movement did not last for long and appeals were made to supporters in England for continuous prayer for true revival. It was in December, 1933, that these prayers were answered and a wider and deeper movement began.'[12] This marked the beginning of the 'Revival Movement' which is also called 'Rwandaism', 'Balokole', 'Saved Ones' or 'Wandugu'.

'From (Rukinga) the movement spread throughout Rwanda and Uganda, southwards to Buhaya and the C.M.S. areas of Tanzania, north to Sudan and eastwards into Kenya where it became particularly strong among the Anglicans of the western region and the Presbyterian and Anglican Kikuyu. Only in areas evangelized by the Catholics, the A.I.M. and the U.M.C.A. has it had less effect.'[13] (The reason the Revival Movement did not really develop in churches of the A.I.M. was that missionaries and pastors of the A.I.M. had always insisted on confession of sin and a personal knowledge of Jesus Christ before church membership was given. Thus in the 1930's there were fewer 'worldly' Christians in A.I.M. churches than there were, perhaps, in some other churches. The Catholics, of course, rejected the

Revival Movement because it was a Protestant movement which called upon a personal form of salvation; the U.M.C.A. being a 'high Church' Anglican mission did not lay as much emphasis upon the need for a personal salvation experience.)

'In 1937 the first envoys of the Revival visited Kenya. This team, as they had come to be called, remained for several days, preaching to Christians around Kabete. Before their departure, a small group of Christians, including a prominent Anglican clergyman, experienced a deep sense of salvation. . . Towards the end of 1938 a second Revival team visited Kenya from Ruanda, holding even more successful preaching services at the Pumwani C.M.S. station in Nairobi.'[14] As the Revival Movement grew some things began to develop which were not so good. Since the movement placed a very high demand upon confession of sin, many people felt it was important to backslide, so that they would have something to confess. Then, too, some of the members of the different evangelistic teams did not always conduct themselves as properly as they should have. Beginning in 1947 the Revival Fellowship began holding large conferences lasting several days in order to help Christians. These conferences attracted from 3,000 to 30,000 people. 'In organization, the Revival is quite different from normal ecclesiastical administrative structures. There are no officials, no executives, no salaried workers; no headquarters, no offices; no bureaucracy, no paperwork, no minutes, no budgets, no membership lists, and no annual subscription fees. Unlike the churches to which virtually all its followers belong, the Fellowship is informal, unstructured, spontaneous, and group-led.'[15]

During the period 1918 to 1939 progress continued in the southern Sudan. The work went slowly because the tribes were quite spread out in that area. However, the C.M.S., which had started the work in 1906 intensified their efforts. The C.M.S. worked among the Moru tribe. 'In 1926 the first converts were received when eight Moru boys were baptized. In 1930 the first Christian women of the tribe, five in number, received the rite. By 1934 there were 125 baptized members of the church with a total Christian community of 414. Biblical translation was carried forward, so that the infant church was before long provided with the Gospel of St. Mark (1928), the Gospel of St. Luke and the Acts of the Apostles (1931), and the Gospel of St. John (1934).'[16] The A.I.M. began work in the southern Sudan in 1949. As soon as a well could be dug for water, a mission station was established. The building up of the A.I.C. in southern Sudan was actually a ministry of Christians from Congo. 'The work in southern Sudan was helped from its earliest days by African missionaries, sent out and partly supported by their home churches in Congo. They had received training in one or other of the Bible Schools in Congo before going to Sudan.'[17]

For Ethiopia, the years 1935 to 1939 were terrible times. On October 3, 1935, Italian soldiers invaded Ethiopia from Eritrea. Their object was to make Ethiopia a colony of Italy. Although the Ethiopians fought bravely, the troups of Haile Selassie were unable to throw back the Italian invaders. On May 5, 1936, the Italian imperialists captured Addis Ababa. After the Ethiopians were defeated the Pope congratulated the Italian army for its victory: ' . . . he declared the pleasure of the Vatican in "the triumphal happiness of a great and good people".'[18] As soon as the Italians were in control of Ethiopia they sent many Roman Catholic missionaries to begin work in the country. Italy is a strongly Roman Catholic country and so once the government in Ethiopia was controlled by the Italians they began at once to expel the six Protestant mission societies working in Ethiopia. By 1938 there were very few Protestant missionaries left working in that country. The development of the churches suffered because of Italian imperialism, but in 1943 the Italians had been pushed out of Ethiopia by the Allied army and a little later Protestant missionaries returned to their churches.

Not all the results of the war were bad. When missionaries of the Sudan Interior Mission returned to Ethiopia in 1943 they met a miracle which God had performed during the Italian occupation. Back in 1928 the S.I.M. had begun work in the Wallamo Province. By 1937, when the Italians forced S.I.M. to leave, there were only forty-eight believers meeting in a handful of meeting places. But these forty-eight people knew the Gospel message and had the Gospel of Mark in their language. Several of these Wallamo men dilligently preached the Good News, with the result that many people believed. By 1943 'There were perhaps 100 separate churches, and probably 10,000 believers in Wallamo. From 48 to 10,000 – an increase of 20,000%'[19] in just seven years. Once again we see that fast church growth does not depend on missionaries nor well-educated pastors, but on the faithful witness of people who have experienced God's transformation in their own lives.

1939–1945

World War Two affected East Africa a little more than it did the parts of Africa we have studied so far. This was because the Allies used Kenya as a base for invading Italian Somaliland and from there they pushed the Italians out of Ethiopia and Eritrea. Thus some of the African battles of the Second World War were actually fought in the northern part of Eastern Africa. The Church in East Africa suffered similar dislocations and problems as the churches in the other parts of Africa during this period. Since we have already listed these problems in other places, we will not repeat them here.

During the war years several of the large denominations in East Africa took positive steps toward autonomy. The Presbyterian Church in East Africa (PCEA) was the result of work done by the Church of Scotland Mission in Central Province in Kenya. In 1946 a small Baptist mission in Central Province, the Gospel Missionary Society, allowed its churches to join the P.C.E.A. 'In 1943, a new constitution was enacted which ensured almost complete independence from the Church of Scotland. Complete independence and unity came, finally, in 1956, and the first African moderator, Charles Muhoro, was elected in 1961. John Gatu became the General Secretary in 1964.'[20]

The Anglican Church in Kenya not only had a large African membership, but there were also large congregations of Europeans, especially in the cities and the 'White Highlands'. As a result, in 1921 the Anglican Church formed two branches of the Church, one for Africans and the other for Europeans. This was later changed at the time of independence. 'In 1953, the first African bishops of the Anglican Church were consecrated. They were Festo Olang and Obadiah Kariuki. . . In 1960, the Anglican Church in East Africa gained its independence from Canterbury to which province all overseas dioceses belong until established as separate provinces. In that year, the Church of the Province of East Africa was established, incorporating all Anglican dioceses in Kenya, Tanganyika and Zanzibar.'[21]

The Africa Inland Church in Kenya actually achieved autonomy or 'independence' from its parent mission before either the P.C.E.A. or the Anglican Church in Kenya received their independence. From 1895 to 1932 the A.I.M. developed and administered the church government. Then in 1933 the Africa Inland Mission Church, as the A.I.C. was called at that time, assumed full responsibility for its own finances and so became self-supporting. In 1940 a committee was formed to draw up a constitution for the A.I.M. Church. This constitution was completed in 1943 and the name of the A.I.M. Church was changed to the Africa Inland Church. In 1952 the A.I.C. central church committee accepted the constitution which had been drawn up in 1943 and the Africa Inland Church then became completely independent from the Africa Inland Mission.[22] After that time the A.I.C. established the Africa Inland Church Mission Board (A.I.C.M.B.) to send missionaries to unreached parts of Kenya. Today these A.I.C.M.B. missionaries are serving in many parts of the Republic. Thus after 1952 the Africa Inland Church was a truly autonomous church in that it was self-supporting, self-governing and self-propagating.

In Tanzania the different Lutheran Churches also moved toward autonomy during World War Two. 'Gradually, dioceses or synods were set up which were independent of the Lutheran churches in Europe. This represented the final phase in the gradual progress from "mission situation" to "local church situation", although missionaries were still invited to help the local church in specific tasks.'[23] Each of these synods was quite independent until June 19, 1963, when the Evangelical Lutheran Churches of Tanzania (E.L.C.T.) was formed. This is not a single church, but a federation of seven smaller Lutheran synods in Tanzania.

In Uganda we have noted that almost from the beginning the Church of Uganda was a self-supporting church. 'The Anglican Church in Uganda is part of the Church of the Province of Uganda, Rwanda, Burundi and Boga-Zaire. It gained independence from Canterbury in 1961...'[24]

The period 1939 to 1945 saw the growth of separatist churches in East Africa and the establishment of new splinter churches. There are not very many separatist churches in Tanzania. The two best known ones are the Last Church of God and His Christ which was founded in 1952 and the African National Church which was established in 1928.

In Uganda there are rather few separatist churches, too. Perhaps the best known separatist church is the Malakite Church. 'Towards the end of 1913, an African teacher, Malaki Musajakawa (ex C.M.S.) joined with a chief in a protest against doctors and medicine. With the tolerance of polygamy in the new church, village churches were half-emptied and by the early 1920's adherents numbered over 90,000. Members resisted vaccination and innoculation and caused much embarrassment to the government. By 1930, numbers had fallen to approximately 60,000 and in 1966 to one thousand.'[25]

The separatist churches in East Africa account for thousands of members. There are now over 180 registered denominations of these churches in Kenya!

1945–1960

After World War Two the Church in East Africa developed on much the same pattern as the Church in West Africa. As we have noted already, after 1945 most of the large denominations in East Africa became fully autonomous. During this time the Christian Councils also took a greater part in expanding co-operation between churches. In East Africa the A.I.C. followed the example of the S.I.M. in Nigeria, by establishing two popular magazines *Kesho* and *Today in Africa* to expand printed evangelism. In the area of radio broadcasts, the Lutheran Church built a radio station in Addis Ababa, called 'Radio Voice of the Gospel' which broadcast Christian programmes to many parts of Africa. The A.I.M. began producing radio programmes for the Kenya Broadcasting Service in 1954. Today the A.I.C.'s *Biblia Husema* Studios prepare many Christian programmes which are used by the Voice of Kenya.

The period 1945 to 1960 was a bright one as the Church prepared for independence. There were only two major areas where the work of the Gospel was hindered. In Kenya there was the Mau Mau Emergency from 1952 to 1960. Most Christians did not feel they could join Mau Mau because of the hate, killing and oaths that were necessary. 'At the grass-roots level there was great hostility between African politcians and some Christians. This fact can be attributed, in large measure, to the Revival. African politicians appeared to the Revivalists as ambitious men whose behaviour often fell short of Christian standards.'[26] Many Christians in Central Province were killed during Mau Mau, but in 1960 the true Church emerged stronger than in 1952 because the weak members had deserted the Church and those people who remained had been strengthened in their Christian life.

Another dark spot was the limitation of work in the Sudan. In 1955 Sudan received independence and in 1958 there was a coup. After that time the Africans in the south began to demand autonomy from the Arab government in the North. The Arabs refused and a guerilla-type war broke out. The Arab government began limiting the movement of missionaries and pastors in 1960 and in 1964 all Christian missionaries were expelled from Sudan. From 1964 to 1970 the Christians in southern Sudan suffered very much at the hands of the Muslims from the north: many Christians were killed, while thousands of others fled across the border into Uganda, Zaire or the Central African Republic.

By 1960 the churches in East Africa were ready for the new

period of political independence which was to follow shortly. In less than eighty years the Church had grown from a small group of believers at the coast, to a large spiritual community for millions of people in East Africa. In fact, after 1960 many books referred to Uganda as a 'Christian country' since more than 50% of her population claimed membership or association with one of the churches within the land. Before 1960 many churches had depended upon mission societies for help in developing the Church, but after 1960 the major responsibility was upon the autonomous Church to complete the task of evangelization.

Questions:

1. What contributions did the Church make to education between 1918 and 1939?
2. Why was a United Christian Church in Kenya not formed in 1923?
3. What was the 'circumcision crisis'? How did it begin?
4. What is the Revival Fellowship? How did it start?
5. Tell when P.C.E.A., Anglican Church and A.I.C. became autonomous.
6. How was the mission of the Church in southern Sudan hindered after 1958?

[1] Groves, C.P., *The Planting of Christianity in Africa*, vol. IV (Lutterworth Press, London, 1958), p. 53
[2] Langley, Myrtle and Kiggins, Tom, *A Serving People* (Oxford University Press, Nairobi, 1974), p. 82
[3] Groves, C.P., *The Planting. . .*, vol. IV, p. 119
[4] Langley, M. & Kiggins, T., *A Serving People*, p. 130
[5] Ibid. p. 152
[6] Ibid. p. 153
[7] Ibid. p. 230
[8] Ibid. p. 231
[9] Barrett, David B. & Others, Ed., *Kenya Churches Handbook* (Evangel Publishing House, Kisumu, 1973), p. 35
[10] Langley, M. & Kiggins, T., *A Serving People*, p. 165

[11] Ibid. p. 166
[12] Ibid. p. 197
[13] Ibid. p. 194
[14] Barrett, D.B., & Others Ltd., *Kenya Churches. . .*, p. 113
[15] Ibid. p. 113
[16] Groves, C.P., *The Planting. . .*, vol. IV, p. 190
[17] Richardson, Kenneth, *Garden of Miracles: A History of the Africa Inland Mission* (Victory Press, London, 1968), p. 225
[18] Groves, C.P., *The Planting. . .*, vol. IV, p. 142
[19] Davis, Raymond, *Fire on the Mountains* (Zondervan Publishing House, Grand Rapids, Mich., 1966), p. 109
[20] Langley, M. & Kiggins, T., *A Serving People*, p. 95
[21] Ibid. p. 89
[22] *Surampya Ya Kanisa – Historia ya Africa Inland Church Kenya* (Africa Inland Church, Nairobi, 1971), p. 26
[23] Langley, M. & Kiggins, T., *A Serving People*, p. 82
[24] Ibid. p. 97
[25] Ibid. p. 221
[26] Ibid. p. 112

32

1960–1975. The first years of political independence

As we bring our study of the development of the Church in Africa to a close, we come to one of the most important periods in African political history: the independence of most African countries from colonial rule. Sudan and Ghana had led the march to independence in sub-Saharan Africa. They were soon followed by the former French colonies of west and central Africa which obtained full independence from France by November, 1960. After that there was a steady stream of British and Belgian colonies which obtained independence. As the countries of Africa became completely autonomous they usually joined the United Nations and so became members of the world community of nations. When each country joined the U.N. it pledged its support for the U.N. charter on Human Rights. One of the provisions of this chapter is freedom of religion for all people. Each U.N. member nation of Africa has now pledged to guarantee freedom of religion for all the people within its borders.

The period 1960 to 1970 saw continued growth of the Church in most parts of sub-Saharan Africa. For most of the churches in Africa this period was a time of putting into use their full autonomy. Throughout Africa the independent governments allowed the churches full freedom to practice evangelism and church growth. The only provision some governments made was that churches were not to participate in 'politics'. This rule hindered many separatist churches which had been founded before independence as political forces. They were usually told not to take sides in local political disputes or rivalries.

While the picture for the Church was generally bright for this period, there were some problems in certain geographical areas. Many Christians in Zaire were killed during the rebellions of 1961 and 1964. In southern Sudan the Arabs continued to persecute the Christians, so that large numbers fled into neighbouring states. In eastern Nigeria thousands of people perished and hundreds of churches and schools were destroyed in the civil war which took place during the last three years of the decade of the sixties. The Church in Angola and Mozambique suffered during the struggle for independence from Portugal, while many church leaders who spoke out against the inequities of apartheid were intimidated by the government or detained.

The period 1970 to 1975 found Christians in many parts of Africa facing differing kinds of oppression. The churches of Rwanda suffered the loss of many Christian leaders and lay people when open warfare broke out between the Watusi and the Bahutu. In Somalia foreign missionaries were expelled by the new Muslim socialist government and many local churches were forced to go underground. When the government of Chad decreed the re-introduction of certain pagan customs in which all citizens were expected to participate, many Christians faced death rather than give up their faith. After the coup in Ethiopia in 1974, the Ethiopian Orthodox Church found itself stripped of political power and in the years that followed some of its property was confiscated. But perhaps the most notorious persecution of Christians during this period was in Uganda. When Idi Amin seized power he shifted Uganda away from its Christian tradition and toward an acceptance of Islam and friendship with certain Arab countries. In 1972 many Christian organizations were banned and in 1977 all churches except the Roman Catholic and the Church of Uganda (Anglicans) were banned. From 1972 to 1979 there was a reign of terror against the population of Uganda. Prominent Christians were often the target of Amin's death squads. The senseless massacres of Christians came to worldwide notice in 1977 when Amin accused Archbishop Luwum of participating in a plot to overthrow the government. The Archbishop of the Church of

Uganda was murdered and in the days that followed many other Ugandans also died. The Church of Africa was again experiencing persecution of the degree suffered by the African Christians of the second, third and fourth centuries.

There were two events which happened during this period which greatly affected the churches in all of Africa. The first one occurred in April, 1963, when delegates from churches in thirty different countries of Africa gathered in Kampala, Uganda. Their purpose was to establish the All Africa Conference of Churches (A.A.C.C.) and work out a constitution for it. At Kampala the delegates discussed such topics as: The Life of the Church: Economic, Social, National and International Responsibilities of the Church; Christian Education and Youth; Formal Education; Literature and Mass Media. As a result, the A.A.C.C. was established and its headquarters placed in Nairobi. According to information provided by the A.A.C.C., the purpose of the organization is to: promote consultation and action among the member churches and council of the A.A.C.C.; to help churches with their leadership training; to provide research and study programmes; and 'without prejudice to its own autonomy, to collaborate with the World Council of Churches (W.C.C.) and other appropriate agencies in such ways as may be mutually agreed.'[1] Since 1963 the A.A.C.C. has received millions of shillings of aid and scholarships from the W.C.C. Today the A.A.C.C. is a major force in Africa. Through its many training courses and scholarships it influences large numbers of African clergy. (Additional information about the A.A.C.C. is available from: P. O. Box 20301, Nairobi, Kenya.)

Before the A.A.C.C. was formed many churches in the newly independent countries of Africa realized that there was a real danger to their future witness of the Gospel. This danger came from outside forces which sought to eliminate evangelism as the main work of the Church. Such forces wished to substitute social issues and politics as areas for total church involvement. Seeing that this would bring trouble, churches in many countries formed 'Evangelical Fellowships' at which true evangelical churches could co-operate in getting out the

Gospel. In 1959 the Sierra Leone Evangelical Fellowship was formed, followed in 1961 by the Evangelical Federation of Upper Volta, and in 1962 by the Evangelical Association of the Ivory Coast. In 1963 'Evangelical Fellowships' were established in Mali, Rhodesia, Zambia and the Congo. After 1963 fellowships were formed in Senegal, Chad, Malawi, Nigeria and Kenya. Members of these national fellowships realized that a continent-wide organization was needed for Africa. In February, 1966, 192 Christian leaders from twenty-three African countries met at Limuru, Kenya, to form the Association of Evangelicals of Africa and Madagascar (A.E.-A.M.). After many meetings to discuss the challenges and issues facing the Church, the delegates realized the need for an organization for all of Africa. 'Rev. Aaron Gamede, the Vice-Chairman of the Bantu Evangelical Church of Swaziland, moved that the ad-hoc conference form a continent-wide fellowship. . . . A 7-man committee drew up a 13-article constitution, which was also unanimously approved by the delegates. Purposes of the fellowship are summed up in Article II, Sections One and Four of the document: "To provide a spiritual fellowship among evangelical Christians who profess the same faith. . . To alert Christians to trends and spiritual dangers which would undermine the Scriptural foundation of the Gospel testimony." Ministries of the fellowship include mutual assistance in evangelism, literature, radio, education, youth work, Bible training schools and women's groups.'[2] The A.E.A.M. established its headquarters in Nairobi. The A.E.A.M. is a smaller organization than the A.A.C.C., but then it does not receive such massive amounts of money from outside sources as the A.A.C.C. does. Nevertheless the A.E.A.M. is playing a greater role each year in assisting its member evangelical fellowships in expanding the Gospel witness (Further infomation about the work and services is available from: A.E.A.M., P. O. Box 49332, Nairobi, Kenya.)

The period 1960 to 1975 was indeed a time of growth and maturity for the Church in Africa. At the Lausanne Conference on Evangelism held in Switzerland in 1974, Africa was singled out as the continent where Christianity is growing faster than anywhere else in the world. Church leaders still see the great need to reach the unevangelized people of Africa, while at the same time doing more to meet the spiritual needs of the congregations.

Questions:

1. What is the A.A.C.C.? When was it established? With what world organization is it closely associated?
2. What is the A.E.A.M.? For what purpose was it established?

[1] *What is the A.A.C.C.?* (pamphlet), no author (A.A.C.C., Nairobi, Kenya, 1974), no page number

[2] *The Africa Evangelical Conference: January 29–February 6, 1966*, no author (A.E.A.M., Nairobi, Kenya, 1966), p. 8

33

The Position of the Church in Africa in 1990

The best way to conclude this book is briefly to survey the situation of the Church in each country of Africa as of 1990. Our study has shown that Christianity started as a candle of light in Africa, but has now grown to a cloud of fire, giving light and direction to a great continent.

How large is the Church in your country? What percentage of the population is Protestant or Roman Catholic? Into how many languages have the Scriptures been translated for each nation in Africa? Here are the answers. (The figures given below reflect the approximate number of people who call themselves Muslims, or Protestants or Roman Catholics. The numbers do not represent actual church membership or the number of people who actively practise their religion.)

WEST AFRICA

LIBERIA

The population of Liberia in 1990 was estimated to be 2,591,000. In Liberia thirty-eight per cent of the people call themselves Christians (Protestants and Roman Catholics). The religious affiliation of Liberians is:

Protestants	932,800	(36.2%)
Muslims	544,100	(21%)
Roman Catholics	46,600	(1.8%)
Followers of Traditional Religions		(41%)

In Liberia there is only one complete translation of the Bible in a local language. However, seven tribes have the New Testament in their own tongue and eight other language groups have at least a portion of the Bible in their language.

CÔTE D'IVOIRE

In 1990 Côte D'Ivoire had a population of about 12,657,000 of which thirty-five per cent were Christians. Ivorians associated themselves with different religious bodies as follows:

Muslims	3,164,300	(25%)
Protestants	2,455,500	(19.4%)
Roman Catholics	1,974,500	(15.6%)
Followers of Traditional Religions		(40%)

Of the seventy languages in Côte D'Ivoire, twenty-eight have copies of some part of the Bible already translated. The New Testament has been translated into fifteen of the local languages and the Bible into three.

GHANA

The estimated population of Ghana in 1990 was 14,488,000. Fifty-two per cent of the population associated themselves with some form of Christianity. The religious percentages for Ghana are:

Protestants	5,099,800	(35.2%)
Muslims	2,463,000	(17%)
Roman Catholics	2,434,000	(16.8%)
Followers of Traditional Religions		(31%)

There are seventy-one different tribal languages in Ghana of which thirty-two have some part of the Bible in print. Twenty-two tribes have translations of the New Testament and five have the entire Bible.

TOGO

In 1990 the Republic of Togo had an estimated population of 3,764,000, of which more than a third considered themselves to be Christians.

Roman Catholics	745,300	(19.8%)
Muslims	715,200	(19%)
Protestants	775,400	(20.6%)
Followers of Traditional Religions		(40.6%)

The people of Togo speak forty-one different local languages. The entire Bible has been translated into three of these languages and another seven have the complete New Testament. There are three other languages which have a part of the Scripture in print.

BENIN

Benin, which used to be called Dahomey, had an estimated population of 4,733,000 in 1990. In Benin only twenty-four per cent of the citizens consider themselves Christians.

Muslims	795,100	(16.8%)
Roman Catholics	757,300	(16%)
Protestants	378,600	(8%)
Followers of Traditional Religions		(59.2%)

There are fifty-one different local languages spoken in Benin. Thirteen of these have some part of the Holy Scriptures reduced to writing. Of these thirteen, twelve have the complete New Testament and four of these have the entire Bible.

NIGERIA

The country with the largest population in Africa is Nigeria. In 1990 it was estimated that 119,812,000 people lived in this West African state. Forty-nine per cent of all Nigerians say they are Christians.

Protestants	49,123,000	(41%)
Muslims	43,132,300	(36%)
Roman Catholics	9,585,000	(8%)
Followers of Traditional Religions		(15%)

There are four hundred and twelve African languages spoken in Nigeria. Scripture portions have been translated into ninety-two of these languages. Fifty-two local languages have the entire New Testament, while fifteen of these have the entire Bible.

NIGER

The population of Niger in 1990 was about 7,366,000. Less than one per cent of the population in Niger are Christians.

Muslims	6,334,800	(86%)
Roman Catholics	14,700	(.2%)
Protestants	14,700	(.2%)
Followers of Traditional Religions		(13.6%)

There are seventeen local languages in Niger. One of these has the complete Bible in print, while four others have only the New Testament. Two additional languages have parts of Scripture in print.

BURKINA FASO

Burkina Faso, which used to be called Upper Volta, has an estimated population of 8,994,000. Sixteen per cent of the people of Burkina Faso are Christians.

Muslims	4,137,200	(46%)
Roman Catholics	899,400	(10%)
Protestants	539,600	(6%)
Followers of Traditional Religions		(38%)

In Burkina Faso the people have seventy-one different local languages. The Bible has been translated into three of them, while twenty local languages have at least one portion of Scripture in writing.

MALI

In 1990 the approximate population of Mali was 8,047,000. Less than two per cent of the people of Mali are Christians.

Muslims	6,518,000	(81%)
Roman Catholics	88,500	(1.1%)
Protestants	48,300	(.6%)
Followers of Traditional Religions		(17.3%)

There are twenty-two local languages in Mali. Nine of these have one part of the Bible in print. Five of these have the entire New Testament and one has the entire Bible.

GUINEA

There were about 6,876,000 people living in Guinea in 1990. Under two per cent of those people considered themselves Christians.

Muslims	4,813,200	(70%)
Roman Catholics	61,900	(.9%)
Protestants	41,300	(.6%)
Followers of Traditional Religions		(28.5%)

There are twenty-seven different African languages spoken by the citizens of Guinea, of which thirteen have some part of the Bible in print. Ten languages have the entire New Testament in writing.

GAMBIA

The Gambia is a nation of about 860,000 people. Nearly three per cent of the population acknowledge that they are Christians.

Muslims	748,200	(87%)
Roman Catholics	18,900	(2.2%)
Protestants	6,900	(.8%)
Followers of Traditional Religions		(10%)

Eighteen different local languages are spoken in Gambia.

Eight of these have part of the Bible in writing. Of these, five have the New Testament in print and the entire Bible is also in one of the local languages.

SIERRA LEONE

In 1990 it was estimated that the population of Sierra Leone was 4,033,000. Ten per cent of the people considered themselves Christians.

Muslims	1,613,200	(40%)
Protestants	334,700	(8.3%)
Roman Catholics	68,600	(1.7%)
Followers of Traditional Religions		(50%)

There are twenty-two local languages. One of these has the complete Bible in print, while ten have the New Testament. Five additional languages have parts of Scripture in print.

SENEGAL

In 1990 the estimated population of Senegal was 7,618,000. Less than five per cent of the citizens of Senegal say they are Christians.

Muslims	6,932,400	(91%)
Roman Catholics	259,000	(3.4%)
Protestants	76,200	(1%)
Followers of Traditional Religions		(4.5%)

Senegal has thirty-six different indigenous languages. Eleven of these have part of a Bible translation available and five also have the New Testament.

GUINEA-BISSAU

The population in 1990 was estimated to be 971,000. Just over six per cent of these people considered themselves Christians.

Muslims	412,700	(42.5%)
Roman Catholics	55,300	(5.7%)
Protestants	6,800	(.7%)
Followers of Traditional Religions		(51.1%)

There are twenty-one local languages in Guinea-Bissau, of which nine have parts of the Bible in print and four have the New Testament.

MAURITANIA

This north-western African state had a population of approximately 1,999,000 in 1990. Less than one per cent of the population are Christians.

Muslims	1,991,000	(99.6%)
Roman Catholics	8,000	(.4%)

There are six Mauritanian languages of which three have the complete Bible in writing and another has a portion of the Bible in print.

CENTRAL AFRICA

CAMEROON

In 1990 it was estimated that the population of Cameroon was 11,935,000. More than half of the citizens of Cameroon (59%) consider themselves Christians.

Roman Catholics	3,580,500	(30%)
Protestants	3,461,200	(29%)
Muslims	2,745,000	(23%)
Followers of Traditional Religions		(18%)

Two hundred and sixty-seven local languages are spoken in Cameroon. Fifty-six of these have part of the Bible in print. Thirty-three have the New Testament in writing and fifteen of these have the complete Bible.

CHAD

The population of Chad was about 5,668,000 in 1990. Thirty-four per cent of the people of Chad say they are Christians.

Muslims	1,983,800	(35%)
Protestants	1,587,000	(28%)
Roman Catholics	340,000	(6%)
Followers of Traditional Religions		(31%)

There are one hundred and sixteen local languages spoken in Chad, of which twenty-six have some part of the Bible in print. Of these twenty-six, twenty-two have the New Testament and four have the complete Bible.

CENTRAL AFRICAN REPUBLIC

The estimated population of the Central African Republic in 1990 was 2,987,000. Nearly ninety per cent of the citizens consider themselves Christians.

Protestants	2,087,900	(69.9%)
Roman Catholics	531,700	(17.8%)
Muslims	98,600	(3.3%)
Followers of Traditional Religions		(9%)

The people of the Central African Republic speak one hundred and four different tribal languages. Four of these have the whole Bible in print, while nine others have the complete New Testament. Four other languages have a portion of Scripture.

GABON

The estimated population of Gabon in 1990 was just over a million (1,273,000). More than eighty per cent of the citizens of Gabon say they are Christians.

Roman Catholics	796,900	(62.6%)
Protestants	247,000	(19.4%)
Muslims	50,000	(4%)
Followers of Traditional Religions		(14%)

There are thirty-seven local languages spoken in Gabon, of which thirteen have at least a portion of the Bible in print. Six of the thirty-seven languages have a complete New Testament and two have the complete Bible.

CONGO

There were over two million citizens (2,447,000) in Congo (Brazzaville) in 1990. Seventy-eight per cent of the population are associated with Christianity.

Roman Catholics	1,150,000	(47%)
Protestants	758,600	(31%)
Muslims	48,900	(2%)
Followers of Traditional Religions		(20%)

There are fifty-six African languages spoken by the Congolese. The Bible has been translated into three of these, while another three have the entire New Testament. Part of the Scriptures have been translated into four other Congolese languages.

ZAIRE

The Republic of Zaire had an estimated population of 34,138,000 in 1990. Ninety per cent of that population is considered Christian.

Protestants	16,044,900	(47%)
Roman Catholics	14,679,300	(43%)
Muslims	477,900	(1.4%)
Followers of Traditional Religions		(8.6%)

In Zaire there are two hundred and eleven tribal languages spoken by the Zairois. Seventy-four of these have part of the Bible already translated. More than half of these have the complete New Testament and twenty-six of those have the entire Bible.

RWANDA

About 7,179,000 people were living in Rwanda in 1990. More than seventy-five per cent of those people associated themselves with some form of Christianity.

Roman Catholics	2,857,200	(39.8%)
Protestants	2,570,100	(35.8%)
Muslims	617,400	(8.6%)
Followers of Traditional Religions		(15.8%)

In Rwanda there are two local languages spoken. One of these has the complete Bible in written form.

BURUNDI

The population of Burundi in 1990 was estimated to be 5,425,000. More than three quarters of the people (86.6%) consider themselves Christians.

Roman Catholics	2,766,800	(51%)
Protestants	1,931,300	(35.6%)
Muslims	54,300	(1%)
Followers of Traditional Religions		(12.4%)

There are two tribal languages spoken in Burundi of which one has the entire Bible.

EAST AFRICA

SUDAN

In 1990 the estimated population was 28,311,000. Less than ten per cent of the population is Christian and lives mostly in the southern part of the country.

Muslims	20,950,100	(74%)
Roman Catholics	1,698,700	(6%)
Protestants	1,075,800	(3.8%)
Followers of Traditional Religions		(16.2%)

There are one hundred and thirty-five different African languages spoken in Sudan. Thirty-five of these have at least one part of the Scriptures in writing. Of that number twenty-four possess the complete New Testament and six have the entire Bible.

ETHIOPIA

The population of Ethiopia in 1990 was estimated to be 50,341,000, of which more than half (52%) are believed to be Christian.

Protestants	25,321,500	(50.3%)
Muslims	17,619,400	(35%)
Roman Catholics	855,800	(1.7%)
Followers of Traditional Religions		(13%)

One hundred and eighteen local languages are spoken in Ethiopia, of which four have the complete Bible in print. Ten other Ethiopian languages have a complete New Testament, while eight others have at least one Gospel.

SOMALIA

The Somali Republic had a population of about 6,695,000 in 1990. There are very few Christians in Somalia (0.2%). Open evangelism is prohibited by the government and so the Church will have difficulty growing rapidly in this country.

Muslims	6,681,600	(99.8%)
Roman Catholics	12,100	(0.18%)
Protestants	1,300	(0.02%)

There are five local languages used in Somalia. One has the complete Bible and two the New Testament, and one other has a portion of the Bible in writing.

KENYA

In 1990 it was estimated that the population of Kenya was 24,821,000. Eighty per cent of the citizens of Kenya are considered Christian in practice or association.

Protestants	13,130,300	(52.9%)
Roman Catholics	6,726,500	(27.1%)
Muslims	1,489,300	(6%)
Followers of Traditional Religions		(12.8%)
Other Religions		(1.2%)

There are fifty-eight African languages spoken by people in Kenya. Some of the Bible has been translated into twenty-nine of these. Of the twenty-nine, there are nineteen complete translations of the New Testament and thirteen complete Bibles.

UGANDA

In 1990 the population of Uganda was estimated to be 16,928,000. Eighty per cent of the people call themselves Christians.

Roman Catholics	7,194,400	(42.5%)
Protestants	6,348,000	(37.5%)
Muslims	846,400	(5%)
Followers of Traditional Religions		(12.2%)
Other Religions		(2.8%)

There are forty local languages in Uganda. The entire Bible has already been translated into fourteen of them, while the New Testament is written in five more. There are six other languages that have at least one part of the Bible in print.

TANZANIA

The approximate population of Tanzania in 1990 was 25,635,000. More than forty-seven per cent of the population of Tanzania feel they are associated with Christianity.

Muslims	83,313,800	(32.5%)
Protestants	7,100,900	(27.7%)
Roman Catholics	5,127,000	(20%)
Followers of Traditional Religions		(19.8%)

There are one hundred and twenty-six tribal languages in Tanzania. Fifteen languages have the Bible in print. Another seventeen have the New Testament. Eleven of the other local languages have at least one portion of Scripture in writing.

SOUTHERN AFRICA

ANGOLA

The population of Angola was approximately 9,978,000 in 1990. Eighty per cent of the population was believed to be Christian.

Roman Catholics	4,280,600	(42.9%)
Protestants	3,701,800	(37.1%)
Followers of Traditional Religions		(16%)
Non-religious		(4%)

In Angola there are forty-one local languages, of which twenty-six have been reduced to writing and now have at least one part of the Bible. Eleven of the languages have the complete Bible and another three have the complete New Testament.

NAMIBIA

The south-west African country of Namibia had an estimated population of 1,288,000 in 1990. Eighty-six per cent of the people consider themselves Christians.

Protestants	901,600	(70%)
Roman Catholics	206,100	(16%)
Followers of Traditional Religions		(11%)
Non-religious		(3%)

There are twenty local languages spoken by the people of

Namibia. Thirteen of these have a portion of the Bible in print. Six of the languages have the entire Bible and another three the complete New Testament.

SOUTH AFRICA

The population of South Africa was estimated to be 38,604,000 in 1990. More than seventy per cent (71.6%) of the population thought of themselves as Christians.

Protestants	23,857,300	(61.8%)
Roman Catholics	3,783,200	(9.8%)
Muslims	463,200	(1.2%)
Followers of Traditional Religions		(20%)
Non-religious		(5%)
Hindus		(1.8%)
Other religions		(0.4%)

There are twenty-five languages in South Africa, of which thirteen have the complete translation of the Bible, as well as the New Testament and portions.

LESOTHO

The population of Lesotho was approximately 1,760,000 in 1990. Ninety-three per cent of the people are associated with Christianity.

Roman Catholics	932,800	(53%)
Protestants	704,000	(40%)
Followers of Traditional Religions		(6%)
Other religions		(1%)

There are three languages used by the citizens of Lesotho. The entire Bible has been translated into two of these.

SWAZILAND

Swaziland had an estimated population of 763,000 in 1990. Seventy per cent of all Swazis consider themselves Christians.

Protestants	490,600	(64.3%)
Roman Catholics	43,500	(5.7%)
Followers of Traditional Religions		(30%)

There are three African languages used in Swaziland. All of these have the New Testament in printed form and two have the complete Bible.

BOTSWANA

In 1990 the population of Botswana was estimated to be 1,303,000, of which slightly more than fifty per cent were believed to be Christians.

Protestants	607,200	(46.6%)
Roman Catholics	49,500	(3.8%)
Muslims	7,800	(0.6%)
Followers of Traditional Religions		(49%)

There are twenty-five local languages used in Botswana. The Bible has been translated into two of these and a third has the complete New Testament. Two other languages have part of the Scripture in print.

ZIMBABWE

The population of Zimbabwe was estimated to be 9,369,000 in 1990. More than fifty per cent (51.6%) is considered Christian.

Protestants	3,972,500	(42.4%)
Roman Catholics	861,900	(9.2%)
Muslims	84,300	(0.9%)
Followers of Traditional Religions		(46.5%)
Non-religious		(1%)

There are seventeen African languages spoken in Zimbabwe, of which ten have a complete Bible in print. Two other languages have a translation of the New Testament, while two more have a portion of the Bible.

MOZAMBIQUE

The east coast state of Mozambique had an estimated population of 15,696,000 in 1990. Only about twenty-two per cent (22.5%) of the people consider themselves Christians.

Roman Catholics	2,370,100	(15.1%)
Muslims	2,040,500	(13%)
Protestants	1,161,500	(7.4%)
Followers of Traditional Religions		(59.5%)
Non-religious		(5%)

There are twenty-one local languages used in Mozambique. Fifteen of these have at least one part of the Scriptures in print. Of that number seven have the entire Bible, while a further three have the New Testament.

MALAWI

The population of Malawi was estimated to be 8,831,000 in 1990. Sixty-eight per cent of the people of Malawi consider themselves to be Christians.

Protestants	3,832,700	(43.4%)
Roman Catholics	2,172,400	(24.6%)
Muslims	1,439,500	(16.3%)
Followers of Traditional Religions		(15.7%)

There are thirteen local languages in Malawi. The New Testament has been translated into eight of these languages and seven of them have the entire Bible. An additional three have a portion of Scripture in print.

ZAMBIA

The Republic of Zambia has a population of approximately 7,912,000. Seventy-seven per cent of the population call themselves Christians.

Roman Catholics	3,054,000	(38.6%)
Protestants	3,038,200	(38.4%)
Muslims	23,700	(0.3%)

Followers of Traditional Religions	(21%)
Non-religious	(1.7%)

There are thirty-five local languages in Zambia. The whole Bible has been translated into fourteen of these, with another eight having the complete New Testament. One other language has a part of the Bible in writing.

NORTH AFRICA

EGYPT

The population of Egypt in 1990 was estimated to be 52,536,000, of which 17.2 per cent were said to be Christian.

Muslims	43,289,700	(82.4%)
Roman Catholics	8,563,400	(16.3%)
Protestants	472,800	(0.9%)
Non-religious		(0.4%)

There are ten languages used by Egyptians. The Bible has been translated into one of these, thrcc others have the complete New Testament and another three languages have a portion of Scripture in print.

LIBYA

Libya had an estimated population of 4,710,000 in 1990. Just over six per cent of the population is Christian.

Muslims	4,394,400	(93.3%)
Protestants	174,300	(3.7%)
Roman Catholics	113,000	(2.4%)
Buddhists	28,300	(0.6%)

There are twelve languages spoken in Libya, but only one has a complete translation of the Bible, although two others have the New Testament and one other has a portion of Scripture in writing.

TUNISIA

The approximate population of Tunisia in 1990 was 8,313,000. The number of Christians is extremely small (0.5%).

Muslims	8,271,400	(99.5%)
Roman Catholics	41,600	(0.5%)

There are eleven languages used by Tunisians and the whole Bible has been translated into one language and the New Testament into two. Another language has a part of the Scripture in writing.

ALGERIA

The population of Algeria was estimated to be 25,350,000 in 1990. Less than one per cent was thought to be Christian.

Muslims	25,223,300	(99.5%)
Roman Catholics	101,400	(0.4%)
Protestants	25,400	(0.1%)

There are eighteen languages used by Algerians. The whole Bible has been translated into two of these, with three other languages having the complete New Testament. Five other languages have a portion of Scripture.

MOROCCO

Morocco had an estimated population of 25,168,000 in 1990. Less than one per cent of the population is Christian.

Muslims	25,067,300	(99.6%)
Roman Catholics	75,500	(0.3%)
Protestants	2,000	
Other Religions		(0.1%)

There are nine local languages in use in Morocco. The New Testament has been translated into two of these and three other languages have a portion of Scripture in print.

Population figures and religions statistics have been compiled from Britannica World Data, Ethnologue (Languages of the World) published by Summer Institute of Linguistics, Dallas, Texas, information supplied by MARC Europe, and other sources.

Bibliography

Anderson, W.B. *The Church in East Africa: 1840–1974*. Central Tanganyika Press, Dodoma, 1972

Baeta, C.G. *Christianity in Tropical Africa*. Oxford University Press, London, 1968

Barrett, David B. ed. *Kenya Churches Handbook: The Development of Kenyan Christianity, 1498 – 1973*. Evangel Publishing House, Kisumu, Kenya, 1973

Barrett, David B. *Schism and Renewal in Africa: An Analysis of Six Thousand Contemporary Religious Movements*. Oxford University Press, Nairobi, 1968

Bartels, F.L. *The Roots of Ghana Methodism*. Cambridge University Press with Methodist Book Depot, Ghana, 1965

Butler, Alfred J. *Ancient Coptic Churches of Egypt*. Clarendon Press, Oxford, 1970

Church, Joe E. *Forgive Them – The Story of an African Martyr*. Hodder & Stoughton, London, 1966

Debrunner, Hans W. *A History of Christianity in Ghana*. Waterville Publishing House, Accra, 1967

Grimley, J.B. &. Robinson, G.E. *Church Growth in Central and Southern Nigeria*. Wm. B. Eerdmans Publishing Co., Grand Rapids, Michigan, 1966

Groves, C.P. *The Planting of Christianity in Africa*. Vols. 1–4 Lutterworth Press, London, 1948

Haliburton, Gordon M. *The Prophet Harris*. Oxford University Press, New York, 1973

Holme, L.R. *The Extinction of the Christian Churches in North Africa*. Burt Franklin, New York, 1969

Kane, J. Herbert, *A Global View of Christian Missions*. Baker Book House, Grand Rapids, Michigan, 1971

Kavulu, David. *The Uganda Martyrs*. Longmans of Uganda, Kampala, 1969

Langley, Myrtle and Kiggins, Tom. *A Serving People*. Oxford University Press, Nairobi, 1974

Latourette, Kenneth S. *A History of the Expansion of Christianity: The Great Century*, Vol. V. Harper & Bros., New York, 1943

MacPherson, R. *The Presbyterian Church in Kenya*. Presbyterian Church of East Africa, Nairobi, 1970

Martin, Marie-Louise, *Kimbangu – An African Prophet and His Church*. Basil Blackwell, Oxford, 1975

Muga, E. *African Response to Western Religion*. East African Literature Bureau, Nairobi, 1975

Noshy, Ibrahim. *The Coptic Church*. Ruth Sloan Associates, Washington, 1955

Oduyoye, M. *The Planting of Christianity in Yorubaland*. Daystar Press, Ibadan, 1969

Ogot, B.A. & Kieran, J.A. (editors). *Zamani: A Survey of East African History*. East African Publishing House, Nairobi, 1968

Oliver, R. & Fage, J. *A Short History of Africa*. Penguin Books, Middlesex, 1962

Oliver, Roland & Atmore, Anthony. *Africa Since 1800*. Cambridge University Press, 1967

Oliver, Roland. *The Missionary Factor in East Africa*. Longman, London, 1952

Olson, Gilbert, W. *Church Growth in Sierra Leone*. Wm. B. Eerdmans Publishing Co., Grand Rapids, Michigan, 1969

Ranger, T.O. *The African Churches of Tanzania*. East African Publishing House, Nairobi (no date)

Richardson, Kenneth. *Garden of Miracles: A History of the Africa Inland Mission*. Victory Press, London, 1968

Simmons, Jack. *Livingstone and Africa*. Hodder & Stoughton Educational, London, 1955

Smith, Noel. *The Presbyterian Church of Ghana, 1835–1960*. Ghana Universities Press, Accra, 1966

Stuart, Mary. *Land of Promises – a Story of the Church in Uganda*. Highway Press, London, 1957

Trimingham, J. Spencer. *A History of Islam in West Africa*. Oxford University Press, London, 1970

Trimingham, J. Spencer. *Islam in Ethiopia*. Oxford University Press, London, 1952

Ullendorff, Edward. *Ethiopia and the Bible*. Oxford University Press, New York, 1968

Welbourn, Frederick B. *A Place to Feel at Home: A Study of Two Independent Churches in Western Kenya*. Oxford University Press, London, 1966

Were, G.S. & Wilson, D.A. *East Africa Through a Thousand Years*. Evans Brothers Ltd., London, 1969

Whitham, A.R. *The History of the Christian Church*. Rivingtons, London, 1968

Wondmagegnehu, Aymro & Motovy, Joachim. *The Ethiopian Orthodox Church*. The Ethiopian Orthodox Mission, Addis Ababa, 1970

Index

Abyssinia. *See* Ethiopia
African National Church, 238
Africa Evangelical Fellowship (South African General Mission), 175, 177, 179
Africa Inland Church, 182, 237–9
Africa Inland Mission (AIM), Cameroons, 211, 215; Congo, 169, 184, 215–6; Kenya, 185–7, 230, 232–3, 239; Sudan, 235; Tanzania, 182; Uganda, 229
African Missionary Societies, EMS 209; AICMB 237
Aggrey, Dr J. E. K., 203
Alexandria, Catechetical School, 9–10
Algeria, 2, 44, 264
All Africa Conference of Churches (AACC), 244
Alphonso, 62
American Board of Commissioners for Foreign Missions, 98, 133–4, 170, 176–7
Amin, Idi, 243–4
Anglicans, Congo, 214; Kenya, 230, 236–7; Liberia, 109; Mozambique, 176; Nigeria, 158, 201; Sierra Leone, 97, 149–50; Uganda, 188, 243–4; Zambia, 178; Zimbabwe, 177. *See* also CMS
Angola, 135, 170–1, 215, 243, 259
Anianus, 7
Apollos, 6
Arius, 12–13; Arianism, 12–14, 40
Assemblies of God, 187, 213
Association of Evangelicals of Africa and Madagascar (AEAM), 245
Augustine, 14–15, 39
Baeta, Rev R. D., 201
Baptists, 80–1; Angola, 170; Cameroons, 132, 162–3, 211; Central African Empire, 212; Congo, 168, 213; Liberia, 104; Malawi, 179; Nigeria, 104; South Africa, 221; Zambia, 178
Basel Mission, 81; Cameroons, 163, 201, 210; Ghana, 91–2, 155–6, 200, 205; Togo, 157, 206
Basutoland. *See* Lesotho
Bechuanaland. *See* Botswana
Belgian Congo. *See* Ziare
Benin, 109, 157–8, 249
Berlin Mission, 86; Berlin Missionary Society, 182; Berlin III, 181
Bible Translation, 23, 105, 133, 178–9, 184; Importance of, 40, 193–4
Booth, Joseph, 219
Botswana, 120, 173–4, 225, 261
Bowen, Thomas, 104
Braid, Garrick S., 204
Bremen Mission, 157, 200–1, 206
Brethren in Christ, 177–8, 212
Byzantine (Eastern) Church, 17, 19, 23, 27
Buganda, 128–30. *See* Uganda
Burkina Faso, 160, 250
Burundi, 256

Cameroons, 132–3, 162–4, 211–2, 217, 253
Carey, William, 80
Carthage, 1, 2, 7–8, 10–11, 14, 27–8
Catholics, 17, 67–8; Angola, 61–2, 170; Benin, 157–8; Cameroons, 132–3, 164, 210; C.A.E., 166; Chad, 166; Congo, 62–3, 135, 166; Ethiopia, 65–6, 190; Gabon

134, 164, 166–7; Kenya, 63–5, 187; Malawi, 179; Mozambique, 176; Senegal, 148; South Africa, 175; South West Africa, 173; Sudan, 190–1; Tanzania, 181–3, 228–9; Togo, 157; Uganda, 129–30, 187–8, 190, 229; Zaire, 167, 213–4; Zambia, 178, Zanzibar, 126–7, Zimbabwe, 177–8
Central African Republic (Empire), 165–7, 212, 254
Chad, 165–7, 243, 254
Chalcedon, Council of, 15, 16
Church of Christ in Zaire, 215–6
Christian Councils, 205–6, 216, 223–4, 231, 238–9
Christian Missionary Alliance, 168
Church Missionary Society (CMS), 81; Benin, 109; Kenya, 122–7, 229–30, 234; Nigeria, 99–103, 158; Rwanda, 233; Sierra Leone, 81–2, 89–90, 96–7, 101, 150, 183, 186; Sudan, 234; Tanzania, 182, 227, 229; Uganda, 129, 187–90, 231
Church, Dr Joe, 233
Church of Scotland Mission, 119, 179, 231–2, 236
Chilembwe, John, 219–20; Chilembwe Rising 219–20
'Circumcision Crisis' in Kenya, 231–3
Clement, 10
Colonialism, 59–65, 87–8, 109, 136–46, 154, 162, 173, 191, 196–8, 207–8, 227
Congo, 165–7, 212–3, 255; River area, 134–5, 167
Constantine, Emperor, 12, 13
Coptic Church, 17–20, 22–3, 27, 29; Egypt, 37, 40–1; Ethiopia, 34, 40–1, 66–7, 130–1, 190, 217, 243
Côte d'Ivoire, 152–5, 202, 248
Crowther, Bishop Samuel, 99–103
Cyprian, 11
Cyrenaira. *See* Libya

Dahomey. *See* Benin
de Graft, William, 92–3, 103–4
de Silveria, 63
Donatists, 14, 40
Dutch Reformed Church, 70, 86, 177–8, 224

East Africa, 51–3, 64–5, 122–31, 226–40
Education, 135, 156, 170, 177, 179, 194, 202–3, 206–7, 215, 217, 224, 227–8
Egypt, 1, 6–9, 11, 14, 15–20, 263 *See* also Coptic Church
Elijah the Second Group, 204
Ethiopia, 3, 5–6, 21–3, 34–7, 40–41, 54, 65–6, 130–1, 190, 235–6, 243, 257
'Ethiopian' Churches (SA), 175, 222
Evangelical Churches of West Africa (ECWA), 159, 209
Evangelical Paris Mission Society, 165

Federation of Evangelical Missions of Cameroons and Equatorial Africa, 217
Finnish Missionary Society, 172
Freeman, Thomas, 103–4, 107
Frumentius, 21–2

Gabon, 133–4, 164–5, 254–5
Gambia, 90, 149, 251–2
German East Africa. *See* Tanzania
Ghana, 45, 72–4, 91–3, 107, 109, 155–7, 200, 205, 248
Glasgow Society, 86
Gold Coast. *See* Ghana
Guinea, 251
Guinea Bissau, 149, 252–3

Hannington, Bishop James, 188

Harris, William W., Prophet, 153–5, 202
Heart of Africa Mission, 169
Holy Ghost Fathers, 135, 149, 166, 170, 187, 211

Islam, 25–30, 54; East Africa, 51–2; Egypt, 19–20, 28–9, 32; Ethiopia, 35–6; Kenya, 53; Mali, 46–7, 160, Niger, 160; Nigeria, 48–9, 159; North Africa, 27–30, 43–4; Senegal, 148; Somalia, 243; 148; Somalia, 243; Sudan, 33–4, 191, 239; Burkina Faso, 160
'Independent' Churches, 175, 204, 214, 222–3, 238
Ivory Coast, *See* Côte d'Ivoire

Jacobus, 17, 18
Jara, Rev. Joseph, 187
Jehovah's Witnesses, 222
John Mark, 6–8
Johnson, William P., 179
Julian, 23
Justinian, Emperor, 19

Kenya, 122–6, 183–7, 228–34 236–7, 239, 258
Kenya, United Church of (proposed), 229–30
Kenya Missionary Council, 229–31
Kimbangu, Simon, 214; Kimbanguiste Church, 214–5
Koi, David, 183
Kongo Kingdom, 61–63
Krapf, Ludwig, 122–126

Last Church of God and His Christ, 238
L'Eglise du Christ au Congo, 216
Leipzig Missionary Society, 182, 184
Lesotho, 221–2, 260
Liberia, 90–1, 109–10, 151–2, 247–8
Libya, 1, 10, 27, 44, 263
Literature, 207–8, 239; African Challenge, 208; Kesho, 239; Today, 239
Livingstone, David, 111–9
Livingstone Inland Mission, 168
Livingstonia Mission, 119, 179
London Missionary Society (LMS), 80, 112–5; Botswana, 120, 173–4, 225; South Africa, 82, 85–6, 112; Tanzania, 181; Zambia, 178; Zimbabwe, 176–7
Longinus, 23
Lutheran Church, 110, 212, 227, 229, 239
Luwum, Archbishop, 243–4

Mackay, Alexander, 129–30, 182
Malakite Church, 238
Malawi, 119, 179, 219–20, 2[illegible]–5, 262
Mali, 46, 160, 251
Mauritania, 2, 253
Mbila, Yohana, 186
Medical work, 170, 194, 215–6, 229
Mendez, 66
Methodists, 81; Benin, 158; Botswana, 174; Congo, 168–9; Gambia, 90, 149; Ghana, 93, 107–8, 156, 201; Ivory Coast, 153, 155, 202; Kenya, 127–8, 183, 187, 230; Liberia, 90, 110, 151–2; Mozambique, 176; Nigeria, 103–4, 158; Sierra Leone, 82, 90, 97–8, 150–1; South Africa, 86; Zambia, 178; Zimbabwe, 177
Moffat, Robert, 85, 112
Mokone, Pastor M., 175
Monophysitism, 15, 16–18, 22. *See* Chalcedon, Council of
Moravians, 71, 82, 85–86, 181–2, 231
Morocco, 264
Mozambique, 115, 176, 225, 243, 262

Muftaa, Dallington, 128–9
Musajakawa, Malaki, 238

Namibia, 259–60
Nicaea, 13–14; Nicaean Creed, 14
Niger, 160, 250
Niger Mission, 102–3, 158
Nigeria, 48, 99–105, 158–9, 201, 205, 208, 249–50
North African Church, 8, 9–20
Northern Rhodesia. *See* Zambia
Nubia, 3, 6, 21, 23, 32–34. *See also* Sudan
Numidia, 2, 7, 15–16
Nyasaland. *See* Malawi

Origen, 10
Owalo, Johana, 187

Paez, 66
Paris Missionary Society, 86, 165, 178, 211–2, 221
Philip (evangelist), 5, 6
Philip, Dr John, 87–8
Political independence, 242
Portuguese influence, 59–68, 170
Presbyterians, Cameroons, 164, 211; Congo, 169; Gabon, 134, 165; Ghana, 203–4; Kenya, 236; Nigeria, 105, 158; South Africa, 221; Zimbabwe, 177

Quaque, Philip, 72–4

Radio, 207, 239; ELWA, 208; Radio Voice of the Gospel, 239
Revival Movement, 233–4, 239
Rhenish Missionary Society, 172
Rhodesia. *See* Zimbabwe
Rwanda, 233, 243, 256

Saker, Alfred, 132, 133
Salvation Army, 156, 177, 229
Schmidt, George, 71, 82
Schweitzer, Dr Albert, 165
Scott, Peter C., 184–5
Scottish Industrial Mission, 183–4 229
Senegal, 147–8, 252
Seventh Day Adventists, 156, 177–9, 213
Sierra Leone, 78, 81–2, 89–90, 95–8, 102, 149–51, 205, 252
Slavery, 75–8, 82, 89–90, 99, 109, 115, 116–7, 127, 183
Slessor, Miss Mary, 158–9
Smith, Joseph, 92
Society for the Propagation of the Gospel (SPG), 71–2, 156
Society of African Missions (RC), 157
Society of the Divine Word (RC), 157
Somalia, 243, 257
South Africa, 49–52, 82–3, 85–8, 111–21, 174–6, 219–25, 260
South Africa General Mission. *See* Africa Evangelical Fellowship
South West Africa, 172–3, 219
Stanley, Henry (explorer), 117, 128–9, 137
Studd, C. T., 169
Sudan, 190–1, 234, 235, 239, 256–7
Sudan Interior Mission (SIM), 159, 208–9, 235–6
Sudan United Mission (SUM), 159, 205
Swaziland, 260–1

Tanganyika. *See* Tanzania
Tanzania, 130, 181–3, 226–7, 231, 237–8, 258–9
Taylor, Rev. J. C., 101–2
Taylor, Rev. William, 152
Tertullian, 10–11, 39
Thompson, Thomas, 72
Togo, 157, 199, 249
Tunisia, 2, 264

Uganda, 128–30, 187–90, 226, 229, 231, 238, 240, 243–4, 258
Uganda, Church of, 189–90

Uganda martyrs, 188–9
Universities Mission, 116, 128, 179, 181, 227, 234
Upper Volta. *See* Burkina Faso

West Africa, 45–9, 72–4, 81–2, 89–111, 147–60, 199–209
West Central Africa, 132–5, 162–71, 211–8
World War I, 200–1, 211–2, 219–10, 226–7; World War II, 206–7, 215–6, 222–3, 236–8

Zaire, 4, 167–70, 214, 215–7, 243, 255
Zambia, 126–7, 178–9, 220, 222, 225, 262–3
Zanzibar, 126
Zimbabwe, 4, 43, 50, 176–9, 261
Zionist Churches, 222–3

Aids Sex And Family Planning

by Dr Kristina Baker and Honor Ward

Mrs Mkhwanazi comes to the Doctor's office, very worried. She is not sure if her only son should enter the University or not for fear that he may catch AIDS, the dreaded disease. How does the Doctor help her?

What about Edred and Phindile, two young people planning to get married. Should they plan on having a child immediately after marriage? This raises the question of family planning and contraceptives for Christians. What should be the Christian's stand on these?

The authors deal with these and many more issues of concern in this book.

How To Communicate The Gospel Effectively

by James F. Engel

Is it possible that, despite the scriptural promise, the Word can, in fact, return void? What is successful evangelism? Does this always mean people will respond to altar calls to receive Jesus Christ?

Applying the principles of Communication theory, Dr Engel answers these provoking questions and more from his rich experiences as a world renowned Christian Communicator and Audience researcher.

JAMES F. ENGEL PH.D is a Professor of Communications, Research and Evangelism at the Wheaton Graduate School, Illinois, USA. He is also the Senior Vice President of Management Development Associates (MDA), a marketing and management consulting firm working primarily with Christians and Christian organizations, worldwide.

He is also an Associate of Daystar University College, Nairobi, Kenya and a senior faculty member of the Asian Institute of Christian Communication.

Dr Engel is an internationally known authority on Christian audience research and the strategy of world evangelization. He has presented seminars in more than 40 countries.

Pastor

by Peter Larom

'For most Christians the local church is the primary place where their Christian growth takes place and the pastor their guide. What a responsibility for those who are called to this ministry!'

So writes the author of this book. Out of his considerable experience, as church leader and lecturer in a theological college in Uganda, he deals in a practical and spiritual manner with the whole range of the pastor's responsibilities.

In his Introduction, written shortly before his death, Bishop Festo Kivengere said he trusted the book would 'produce profound results in the ministry of those who will read it'.

PETER LAROM is a lecturer at Bishop Tucker College, Mukono, Uganda.